PENGUIN CANADA

THE PENGUIN BOOK OF MORE CANADIAN JOKES

John Robert Colombo is nationally known as the Master
Gatherer for his compilations of Canadiana. He is the author,
compiler, or translator of over 150 books, including collections
of fantastic literature, poetry, essays, and such popular reference
works as *Colombo's Famous Lasting Words* and *The Penguin
Treasury of Popular Canadian Poems and Songs*. The present
volume is a successor and sequel to his successful collection
The Penguin Book of Canadian Jokes, books compiled to make
Canadians laugh.

As Peter C. Newman wrote about John Robert Colombo: "In
a very real way you have become the guardian of perpetuating
the Canadian psyche—in a fascinating and readable fashion."

Also by John Robert Colombo

The Penguin Book of Canadian Jokes

The Penguin Treasury of Popular Canadian Poems and Songs

1000 Questions About Canada

Ghost Stories of Canada

John Robert Colombo's Famous Lasting Words

Mysteries of Ontario

Colombo's All-time Great Canadian Quotations

Colombo's New Canadian Quotations

Singular Stories

The UFO Quote Book

Marvellous Stories

the Penguin Book of more canadian jokes

JOHN ROBERT COLOMBO

PENGUIN
CANADA

PENGUIN CANADA

Penguin Group (Canada), a division of Pearson Penguin Canada Inc.,
10 Alcorn Avenue, Toronto, Ontario M4V 3B2

Penguin Group (U.K.), 80 Strand, London WC2R 0RL, England
Penguin Group (U.S.), 375 Hudson Street, New York, New York 10014, U.S.A.
Penguin Group (Australia) Inc., 250 Camberwell Road, Camberwell, Victoria 3124, Australia
Penguin Group (Ireland), 25 St. Stephen's Green, Dublin 2, Ireland
Penguin Books India (P) Ltd, 11, Community Centre, Panchsheel Park,
New Delhi – 110 017, India
Penguin Group (New Zealand), cnr Rosedale and Airborne Roads, Albany, Auckland 1310,
New Zealand
Penguin Books (South Africa) (Pty) Ltd, 24 Sturdee Avenue, Rosebank 2196, South Africa

Penguin Group, Registered Offices: 80 Strand, London WC2R 0RL, England

First published 2003

1 2 3 4 5 6 7 8 9 10 (WEB)

Manufactured in Canada.

NATIONAL LIBRARY OF CANADA CATALOGUING IN PUBLICATION

The Penguin book of more Canadian jokes / compiled by John Robert Colombo.

ISBN 0-14-301490-0

1. Canadian wit and humor (English)   2. Canada—Humor.
I. Colombo, John Robert, 1936-

PS8375.P452 2003   C818'.60208   C2003-902582-9
PN6178.C3P45 2003

Visit the Penguin Group (Canada) website at **www.penguin.ca**

To Debbie & Joel Bonn

Contents

Preface

This is a brand-new collection of Canadian jokes, anecdotes, and lore. It follows in the wake of *The Penguin Book of Canadian Jokes*, my earlier collection, which proved to be so popular with the reading public that I felt I should keep my files open and compile a fresh new book of light humour.

But the people at Penguin Group (Canada) are a wary and responsible colony of people. (The collective of penguins is a colony.) They asked me to assure them that the new collection "measures up" to the standard established by the previous collection. They added a proviso: "We will publish another collection, but you have to come up with good jokes, with new jokes, and with jokes that are not just variations on the ones in the first book."

"No problem," I replied. "Scout's honour! *Certainement!*"

The result is *The Penguin Book of More Canadian Jokes* . . . a spanking new book . . . full of lively content with a Canadian slant.

A joke is a funny story. It is fictitious, it is short, and it surprises its reader or listener. It has to leave its audience laughing, or at least smiling.

An anecdote is also a funny story. But it is not entirely fictitious, for the reason that it is told about a real-life person. It is
"told as true," though it is manifestly false. The subject of the
anecdote may be a character from history (like Sir John A.
Macdonald, our first prime minister), or a present-day personality (like singer-songwriter Marie-Lynn Hammond). Jokes and
anecdotes are similar in structure, so much so that anecdotes are
sometimes called "anecjokes."

And lore is something else again. It is not a story, real or fictitious. In place of a narrative structure, it offers a bald statement
that strikes the reader or listener as ridiculous. I have in mind
such lore as graffiti, road signs, public notices, instances of
"admirably awful writing," and so on. Lore is often heart-
warming, sometimes sharp-edged, inherently odd, amusing, and
funny. Lore is ephemeral and fleeting, and therein lies its charm.

Although the jokes, anecdotes, and lore that make up this
collection are easily defined, it is harder to define the two other
words that I used: "Canadian slant." The items in this book are,
I believe, inclined that way.

They are quite Canadian. I have in mind the greater part of the
country, the English-speaking part. Quebecers laugh at these jokes,
too, and they have some of their own jokes, but few manage to
survive the hurdle of translation from French into English.

So in that sense, you might ask, "How Canadian is the material in this book?" I am tempted to say that it is "as Canadian as
possible under the circumstances" (to recall that ever-fresh
expression once heard on CBC Radio's old *Morningside*
program—found among the twenty-four classic Canadian jokes
in the last chapter of this book). I also recall Don Harron (in the
guise of the old farmer Charlie Farquharson) punning: "The only
thing quintessentially Canadian is the Dionne quintuplets!"

Nevertheless, I am convinced that a distinctive Canadian
humour exists. It receives its fullest expression in our small talk.
(I made this suggestion at some length in the preface to the first
book of jokes.) It finds its most direct expression in our jokes,

anecdotes, and lore—in our occasional humour. It is also the product of a columnist like Eric Nicol, a comic like Dave Broadfoot, an entertainer like Don Harron, a group like the Royal Canadian Air Farce, a broadcaster like Bill Richardson, a personality like Mary Walsh or Stuart McLean. It is to be found in our literature, especially in the novels of Robertson Davies and Mordecai Richler. It is embedded in the very rhetoric of Stephen Leacock (gone now for half a century yet still our funniest and most influential humourist). It is a pleasure to note that after all these years, a dozen or so of his books remain in print—including the classic *Sunshine Sketches of a Little Town*. I also find lively occasional humour in stage presentations, like the Spring Thaw routines of the past and Michel Tremblay's present-day plays. Nor can I overlook those popular ex-pat Canadian comedy performers, including Lorne Michaels, Jim Carey, and John Candy. Or those lovely, lively at-home singer-performers Anna Russell, Nancy White, Marie-Lynn Hammond, and Mary-Lou Fallis. (Long may these women follow in the giant footsteps of the inimitable Toronto-born entertainer Beatrice Lillie.)

As amusing, as irreverent, as witty, and as Canadian as these writers and performers are, or were, I would like to argue that our funny bone is our willingness to rib ourselves. Our humour is light wit, a self-conscious mockery, and it is most endearingly our own when it refers to people, places, things, and ideas that are recognizably Canadian. Let me elaborate. A joke about a fellow Canadian (Anne Murray, Céline Dion) is Canadian without any qualification on anyone's part. A joke told at the expense of head of government (Brian Mulroney, Jean Chrétien) may resemble one that was earlier told about a foreign head of government (Margaret Thatcher, Ronald Reagan), but it becomes Canadian in my book if, like a tailor-made suit, it really fits Brian or Jean.

Similarly, jokes about Canadian places (Medicine Hat, Moose Jaw) attract our attention and sustain it in a way jokes about American places (Peoria, Dubuque) do not. Some place names are showstoppers.

As well, there are things that may be specifically Canadian. All someone has to do is mention a few objects that have a special place in our affections—the Maple Leafs, beavers, snow, climate, and other innumerable commonplaces of our national existence—and we are ready to smile.

Then there is a set of ideas that, while not patented in this country, have a Canadian patina to them. These ideas bring to mind characteristics we share and qualities we treasure. (I have in mind peacekeeping, multiculturalism, bilingualism, transfer payments, and other pleasures and annoyances.)

Over and above these categories—people, places, things, ideas—there are some distinctive attitudes that we have that are traditionally associated with our country and its people. Edgar Z. Friedenberg, a political scientist, noted that we possess an exaggerated "deference to authority." "The Canadian genius," according to essayist and travel writer Jan Morris, "is essentially a deflationary genius." Indeed, we like to think of ourselves as every day being summoned to the Senate, prepared to give every proposed course of action "a sober second thought." Whether rightly or wrongly, we view ourselves as a gentle and genteel people. Inevitably there is the church-basement feel to our public policy, the Boy Scout approach to our foreign policy. The humour we enjoy, however tentative, however thoughtful, reflects these characteristics, as does the humour of no other people in the world.

At the same time, our approach to life is one that takes into account our "gateway to the north," our "social safety net," our "longest unguarded border" (until 9/11 at least), our gigantic cultural complexes (the world's leading public film board, the world's largest broadcasting system), and so forth. To match all this, we have a humour that is progressive, generally positive, and decidedly our own.

Inevitably some of the oral or written humour in this book may be described—at best or at worst—as marginally Canadian. These stories are ones that are making the rounds in our provinces and territories in the spirit of mockery or mirth. In the past I enjoyed many conversations with the folklorist Edith Fowke about national cultural expression and regional variation. She used to maintain that there is nothing regional about folklore; it is a global phenomenon. (To adapt a catchphrase from the 1960s, folklore thinks globally yet acts locally.) She took great delight in its local variations, collecting and publishing our own variety of the world's legends, songs, traditional humour, and oral lore. Canadian humour is an attitude to life that embraces the humour of people from other countries of the world.

If some of the jokes in this collection lack specific national reference, be assured that they are nevertheless Canadian—they were found in circulation in one or more of our provinces and territories—and that the attitudes they express are consistent with the national characteristics observed by Friedenberg, Morris, and countless other commentators (whose interpretations are to be found in such indispensable reference works as *Colombo's All-time Great Canadian Quotations* and *Colombo's Famous Lasting Words*). While some of the jokes in these pages may also be heard elsewhere in the English-speaking world, notably the United States, the United Kingdom, Australia, and New Zealand, why should we hesitate to claim them as our own? Let us be bold. Let us assume that our versions of these jokes are the original versions, ones that originated here and there across the country—perhaps at its geographical centre, near Starbuck, Manitoba! We have our own humour. Let's laugh along with it.

A word of caution. "Viewer discretion is advised." There is no X-rated chapter in this collection, but there are some jokes that some people may regard as somewhat offensive. This reaction does not bother me. Is it necessarily a bad thing if some jokes are deemed offensive? Is it always impolitic—inappropriate—to be politically incorrect? For instance, would any collection of Canadian humour be complete without its quota of Newfie jokes? (There *are* no Newfies, so no apologies are in order. At the same time, I have met many fine men and women from Newfoundland and Labrador, and they are generally the best bearers of the tales of these imaginary, benighted characters.) There are no jokes in these pages that are blasphemous or sacrilegious; I failed to find any of this sort that were even vaguely relevant to the country. Nor are any jokes included that display crudity of language; coarse language is not required for the telling of jokes—except for a handful that are about rough language. No jokes play on any private person's incredulity, but public personalities are deemed fair game, being able to defend themselves with their thick skins and sharp tongues.

I acknowledge that I have included some jokes that are problematical in the sense that they raise issues some readers may find disturbing. So let me ask a relevant question: "Why shouldn't jokes disturb?" Ted Cohen, a professor of philosophy at the University of Chicago, is the author of a study of Kant's aesthetics. He is also the author of a deeply considered study of humour. In his book *Jokes: Philosophical Thoughts on Joking Matters* (1999), he tackles the problem of what he calls the "mean joke." His analysis leads him to face the much larger issue of what he calls "the mean world," along with our sad reluctance to recognize that nature and humanity are not always what we would like them to be. Nature and humanity seldom behave the way we feel and think they should behave. Here is how Cohen expresses the discrepancy between what we want and what is:

> Wish that there were no mean jokes. Try remaking the world so that such jokes will have no place, will not arise. But do not deny that they are funny. That denial is a pretense that will help nothing. And it is at least possible, sometimes, that the jokes themselves do help something. Perhaps they help us to bear unbearable affronts like crude racism and stubborn prejudice by letting us laugh while we take a breather.

These jokes—in fact, all jokes—help us articulate our concerns as human beings. They have value as the valve that helps us let off steam. From another point of view, they require us to admit the existence of conditions and behaviours that make us feel uneasy. And all this (as far as jokes are concerned) is to the good. They reconcile us to our lives and to our fates. They add to the advancement of learning as well as to the gaiety of nations.

On a personal note, I have been collecting Canadian lore, mainly quotations and references but also jokes and anecdotes, since the centennial year of 1967. For decades I told people that one day I would compile a book devoted solely to Canadian jokes. Friends and acquaintances who had heard me make this boast expressed incredulity, their responses being dismissive or sceptical.

Dismissive: Are there any Canadian jokes?
My response: As it happens, that's the first joke in the book.

Sceptical: That will be a short book.
My response: As it happens, that's the last joke in the manuscript. It will appear on page 500 of the book.

So, after thirty-four years of collecting, *The Penguin Book of Canadian Jokes* was duly published in September 2001. (The first radio interview to promote the book was scheduled for September 11; it was hastily cancelled.) To my initial disappointment, the first book fell some pages short of 500. There were only 488 numbered pages in the book. But looking into the matter, I realized that there were, in addition to the numbered text pages, 16 preliminary pages. So with a bit of addition (xvi + 488), the total number of pages came to 504. I had found more instances of popular humour than even *I* had imagined I would find!

In fact, the day the Penguin editors "put the book to bed," as publishers are wont to say after approving the proofs and releasing the text to the printer, I found I had amassed some 65 pages of entirely new jokes. And that was only the beginning. A little birdie told me that this new material would form the nucleus of a new book of Canadian humour—the current collection.

When I met with Michael, the editor of the manuscript that became *The Penguin Book of Canadian Jokes,* an interesting conversation took place in the publisher's boardroom. Michael is a thoughtful person. He introduced me to Debby, the Associate Publicity Director. Debby is outgoing and right away asked, "John Robert, why did you decide to collect and publish a book of Canadian jokes?"

I grimaced and on autopilot replied, "Well, I have been collecting Canadian lore and literature since 1967 and publishing it in books because most of it is being overlooked and forgotten and I wanted to preserve it. Jokes are part of this slighted heritage."

But as I listened to the drone of my own voice, I realized that while what I was saying was perfectly true, it was not really the kind of answer that would excite a publicity director. So in mid-sentence I changed course. I stopped justifying my work and turned the tables. I asked Debby a question: "Why is Penguin publishing this book?"

"We want to sell a lot of copies and make a lot of money!" she replied with conviction in her voice and a smile on her face.

"Now that is a positive answer!" I said.

Both of us turned to Michael, who had been quiet, but observant, all the while. He looked around, owlishly, and then said, "We are publishing this book because we want to make Canadians laugh."

"That's it! That is the most positive answer of all!" I said.

Indeed, it is the reason I compiled the first book, and the second. And with the help of readers like you, in the course of time, I hope to compile a third, a fourth, and perhaps even a fifth.

acknowledgments

For assistance I am especially grateful to two friends, Alice Neal, my researcher, and Philip Singer, librarian with the Toronto Public Library System. Thank you, Alice. Thank you, Philip.

I would be remiss if I did not single out for acknowledgment a cluster of contributors who at any hour of the day—or night— might be expected to phone, fax, mail, or e-mail to my attention the latest joke that is making the rounds. Joel Bonn of Quebec's Eastern Townships is proficient in this practice. (He teaches speed-reading; he should instruct in speed-speaking as well!) For a good many jokes, particularly ones from the Maritime provinces, I am in the debt of Ed Butts, journalist, novelist, and jokesmith. Doug Cunningham is a Toronto lawyer who always has a trenchant joke to share. The eminent sociologist Marcello Truzzi has an informed sense of humour and is a magnet for material that he knows will be of interest to me. Cyril Greenland, R. Ritchie Benedict, and Dwight Whalen contributed to the flow of rich anecdotal material. Peter Urs Bender and George Torok do not tell jokes—they are public speakers—but they saved a few for me. Eric McLuhan and Fraser Sutherland supplied numerous amusing musings, as did bibliophiles Ann and David Skene-Melvin. I owe the late F.R. Scott, legal scholar, poet, and royal commissioner, a debt of gratitude for many things, including the gift of a slew of jokes about bilingualism and biculturalism; these stories have yet to grow stale with the passage of the years, despite the fact that they were originally published decades ago as "B&B Stories" in the last issue of *The Tamarack Review*, Winter 1982. Other material came via the internet, where authorship has been eroded to the point of anonymity: the cyberspace equivalent of Anon. and Ibid.

Again I am in the debt of Cynthia Good of Penguin Group (Canada), a publisher whose abilities and enthusiasms are fabled throughout the book trade. Michael Schellenberg very capably arranged for a proposal to be turned into a manuscript. Editor Judy Phillips ably and expeditiously undertook to transform the manuscript into a book.

But, over all, the first and last acknowledgment must be to my wife, Ruth—my first reader, who groaned and giggled her way through the collection.

Readers who would like to forward to me their own Canadian jokes and anecdotes for future use are encouraged to do so: through e-mail at **jrc@inforamp.net**; through the internet at **www.colombo.ca**; or through the post, addressed to me, care of the Editorial Department, Penguin Group (Canada), 10 Alcorn Avenue, Suite 300, Toronto, Ont., M4V 3B2, Canada.

O Canada!
Oh Canada!

The majority of the jokes I have been collecting fit readily into different categories—hockey, politics, weather, and so on. But a minority of jokes seem to fit nowhere, or they fit everywhere. For those jokes I created this chapter.

"O Canada! Oh Canada!" has jokes, anecdotes, and lore that "defy categorization." Nevertheless, they are all-Canadian; they tell us a lot about the national characteristics of the thirty million inhabitants of this land of almost ten million square kilometres. Is it no wonder that we are a modest people and that our wit has been described as diffident?

The Naming of Canada

How was Canada named?

No historian, French or English, credits the following account of how Jacques Cartier named the new land in 1534. But the story persists because of its popular appeal.

Cartier and his crew sailed up the St. Lawrence in their little ships. From the deck of his ship, he surveyed the bleak northern shore of Labrador. He shook his head.

Under his breath, a Portuguese crew member complained, "Aca nada."

Cartier overheard him and took the words to be the name of the new land. It was only later that he realized that the words are Portuguese for "Nothing here."

Naming Canada

Here is the story about how the Dominion of Canada acquired its present name.

When the future Fathers of Confederation met to establish this country, they faced the problem of no one knowing what to call it. Then John A. Macdonald, not yet Sir John A., had a great idea.

"Let's drop all the letters of the alphabet into a hat and draw three of them. The first three letters will form the new name of the new country."

So they did so.

The first letter was pulled and one of the future Fathers shouts, "C, eh?"

The second letter was pulled and one of the future Fathers shouts, "N, eh?"

Then the third and last letter was pulled and the third future Father shouts, "D, eh?"

And that is how "Canada" was named.

New Element

Q. What is the name of the new element in the Canadian Periodical Table?

A. Canadium Eh. It is similar to Americium but a little denser. Much more rigid. Often called Boron.

Pink on the Map

Q. Why is Canada always pink on the map?
A. From embarrassment.

Geography Lesson

Q. Why does the world need Canada?
A. If Canada didn't exist, the Chinese could sail right across the Pacific and invade Denmark.

Quickies

Q. What's a WASP's idea of open-mindedness?
A. Dating a Canadian.

Q. What do they call a witty man in Canada?
A. A tourist.

Ten Favourite Canadian Whines

These are from Peter Urs Bender and George Torok, authors of Secrets of Power Marketing.

1. Complaining about the Americans.
2. Complaining about the U.S. dollar exchange rate.
3. Complaining about the demise of the "Avro Arrow."
4. Complaining about the government and the "idiots" who voted them in.
5. Complaining about the Canadian Football League (CFL).

6. Complaining about Canadian senators—the politicians, not the hockey team.

7. Complaining about customer service, or lack thereof.

8. Complaining about their neighbour.

9. Complaining that there is nothing on TV anymore (while they click away).

10. Complaining about the weather.

National Emblems

Canada's national symbol, I have often thought, should not be the beaver, but the carp.

—Mavor Moore, theatre personality,
Reinventing Myself: Memoirs (1994).

What Is It?

Q. What is made in Canada, rolls over, and makes old faces new?
A. A Canadian coin.

Capital

Q. What is the capital of Canada?
A. About $18.67.

Income Tax

If you ask the Canada Customs and Revenue Agency, this country is a land of untold wealth and untapped treasure.

Some "Cross" Jokes

He crossed a beaver with a dog and got a beaver retriever.

He crossed a maple with a leaf and got an excuse for a hockey team.

He crossed a maple with a syrup and got a sap.

He crossed a road with a chicken and got the answer we have all been looking for.

One-liners

Stop me if you've heard this one . . .

Did you hear the one about the Newfie Nobel laureate?

Did you hear the one about the Canadian peacekeepers who were summoned to bring peace to the caucus of the Canadian Alliance?

Did you hear the one about the rainmaker who moved to Vancouver to find a job but found, instead, that nobody there would hire him?

Did you hear the one about the referendum on Canadian sovereignty?

Did you hear the one about the graduate of Wawa U.?

Did you hear the one about good government in Canada?

Some Cool Things about Canada

From the internet, March 2001

1. Lacrosse.
2. Hockey.
3. Basketball.
4. The biggest flags ever seen at the Olympic closing ceremonies were Canadian (twice—the second one was smuggled in against a rule that was passed because of the first one).
5. Beer commercials.
6. MuchMusic.
7. Tim Hortons.
8. During the War of 1812 we burned the White House and most of the city of Washington.
9. Canada has the largest French population in the world that never surrendered to Germany.
10. Our "civil war" was led by a drunken, insane William Lyon Mackenzie.
11. Our "civil war" was a bar fight that lasted a little under one hour.
12. The only person arrested and hanged after our "civil war" was an American mercenary who slept in and missed the whole fight, showing up just in time to get caught.
13. The Hudson's Bay Company once owned one-eleventh of the earth's surface.
14. The average dogsled team can kill and devour a grown human in less than three minutes.
15. We wear socks with our sandals.
16. We know what holds the country together—medicare.

Prepositions

Q. How do Canadians avoid ending their sentences with prepositions?

A. They say things like this: "Where do you come from, eh?"

International Convention

A Canadian at an international convention found himself sitting next to an American who spoke with a Southern accent.

"Where are you from?" the Canadian asked.

"Why, son," the man said loudly, "I'm from the greatest country on earth."

"Oh? That's funny—you don't sound Canadian."

Border Story

An American friend of a friend of a friend writes as follows . . .

Shortly after arriving at the University of Washington, I joined some new friends on a trip to nearby Vancouver, British Columbia. It was my first trip outside the United States.

At the border, a guard asked how long we would stay in Canada. Knowing it would be after midnight when we returned, I asked, "How late will we be able to get back across the border?"

"Any time, ma'am," the guard replied. "We never close Canada."

High and
Low Society

Jokes and anecdotes about Canadian society appear in this chapter. "High and Low Society" embraces what the media now call "the Canadian way" (to distinguish it, no doubt, from Superman's "American way"), so this chapter includes funny material on ethnicity, multiculturalism, bilingualism, medicare, national occupations and preoccupations, and conceptions and preconceptions of "what it means to be a Canadian."

In many ways this chapter is the heart and core not only of this collection but also of the Dominion of Canada. (Yes, Canada remains a dominion. It always has been a dominion and it will always be a dominion, not being a republic, a people's republic, or an out-and-out monarchy.)

The poet Irving Layton had a one-sentence definition of a Canadian: "A Canadian is someone who asks himself what it means to be a Canadian."

Preston Manning, now that he is retired from politics, convulsed an ideaCity conference in Toronto in June 2002 with the wisecrack: "Canada is the only country founded on the relentless pursuit of the rodent."

New Canadians

An Italian couple immigrated to Canada. After three years they successfully applied for citizenship.

Proudly holding the papers, the husband said, "Maria, we're Canadians now."

She shoved an apron at him and said, "Good. Now you do the dishes."

Qs & As

Q. What does a Canadian say when you step on his foot?
A. Sorry.

Q. What do you call a Canadian fireman?
A. A hoser.

Q. What's another name for a Canadian Mountie?
A. Canadian bacon.

Q. Why does hockey only have three periods?
A. Canadians can't count to four.

Q. How do you empty a swimming pool of Canadians?
A. "Excuse me, could everyone please get out of the pool?"

Q. Why did the Newfie want Quebec to separate?
A. He wanted to be closer to Ontario.

Q. Why did the Canadian cross the road?
A. He saw some American do it on TV.

Q. Why did the Canadian cross the road?
A. Because the sign said "Walk."

Q. Why did the Canadian chicken say "Meow!"?
A. Because it was learning to speak French.

Letter of Complaint

According to the Correctional Update *bulletin from the Ontario Ministry of Correctional Services, after a ministry official opened a letter addressed to Mr. Hamilton Jail from the marketing manager of American Express, this reply was sent:*

Dear American Express:

Thank you for your recent letter offering me the opportunity to apply for an American Express Card. You say it is designed for a person who travels and entertains extensively.

To tell the truth, I don't get around much and, now that I'm 103 years old, I'm not in very good shape. In fact, I can see the writing on the wall. Although I've entertained more than you probably realize through the years, those days are coming to a close.

Perhaps my young successor, Hamilton-Wentworth Detention Centre, might be more interested in your offer.

Yours truly,
(Mr.) Hamilton Jail

The source of this item is Zena Cherry's column, The Globe and Mail, *July 22, 1978.*

Santa on Trial

You are accused, Mr. Santa Claus, alias Saint Nick, alias Kris Kringle, age unknown, of no fixed abode, with the following charges:

Failing to apply for landed immigrant status when entering Canada and taking up residence at or near the North Pole;

Crossing the Canada–United States border illegally on December 25 of each year as far back as records go;

Failing to operate a union toy shop, denying your elves and dwarfs the minimum wage, ignoring the provisions for paid vacations and wages at time-and-a-half for workweeks of more than forty hours each, and disregarding the requirement to meet the standards of the Workers' Compensation Boards; and

Failing to transmit unemployment insurance payments, income tax deductions, and Canada Pension payments to the proper authorities on behalf of your employees.

You are accused of the illegal entry of millions of Canadian homes on December 25 of each year;

Violating the Federal Anti-Combines Investigation Act by operating a tight monopoly;

Failing to file a flight plan for your travels;

Failing to equip your vehicle with seatbelts or properly fitting your reindeer with emission-control devices;

Failing to declare as taxable income the cookies and milk left for you by millions of families each year;

Illegally competing with the Canadian Post Office, and possible violation of drug laws by administering an unauthorized substance to Rudolph the Reindeer to make his nose light up; and, finally,

Parking in no-parking zones, namely rooftops, and operating a vehicle without either a driver's or a pilot's licence, there being no record of said permit ever being issued in the name of a Mr. Claus in any of the country's provinces or territories;

Faced with all these accusations, and understanding their severity, have you any statement to make . . . before I wish you a . . . Merry Christmas and a Happy New Year—and dismiss these charges?

The Canada Council of Commonwealth Relations

December 1976

Dear _____,

As part of our programme for fostering great world understanding, the Council has selected your family as a participating household on our new Lend a Helping Hand Plan.

You will be pleased, we are sure, to know that we have assigned a typical family group from Pakistan to be guests in your home for the next few months.

These people have suffered a tremendous social upheaval and it will take some time for them to adapt to our way of life. We are sure you will do everything possible to help them make the transition as pleasant as possible, even if it means some minor re-organization in your home and in your personal habits.

The family will consist of the father, mother, nine children, wife's brother, husband's grandmother and her sister, four goats, one sheep, and bullock. We have been informed that you have suitable rough pasture for the animals, and could erect temporary quarters for them adjoining the house.

Within the next seven days we shall be able to inform you of the arrival date, routing, and names of your selected family... we shall include some recipes for Pakistani dishes (they love rice). No doubt you will wish to meet them at the airport—we suggest you rent a truck.

While this may seem like only a small gesture, we are convinced that it is only by such brotherhood that the world will become one big happy family. Bless you.

Yours in friendship,
Canada Council for Commonwealth Relations

J. Bull
BS/uy

This letter, with its distinctive letterhead, outlines a government program whereby Pakistani families are to be billeted in Canadian homes. "In so doing it satirizes Canadian immigration policy, particularly in the 1970s when the Liberal government under Prime Minister Trudeau encouraged what was called by some the 'open door' policy," *explains Jennifer J. Connor of the University of Western Ontario in a study titled* Parodies of Administrative Communications: Some Canadian Examples.

"The letter preys on WASP (white Anglo-Saxon Protestant) fears of loss of control through loss of dominance in Canada. Note the references to the extended family arriving from Pakistan, and the signature 'J. Bull' (John Bull, the Englishman) . . . Clues to the letter's humorous intent—for Anglo-Saxon readers   lie in the initials 'BS/uy'; it takes little imagination for the alert reader to determine what they stand for."

Odd Joke

A blond, a brunette, and a redhead . . . a vicar, a priest, and a rabbi . . . two giraffes and a duck . . . a farmer, a lawyer, and an accountant . . . a Newfie, a French Canadian, and an Ontarian . . . a homosexual and two lesbians . . . an Englishman, an American, and a Canadian . . . all of these people walk into a bar.

The bartender looks up and says, "Hey, what kind of joke is this?"

How the Lord Came to Noah
in Canada in the 2000s

It is the old story.

The earth is wicked, Noah is ordered to build the Ark and save two of every living thing, along with a few good humans.

"Here's the blueprint," said the Lord, handing Noah a long and detailed list of specifications. "But hurry up! In six months, I start the rains."

Six months later, the rains came down.

The Lord looked down upon the earth and saw Noah weeping in his yard. There was no Ark.

"Noah," the Lord roared, "where is my Ark?"

"Forgive me, Lord," begged Noah, but things have changed. I needed a building permit.

"I've been arguing with the inspector about the need for a sprinkler system.

"My neighbours claim I have violated the neighbourhood zoning law by building the Ark in my own backyard.

"We had to go to the Developmental Appeal Board for a decision on the matter.

"Getting wood was another problem. There's a ban on cutting trees to save the spotted owl. I tried to convince the environmentalists I needed the wood to save the owls. No go. I gathered the animals, but got sued by an animal rights group. They insisted I take more than two of each kind.

"Environment Canada decided I could not build the Ark without filing an Environmental Impact Statement on your proposed flood.

"I'm still trying to resolve a complaint with the Human Rights Commission on how many minorities I'm supposed to hire for my building crew.

"The Canada Customs and Revenue Agency has seized my assets, claiming I'm trying to leave the country illegally.

"So, forgive me, Lord, but it would take about five years to finish this Ark of yours."

The skies cleared, the sun began to shine, and a rainbow arched across the sky. Noah looked up in wonder. "You mean you're not going to destroy the world?" he asked the Lord.

"No," replied the Lord. "The government already has!"

Metrification

Canada went officially metric in the year 1971.

Coincidentally, the system was introduced at about the same time as the diet drink called Metrical appeared on the market.

It is largely a numbers game.

The Metric Commission wanted every Canadian to think in the new metric system rather than in the old imperial system. But it was easier to say than to do.

One official was quoted as declaring, "From now on, I want members of the public to think millimetres, talk millimetres, and dream millimetres—every inch of the way."

Managed Health Care

Canada is moving toward private hospitals.

Before being admitted to a private hospital, a prospective patient receives immediate attention not from an orderly or a nurse but from a specialist.

It is the specialist's responsibility to determine what sort of illness the prospective patient can afford.

Medical Services

The Ontario Minister of Health is opening a brand-new medical facility in Hamilton, Ont. Here is what he has to say on that occasion:

"Since the people of Ontario elected the Conservative government, the province has made tremendous advances in the delivery of medical health services.

"Because of the unstinting work of the Ministry of Health and the selfless dedication of the Ontario College of Physicians and Surgeons, we now have well-funded hospitals with the most sophisticated equipment that money can buy. No other jurisdiction in the world can match the extent and level of services currently being offered in the province of Ontario. This is an enviable achievement of which we Conservatives are particularly proud.

"Now, ladies and gentlemen, I do not wish to prolong my talk. In fact, I am unable to do so, for, as you know, I've been plagued with a serious spinal cord problem. I will be leaving for Buffalo shortly for surgical treatment."

Black Box

The Canadian Transportation Safety Board recently acknowledged that for the past five years, the Board had secretly funded a study with Ford of Canada.

The Ontario-based automaker installed tiny "black boxes" in all of its four-wheel-drive pick-up trucks in an effort to determine the cause of fatalities in accidents. The results were broken down by province.

The Safety Board learned that in all provinces but one, the last words of the drivers, in 61.2 percent of fatal crashes, were the following: "Oh, shit!"

Only in the province of Alberta were the last words of the drivers different. There the final words, 89.3 percent of the time, were: "Hold my beer and watch this!"

Bilingualism

"I'll tell you what bilingualism is," the speaker says. The audience listens carefully.

"When I speak to you in English, the French-speaking members of the audience will understand not a single a word of what I say.

"When I speak to you in French, the English-speaking members of the audience will understand not a single word of what I say.

"For this reason, I have to say everything twice, once in English and once in French. That's bilingualism."

Press Freedom

Press freedom became an issue following the acquisition of the Southam newspaper chain by CanWest Global Communications, the media conglomerate owned and operated by the Asper family of Winnipeg.

CanWest began to dictate editorial policy. Press freedom came to a head when Leonard Asper fired Russell Mills, publisher of the *Ottawa Citizen*, for writing and publishing an editorial critical of Prime Minister Jean Chrétien without first consulting the paper's owners.

Newspaper columnists took notice, some of them even suggesting that the federal government should intervene.

"There's an easy solution!" wrote columnist Orland French in *The Globe and Mail*, June 18, 2002. "Take two Aspers and call Winnipeg in the morning."

The Economy

According to all the reports and studies released by the C.D. Howe Institute, Canada is closer to receivership than to leadership.

Bad Manners

"Bad manners."

Noun. What Americans call eccentricity, and Canadians call rudeness.

Politeness

You'll know a Canadian when you meet one. We all say "thank you" to our bank machines and "good night" to our TV news anchors.

Jokes

Canadians are the only people who tell Canadian jokes.

Canadian, American

"You do know what a Canadian is, don't you?"

"A Canadian is an unarmed American with a health plan."

Canadian Survivor Contestants

Canadian Survivor Contestants wanted!

CBC Television is developing a version for viewers in Alberta of the popular U.S. television show *Survivor*. The rules are very simple and straightforward.

Each contestant must travel from Edmonton to Fort McMurray through High Level, Grand Prairie, Peace River, Hinton, Edson, Jasper, Banff, Red Deer, Calgary, Lethbridge, Medicine Hat, Brooks, Drumheller, Lloydminster, and back to Edmonton again while driving a Volvo with a bumper sticker that reads:

"I voted for Chrétien, I'm gay, and I'm here to take your guns away from you."

Continentalism

Two bureaucrats in Ottawa are discussing the latest continental trade agreement between Canada and the United States.

"It's really quite equitable," says the first bureaucrat, Jean-Pierre.

"Yes, I know," says the second bureaucrat, Pierre-Jean. "We give them our water and in exchange they take our oil and natural gas."

Hell

So cold is it in the Great White North that when a Canadian thinks about Hell, he wonders what the heating bill must be.

Psychiatric Hotline

This piece of photocopy lore was in circulation at the Clarke Institute of Psychiatry, Toronto, August 2002.

Hello. *Bonjour.* Welcome to the Psychiatric Hotline.

If you are obsessive-compulsive, please press 1 repeatedly.

If you are co-dependent, please ask someone to press 2.

If you have multiple personalities, please press 3, 4, 5, and 6.

If you are paranoid-delusional, we know who you are and what you want. Just stay on the line so we can trace the call.

If you are schizophrenic, listen carefully and a little voice will tell you which number to press.

If you are manic-depressive, it doesn't matter which number you press. No one will answer.

If you are anxious, just start pressing numbers at random.

If you are phobic, don't press anything.

If you are anal-retentive, please hold.

Goodbye. *Au revoir.*

I Am Thankful

I am thankful to Ann and David Skene-Melvin for sending to me via e-mail the following homily on life's blessings, Valentine's Day, February 14, 2002.

I am thankful for my wife, who says, "It's hot dogs tonight," because she is home with me, not with someone else.

For the teenager who is complaining about doing dishes, because that means she is at home, not on the streets.

For the taxes that I pay, because it means that I am employed.

For the mess to clean after a party, because it means that I have been surrounded by friends.

For the clothes that fit a little too snug, because it means I have enough to eat.

For my shadow that watches me work, because it means I am out in the sunshine.

For a lawn that needs mowing, windows that need cleaning, and gutters that need fixing, because it means I have a home.

For all the complaining I hear about the government, because it means that we have freedom of speech.

For the parking spot I find at the far end of the parking lot, because it means I am capable of walking and that I have been blessed with transportation.

For my huge heating bill, because it means I am warm.

For the lady behind me in church who sings off key, because it means that I can hear.

For the pile of laundry and ironing, because it means I have clothes to wear.

For weariness and aching muscles at the end of the day, because it means I have been capable of working hard.

For the alarm that goes off in the early morning hours, because it means that I am alive.

And finally . . . for too much e-mail, because it means I have friends who are thinking of me.

Send this to someone you care about . . .
(I just did.)

3
Ordinary People,
Celebrated People

This chapter is devoted to the experiences of ordinary people as well as to the exploits of famous or celebrated people.

As everyone knows by now, Canada is a mix of peoples from around the world. We like to see ourselves as forming a mosaic of cultures, rather than a melting pot of peoples (as in the United States). In point of fact, since the 1980s, the "mosaic" has been turning into a collage of cultures, with more "unassimilable elements" and "unmeltable ethnics" than ever before.

Canada is changing . . . and these jokes and anecdotes are witnesses to that change.

Quickies

Q. What name would you give the typical Canadian?
A. Jean-Luigi McGregorchuck.

Q. What do you call a gentle Assyrian from Manitoba?
A. Urgentle Man.

Q. How can you spot the West Vancouver matron at the funeral?

A. She's the one in the jogging suit.

Q. What do you get if Anna Maria Alberghetti married Lorne Green and then Clark Gable?

A. The all-Canadian girl, Anna Green Gable.

Alexander Graham Bell

Alexander Graham Bell invented the telephone. At Baddeck, Cape Breton Island, he also pioneered heavier-than-air flight.

A reporter once asked him, "Can you telephone from an aeroplane?"

"Certainly," he answered. "Anyone can tell a phone from an aeroplane."

Royal Ball

It is said that Prince George, later King George V (1910–1936), and his brother Albert, Duke of Clarence, paid a visit to Canada. It is further said that in Quebec City, they attended the ball that was held in their honour.

Prince George grew annoyed when he saw his younger brother devoting all his time to dancing with the pretty young ladies, rather than attending to his ducal duties. Prince George approached him in private and complained about it.

Albert replied, "That's all right. There are two of us. You go and sing 'God Bless Your Grandmother,' while I dance with the pretty young ladies."

Royal Visit

The mayor of a small town that was overlooked on the schedule for the 1939 royal visit of Their Majesties King George VI and

Queen Elizabeth sent Prime Minister Mackenzie King a personal letter in which he explained that all the members of the community were of British extraction and that each and every one of them strongly supported the monarchy. He concluded with the humble request that the Royal Blue train stop there.

Mackenzie King was so moved by the letter and the plea on behalf of loyal Britishers in the town that he rescheduled the western leg of the trip to arrange a short stopover.

The Royal Blue train with Their Majesties rolled into the small town at 4:30 in the afternoon of a rainy day. On the dot, the King and Queen alighted and stood on the platform, peering into the dense fog. They saw a lantern light in the distance as it approached them. Soon the mayor and his wife came into view in the company of a great many members of their family. When the family members reached the royal couple, they just stood there, staring, as if to assure themselves that the royal visitors were the real McCoy, the King and Queen of Great Britain.

"Your Worship, do you not have a chain of office?" asked King George, puzzled, but also hoping to break the ice.

"Oh, yes," replied the mayor, "but I wear it only on special occasions."

British Empire

During the darkest period of World War II, an American financier visiting London was granted an audience with the King of England.

King George VI was despondent: "London is being bombarded nightly. Rommel may capture Suez. Hong Kong has fallen, India is in ferment, and Japan menaces Australia. What is it I can do?"

The financier pondered the question for a moment and then answered it. "Your Majesty," he suggested, "if I were you, I would put Canada in the Queen's name."

Queen Mom

Queen Elizabeth II told the following story about the late Queen Mother and King George VI during an official speech at her Golden Jubilee celebration at a banquet in Vancouver, October 7, 2002. I have it courtesy of columnist Christie Blatchford of the National Post, who printed it the following day. Queen Elizabeth concluded the story with the remark, "I know exactly how she felt." She received a standing ovation.

I am told of a story about my mother during her visit to Canada in 1939.

My father and mother were scheduled to visit a veterans' hospital in the province of Quebec during their six-week tour. Two Boer War veterans, both of Scots heritage, argued for weeks before my parents' arrival.

One said, "She was born in Scotland, so I say she's Scots."

The other said, "She married an English man, so I say she's English."

They decided to let Queen Elizabeth settle their cultural differences. When the two were presented to Her Majesty, they asked, "Are you Scots, or are you English?"

My mother paused, and then replied, "Since I have landed in Quebec, I think we can say that I am a Canadian."

Sam and Edgar

Peter C. Newman in his book *The Bronfman Dynasty* (1978) records the following exchange. It took place in 1967, the year Edgar Bronfman decided to acquire effective control of the Metro-Goldwyn-Mayer film studio, using his Seagram's stock as leverage. Edgar's father, Sam, was sceptical of the wisdom of such a move.

Sam asked, "Tell me, Edgar, are we buying all this stock in M-G-M just so you can get laid?"

Edgar replied, "Oh, no, Pop. It doesn't cost $40 million just to get laid."

Good Advice

Oswald Avery, the Canadian-born bacteriologist, was one of the founders of immunochemistry and one of the discoverers of the genetic properties of DNA. He worked at the Rockefeller Institute in New York City. Although he made many experimental predictions that proved to be right, he also made many that proved to be wrong.

He used to say, "Whenever you fall, pick up something."

Mathematics

On one occasion, the eccentric, Hungarian-born mathematician Paul Erdös met another mathematician and asked him where he was from.

"Vancouver," the mathematician replied.

"Oh, then you must know my good friend Elliot Mendelson," Erdös said.

The reply was, "I am your good friend Elliot Mendelson."

Jack Kent Cooke

Jack Kent Cooke was a crackerjack salesman. With a prospect, he would never take no for an answer. He trained other salesmen, and he was as hard on them as he was on himself.

Salesman: Mr. Cook, I made some very valuable contacts today.

Cooke: I see. What you are telling me is that you didn't make a single sale.

Lord Beaverbrook

In his day, Canadian-born Maxwell Aitken, Lord Beaverbrook, was the most feared of Britain's "press lords."

He was in the washroom of his favourite London club when he encountered Edward Heath, future prime minister, who was then a young member of Parliament. Beaverbrook recalled that he had printed a nasty editorial about Heath a few days earlier.

"My dear chap," said Beaverbrook. "I've been thinking it over, and I was wrong. Here and now I wish to apologize."

"Very well," replied Heath. "But next time, I wish you would insult me in the washroom and apologize in your newspaper."

The Beaver

Lord Beaverbrook was not a believer. But then again he was not a disbeliever.

Lady Beaverbrook asked him on his deathbed if he wanted the comfort of a confessor.

"No," he said.

"Do you want anyone to be here at this time?"

"Yes," he replied, mischievously. "I want my lawyer and my doctor to be by my side."

"Why?"

"I want to die like Jesus Christ on the Cross with a thief on either side."

The Aged Beaver

The financier and publisher Maxwell Aitken, Lord Beaverbrook, celebrated his seventy-second birthday on May 25, 1915. CBC Radio, to mark the occasion, had its London correspondent interview him.

"You're to be envied, Lord Beaverbrook," the correspondent said, having in mind the man's illustrious career in the worlds of finance, politics, and newspapers.

The Beaver replied, "Nobody at seventy-two is to be envied."

Lord Thomson of Fleet

Roy Thomson, Lord Thomson of Fleet, was an immensely wealthy "press baron" and a notorious skinflint. His title was conferred soon after he became publisher of the *Times of London* in 1963. His son Ken, joint chairman of the Thomson Organization, was invariably known in those days as Young Ken.

One day the company limousine was transporting Roy and Young Ken to their newspaper's headquarters. Young Ken took out a copy of the *Times*, opened it, and began to read.

"Where did you get that copy?" snapped Lord Thomson.

"At the shop around the corner," replied Young Ken.

"Well, Ken," said the father, "you take it right back and let someone else buy it. You can read my copy when I've finished with it."

Thomson the Skinflint

Roy Thomson, the son of a Toronto barber who purchased the *Times of London*, came to great wealth late in life. In many ways he remained boyish or "boily." In 1963 he was created a peer: Lord Thomson of Fleet.

When an elderly dowager in London persisted in referring to him as "Mr. Thomson," he barked at her: "Madam, I've paid enough for this goddamn title, you might have the good grace to use it."

Lord Thomson and Happiness

Lord Thomson and Sir Charles Forte, the British catering magnate and proprietor of the Trust-Forte chain of hotels, were deep in conversation.

"You know, Roy, it's happiness that really counts," Sir Charles said.

"Ah yes, but happiness cannot buy money," replied Lord Thomson.

Buckley and Galbraith

William F. Buckley, the Conservative columnist, phoned John Kenneth Galbraith, the Canadian-born economist, and tried to schedule a meeting during a particular week in June.

"Bad timing, Bill," said Galbraith. "That week I'll be teaching at the University of Moscow."

"Oh? What do you have left to teach them?" inquired Buckley.

Authority

James (the Amazing) Randi, speaking at a meeting of the Committee for the Scientific Investigation of Claims of the Paranormal held in Toronto, November 14, 1987, reminisced about his past. He said that although he was born and raised in Toronto, he did not "grow up" in Toronto.

"I never did grow up," he explained.

Then he recalled his boyhood in Toronto. He said that as a youngster, he had clambered all over the Don Valley. He came upon a rock on which someone had printed two words: "Question Authority!"

To these, he added three words of his own: "Why should I?"

Fortune Teller

David Gower, the noted sceptic who helps host the annual Psychic UnFair in Toronto, visited a fortune teller.

"You will be poor and unhappy until you are fifty," predicted the fortune teller, after consulting her crystal ball, her tarot pack, David's cranium, and then the palm of his left hand.

"And then?" asked the bemused David.

"Then you'll get used to it," snapped the fortune teller.

Bribery

In a private club, a man dressed in a dark suit approaches the businessman Karlheinz Schreiber and on the sly hands him a thick envelope stuffed with hundred dollar bills.

"Thanks," says Karlheinz.

"Don't mention it," says the man as he leaves.

Tom Swifties

"I wanted the balance sheet of the *National Post* to be in the black," said Conrad blackly.

"I wanted the *National Post* to be read, not to be in the red," said Conrad blackly.

"You should read Tom Swifties swiftly," said Tom quickly.

Conversation

Two Cape Bretoners, McTavish and Macdonald, who had not seen each other for several years, happened to meet in a bar.

McTavish: I got married since I last saw you.

Macdonald: Oh? That's good.

McTavish: No, not so good. She was a shrew.

Macdonald: Oh, that's bad.

McTavish: No, not so bad. She was rich.

Macdonald: Oh? That's good.

McTavish: No, not so good. She was tight with money.

Macdonald: Oh, that's bad.

McTavish: No, not so bad. She built us a house with it.

Macdonald: Oh? That's good.

McTavish: No, not so good. The house burned down.

Macdonald: Oh, that's bad.

McTavish: No, not so bad. She was in it.

The Ukrainian and the Tractor

A Ukrainian farmer is charged, no doubt unjustly, with theft. He goes to Vegreville to see a lawyer.

"Do you have enough money to cover my retainer?" asks the lawyer.

"Sir, I am a poor Ukrainian, not long in this country. All I have is my reputation and a tractor," replies the farmer.

"I don't know about your reputation, but if you have a tractor, you can't be very poor. I believe that you can raise enough money to cover my retainer," says the lawyer. "By the way, what were you accused of stealing?"

"Sir, the tractor."

Pool Manners

A guest registered at a fancy hotel in Calgary is enjoying the use of the swimming pool when the manager appears and tells him quite bluntly to get out of the pool.

When the guest asks the reason, the manager says, "Because you peed in the pool."

Well," replies the guest, "lots of people do that."

"True," answers the manager, "but not from the diving board."

Two Old Ladies

Two old ladies live alone in an old house. Their names are Mary and Martha and they are growing forgetful.

Mary says, "Martha, I'm tired. I'm going up to sleep."

Mary climbs up the stairs and crawls into bed. No sooner is she in bed than she yells downstairs, "Martha, I'm confused. Am I going to sleep or am I waking up?"

Martha yells back, "You're going to sleep."

Half an hour later, Martha decides that she should go to bed. So she begins to climb up the stairs. But so tired is she that she has to stop at the landing. She becomes confused and yells out, "Mary, wake up! Am I going up the stairs or down the stairs?"

Mary wakes up and yells back, "You're going up the stairs."

Martha sits on the landing for a few minutes. "I'm a little confused," she says to herself. "But I'm not as confused as poor Mary. I'm going to knock on wood so that I'll never be as confused as Mary."

So she knocks three times on the wooden floor of the landing.

Mary hears the noise and asks, "What's that knocking?"

Martha says, "I don't know. I wonder if somebody's at the front door or the back door."

Two Ladies

Two elderly ladies who had been friends since childhood were playing cards one afternoon on the porch of their nursing home.

One of the old girls suddenly said to the other, "Oh dear, I don't know how to say this to you, but, even though we've been friends for almost eighty years, I find that I can't remember your name. This is terribly embarrassing, and I do hope you aren't offended, but could you please tell me your name."

The other old girl's eyes widened and her mouth opened wide in shock. She glared at her companion, and then said, "How soon do you need to know?"

Locked Out

A man and his wife found themselves locked out of their car. The man said it was no problem, as he could jimmy the door open with a wire coat hanger. He went into the mall where they had been shopping and, after asking at several stores, he finally got a wire coat hanger. He took it out to the car and in a matter of minutes had the car door open. Before getting into the car, he bent down and slid the hanger under the driver's seat, telling his wife he was putting it there just in case they locked themselves out of the car again.

Stuttering Sailor

There was a sailor who had a bad problem with stuttering. He could barely put two words together. The only way he could make himself understood was to sing what he wanted to say. It seemed that whenever he sang, the stutter disappeared.

One day he ran up to the captain, obviously distraught about something. He stuttered: "Th-th-th-th muh-muh-muh . . ."

The captain couldn't understand a thing the sailor was saying. "Settle down," the skipper said, "Take your time. Take a breath, and sing what you want to tell me."

So the sailor took a deep breath and began to sing:

Let old acquaintance be forgot
That ever come to mind;
The second mate fell overboard,
He's half a mile behind.

Irish and Scots

Q. What's the difference between an Irishman from Newfoundland and a Scotsman from Nova Scotia?
A. The Scot can swim.

Bank Robbers

It seems there was this pair of would-be Prairie bank robbers named Tom and Lee.

Now, all they knew about robbing banks they had learned from the movies. So the first thing they decided they needed was guns.

"But I don't want to carry a gun," objected Lee. "I don't like 'em, don't know how to use 'em, and I wouldn't be able to shoot anyone anyhow."

"No, you have to have a gun," Tom told him. "If you don't have a gun, they don't take you seriously."

Lee continued to object, but finally they agreed on a compromise. Tom would carry a real gun, in case they actually had to shoot somebody, and Lee would carry a blank pistol, purely for effect.

Now, as everyone knows, handguns are fairly hard to come by in Canada, especially compared with the United States. Tom managed to cross the border and purchase a pistol in an American pawn shop, but he knew that he would only be able to pull that trick once and that Lee couldn't do it at all, since he had a criminal record (though not a very distinguished one) in the United States. So they decided that they would break into a local theatre that was staging a production of *The Wild Dogs* and steal a stunt gun from the props room.

That done, they prepared to make the heist. The day of the robbery, as you might expect, nothing went right. It was raining, the getaway car had engine trouble, and unknown to them, while they were planning the robbery, a Royal Canadian Mounted Police detachment had been relocated directly across the street from the branch of the bank that they had chosen to knock off.

Now, any bank robber with half a brain in his head would have decided to quit and grow prize tomatoes at this point. But these two decided to carry through, since they'd gone to the trouble of memorizing the floor plans for the bank building.

So they broke in, in broad daylight, and it seemed that everything was going to work after all, until they tried to leave the building with their sacks of cash. At some point they must have triggered a silent alarm, because as they tried to make their getaway, they tried to open the front doors but they found that they were locked.

Mounties were pouring out of the detachment across the street, taking up positions on the street, and advancing on the bank.

Tom and Lee quickly dove behind a desk, and Tom popped his head up just long enough to shout, "Eat lead, coppers!" It was just like in the movies. He fired wildly at the plate-glass window that separated him from the street outside, then ducked back down.

A minute later, he poked his head up to survey the damage, only to find the window still intact. Realizing that somewhere along the line their guns must have gotten switched, he ducked back down behind the desk and announced disgustedly, "Dud! Lee, do right—off the Mounted Patrol!"

Medium

A woman goes to a medium hoping to contact her dearly departed Ukrainian grandmother. The medium assures her that she (the medium) can call up the dead, and then seems to go into a trance.

After a minute she begins to moan, and then says in a creaky voice, "Is that you, granddaughter?"

The woman says, "Grandmother, is it really you?"

"Yes, my dear. It is I. What do you wish to ask me?"

"What I'd like to know, Grandmother, is, when did you learn to speak English?"

Told in New Delhi

The following story is told in New Delhi.

Sardar Tehl Singh, newly arrived in Canada, earned enough money to buy himself a new car. He was driving along the highway when a traffic officer tailed him, signalling for him to slow down and stop.

"Why are you going from one side of the road to the other?" the officer demanded.

"I am learning how to drive," replied Tehl Singh.

"You have to have a driving instructor sitting beside you when you are a learner. May I see your licence?"

Tehl Singh pulled an envelope from the glove compartment of his car. "I have a learner's permit. I am learning how to drive by correspondence."

Shipwrecked

A male engineer from Toronto was on a cruise ship in the Caribbean for the first time. It was wonderful, the experience of his life. He was being waited on hand and foot. But it did not last. A hurricane came up unexpectedly. The ship went down almost instantly.

The man found himself, he knew not how, swept up on the shore of an island. Nothing else was anywhere to be seen. No person, no supplies, nothing. The man looked around. There were some bananas and coconuts, but that was it. He was desperate, and forlorn, but decided to make the best of it. So for the next four months he ate bananas, drank coconut juice, and mostly looked to the sea mightily for a ship to come to his rescue.

One day, as he was lying on the beach stroking his beard and looking for a ship, he spotted, out of the corner of his eye, movement. Could it be true, was it a ship? No . . . from around the corner of the island came a rowboat. In it was the most gorgeous woman he had ever seen, or at least seen in four months. She was tall and tanned, and her blond hair flowing in the sea breeze gave her an almost ethereal quality. She spotted him also as he was waving and yelling and screaming to get her attention. She rowed her boat toward him.

In disbelief, he asked, "Where did you come from? How did you get here?"

She said, "I rowed from the other side of the island. I landed on this island when my cruise ship sank. I'm from Montreal."

"Amazing," he said, "I didn't know anyone else had survived. How many of you are there? Where did you get the rowboat? You must have been really lucky to have a rowboat wash up with you."

"It is only me," she said, "and the rowboat didn't wash up, nothing did."

"Well then," said the man, "how did you get the rowboat?"

"I made the rowboat out of raw material that I found on the island," replied the woman. "The oars were whittled from gum tree branches, I wove the bottom from palm branches, and the sides and stern came from a eucalyptus tree."

"But, but," asked the man, "what about tools and hardware; how did you do that?"

"Oh, no problem," replied the woman. "On the south side of the island there is a very unusual strata of alluvial rock exposed. I found that if I fired it to a certain temperature in my kiln, it melted into forgeable ductile iron. I used that for tools, and used the tools to make the hardware. But, enough of that," she said. "Where do you live?"

At last the man was forced to confess that he had been sleeping on the beach. "Well, let's row over to my place," she said. So they both got into the rowboat and left for her side of the island.

The woman easily rowed them around to a wharf that led to the approach to her place. She tied up the rowboat with a beautifully woven hemp rope.

They walked up a stone walk and around a palm tree. There stood an exquisite bungalow painted in blue and white.

"It's not much," she said, "but I call it home. Sit down, please. Would you like to have a drink?"

"No," said the man, "one more coconut juice and I will puke."

"It won't be coconut juice," the woman replied. "I have a still. How about a piña colada?"

Trying to hide his continued amazement, the man accepted, and they sat down on her couch to talk. After they had exchanged their stories, the woman said, "Tell me, have you always had a beard?"

"No," the man replied, "I was clean shaven all my life, and even on the cruise ship."

"Well, if you would like to shave, there is a man's razor upstairs in the cabinet in the bathroom."

So, the man, no longer questioning anything, went upstairs to the bathroom. There in the cabinet was a razor made from a bone handle. Two shells honed to a hollow ground edge were fastened to its end inside a swivel mechanism. The man shaved, showered, and went back downstairs.

"You look great," said the woman. "I think I will go up and slip into something more comfortable." So she did.

The man continued to sip his piña colada. After a short time, the woman returned wearing fig leaves strategically positioned and smelling faintly of gardenia.

"Tell me," she said, "we have both been out here for a very long time with no companionship. You know what I mean. Have you been lonely? Is there anything that you really miss? Something that every man and every woman needs? Something that it would be really nice to have right now?"

"Yes, there is," the man replied, as he moved closer to the woman while fixing a winsome gaze upon her. "Tell me . . . do you happen to have an . . . internet connection?"

Italian Conversation

At the corner of Bloor and Lansdowne, in Toronto, the bus stops and two Italian men get on. They seat themselves and engage in animated conversation.

The Anglo-Saxon lady sitting behind them ignores them at first, but her attention is galvanized when she hears one of the men say, "Emma come first. Denna I come. Two asses, they come together. I come again. Two asses, they come together again. I come again and pee twice. Then I come once-a-more."

"You have a foul mouth," retorts the lady with great indignation. "In Canada we don't talk about our sex lives in public."

"Hey, calma down, lady," says the man. "Imma just tellun my friend howda to spell Mississippi."

The Silent Treatment

A man and his wife were having some problems at home and giving each other the silent treatment.

Later that week, the man realized that he would need his wife to wake him at 5:00 a.m. for an early-morning business flight to Toronto. Not wanting to be the first to break the silence (and lose the fight), he wrote on a piece of paper, "Please wake me at 5:00 a.m."

The next morning the man woke up, only to discover it was 9:00 a.m. and that he had missed his flight.

Furious, he was about to go and see why his wife had not awakened him, when he noticed a piece of paper by the bed. The paper said, "It is 5:00 a.m. Wake up."

Lifetime

I met a guy the other day and asked him if he had lived in Canada all his life.

"Not yet," was his answer.

eskimos, inuit, indians, Natives

A few words about nomenclature. It has been customary (since the 1960s) to refer to all Eskimos as Inuit and to one Eskimo as an Inuk. It has been the government's practice (since the 1970s) to refer to all Indians as Native Peoples or as members of First Nations. Yet for the purposes of joke-telling, the old nomenclature persists.

No disrespect is intended because no living "Aboriginal Person" is meant—to employ the cumbersome term adopted by the Royal Commission on Aboriginal Peoples of 1996 co-chaired by René Dussault and Georges Erasmus. Besides, who in his or her right mind would dream of beginning to tell a joke this way: "A Native Person was walking down the street . . ."?

Riddles

Q. What did the Eskimo say when told his ancestors were Mongolian?
A. "I knew it." (Inuit)

Q. What's Eskimo fellatio?
A. Inuk-suck. (Inukshuk, a stone figure)

Q. Why have the Eskimos been ahead in the space race for a long time?
A. Because they have had ICBMs for centuries.

Q. Have you heard the Eskimo national anthem?
A. It's "Freeze a Jolly Good Fellow."

Q. Is it true that Eskimos eat whale meat and blubber?
A. Yes, but then you'd blubber too if you had to eat whale meat.

Q. What do Eskimos get from sitting on blocks of ice?
A. Polaroids.

Q. Why do Eskimo women wash their clothes in Tide?
A. Because it's too cold out-tide.

Q. Why do Eskimos have bad luck?
A. Because they wear mukluks.

Icebergs

Q. What did the mother and father icebergs call their baby daughter?
A. Floe.

Ice Floe

An Eskimo man and an Eskimo woman were trapped on an ice floe.
   They were stuck on it for years, living off fish they caught.
   They had a baby boy.
   The boy grew to young manhood.
   On his eighteenth birthday his mother said, "What would you like for your birthday?"
   The boy replied, "Not another damn icicle!"

Claiming the Land

Jacques Cartier made his celebrated landfall on July 24, 1534, planting the flag of France on the shore of the Gaspé, with the following speech: "I claim this land for François I, King of France."

The ceremony was observed by a band of Iroquois led by their chief Donnacona. The chief was greatly surprised by Cartier's speech because he had not even known that their place was listed on the market.

Indians

Q. How do whites treat Indians?
A. With reserve.

Q. What do you call a family of way-out Indians?
A. All gone kins. (Algonkians)

Q. What's the last word in Prairie Indian?
A. The dernier Cree.

Q. What does an Indian bookie say?
A. "You're on!" (Huron)

Q. Which Middle East country was like the Indian nation?
A. Iraq was. (Iroquois)

Q. How many pharmacies does an Indian need?
A. One IDA. (Oneida, Independent Druggists Association)

Q. How do Indians like their fish?
A. Saltish. (Salish)

Q. What happened to the Indian who drank too much tea?
A. He drowned in his "teapee."

Q. What did the little Indian boy say when he slipped and fell onto fresh asphalt?
A. He said, "Tar-on-toe, Tar-on-toe!"

Q. Where do Indians shop?
A. Tsimshians. (Simpsons)

Q. What does an Indian lawyer do?
A. Sioux. (sue)

Fate of the Missionary

In the early days of the opening of the Western Prairies, a mission-ary angers the chief of the Blackfoot people. The chief summons his warriors, who surround him, waving their bows and arrows.

Upon surveying his situation, the missionary says quietly to himself, "I am going to die. I must pray to God."

With that, a magnificent ray of light appears in the heavens, and a mighty voice booms out: "No, you are not going to die. Pick up that rock lying on the ground at your feet and bash in the head of the chief!"

The missionary does as he is told. He picks up the rock and proceeds to bash in the head of the chief. He breathes heavily, all the while standing over the chief's lifeless body.

The warriors surround him with a look of shock on their faces.

The voice booms out again, "Okay... *now* you are going to die!"

Devil and Chief

The Devil was trying to cheat an old Indian chief of his soul. He told the Indian that he was going to test his memory, and if the old man failed, he would lose his soul. He asked the chief, "Do you like eggs?"

The chief said he did. The Devil went away.

Twenty years later, the old chief was dying, and the Devil figured he could collect. He went to the chief's bedside and extended his hand in what he supposed was the standard Indian salutation and said, "How!"

Without a moment's hesitation the old chief said, "Fried."

Heap Big Medicine

A Blackfoot chief was feeling very sick. Being a traditional chief, he summoned the band's medicine man. After a brief examination, the medicine man took out a thin strip of elk hide and gave it to the chief.

"Chief," he said, "every day I want you to bite off a piece of leather, a thumbnail-sized piece. Chew it and then swallow it. I'll visit you again in a week to see how you are feeling."

A week later, the medicine man returned to see the chief. "How are you?" he asked.

The chief shrugged and explained, "The thong is ended, but the malady lingers on."

Canadian Wisdom Chant

I would like to share an old Native Canadian chant. Each year during the first week of April, the Native Canadians would wake up at sunrise and repeat their chant over and over. They say this powerful chant primarily for three important reasons:

1. To ensure that their crops are bountiful and will keep them and their families fed all year;
2. To ward off harm and evil;
3. To gain great wisdom.

It goes like this:

Oooooh waaaaah (pause)
Taaaaa foooooo (pause)
Lie aaaammmm (pause)

Now repeat it without the pause. As you repeat it more often and more quickly, its message becomes clear and you will become wise.

Try it. It works very well and very quickly!

Indian Talk

A fellow meets a Cree Indian.

The fellow says, "How!"

The Cree replies, "How!"

The fellow again says, "How!"

The Cree again replies, "How!" Then he adds, "I didn't know you could speak Indian."

"It's easy," the fellow says, "when you know how."

Shaman's Reply

An anthropologist who was studying Native ways in Alberta in the 1940s asked the local shaman how he would act if he wanted to contact Mikinak, the spirit of the Great Turtle, whose voice was once heard throughout the land.

"I would address my question to an empty tent," the shaman replied. He was alluding to the performance of the traditional rite of the Shaking Tent, the oracle of the Indians.

"Why would you do that?" asked the anthropologist.

"Because I am poor. If I were wealthy like the anthropologists who visit us, I would have a telephone."

Indian Leader

An Indian leader came to Ottawa to plead his band's cause. The band members wanted the right to handle their own affairs.

The head of the Department of Northern Affairs said, "We can't give you those rights. Indians aren't smart enough to take care of their own business."

The Indian leader said, "Are you saying that I don't have much brains?"

The government man said, "I'm talking about the average Indian. You were sent here because you're one of the smartest Indians."

The Indian said, "I'm just an average Indian. We do the same as the rest of the citizens of Canada. We never send our smartest people to Ottawa."

Apollo Project

When NASA was preparing for the Apollo project that would take man to the moon, some of the training of the astronauts took place outside Sudbury, Ont., not far from an Ojibwa reserve.

One day, an Ojibwa elder and his son were out hunting when they came across the space crew. The old man, who spoke only the Algonkian language, asked the astronauts a question that his son translated.

"What are these guys in those big suits doing?"

A member of the crew said they were practising for their trip to the moon.

The elder got all excited and asked if he could send a message to the moon with the astronauts.

Recognizing a promotional opportunity, the NASA representatives found a tape recorder and recorded the elder's message. Then they asked his son to translate it. He refused.

The NASA representatives brought the tape recording to the reserve, where the rest of the tribe listened and laughed, but they refused to translate the message the elder had delivered to be taken to the moon.

Finally, the NASA representatives called in an official government translator. His translation of the old man's message went like this: "Watch out for these guys; they have come to steal your land."

5
Why We teLL
Newfie jokes

To answer the question asked in the title of this chapter, we tell Newfie jokes because they are there.

"They" refers to the jokes, not to the Newfies. There is no Newfie any more than there is a Santa Claus or a tooth fairy. There are Newfoundlanders and Labradorians, but these fine people (there are some 555,000 of them) have nothing in common with Newfies. What we call "Newfies" are fictitious beings, stupnagels. (By the same token, there are no Mainlanders either. The clueless Mainlander is the object of some choice Newfie humour.)

Every country has a group of people who become the butt of their jokes and jibes. In the United States, it is the Okies and Val gals—people from the Ozarks or San Fernando Valley girls. The English tell their stories against the Scots and the Irish, whereas in Scotland and Ireland, they joke about the English. The French ridicule the Belgians, the Belgians the people of Flanders. Germans enjoy downgrading Prussians, and so on. (Sometimes I think ethnic jokes are the people's way of being international-minded. It is the people's United Nations.)

In tiny Bulgaria, I found the butt of Balkan storytelling to be the poor benighted folk who live in the picturesque town of Gabrovo in the interior of that country. The Gabrovitsi have taken their revenge on their fellow countrymen by erecting a House of Humour, the world's first, with a lecture hall, an art gallery, a library, and a publishing wing. It is like the Stephen Leacock Memorial Home in Orillia, Ont., combined with Montreal's Just for Laughs festival. Its motto is "The world survives because it laughs."

Folklorists who collect the lore of the people know such humour as "stupnagel jokes." Stupnagel is a general term for a dull-witted fellow (seldom a woman) who falls for all ruses. Yet on occasion the half-wit will outwit his with-it abusers. In East European countries he has a name: Sly Peter. He "bests" everyone in sight. The Arab incarnation of the figure is the Mullah Nasruddin, whose seeming simplicity is a recognition of inarguable complexity: Nothing is what it seems. In our own country, we have the Trickster, the Algonkian character who answers to the name of Nanabozo or Nanabush, whose psychology encapsulates the essential duality and perversity of mankind.

For fun I checked the anagram generator on the internet. I asked it to find for me an anagram for the six letters of the word NEWFIE. I wanted it to add to the longest chapter of this collection.

The anagram generator found: WE FINE.

Newfie Jokes

A Newfie is addressing a Mainlander. "Do you know why Newfie jokes are so simple?"

The Mainlander replies, "No. Why?"

The Newfie answers, "So Mainlanders can understand them."

Ontario Plates

A Newfoundlander and his son ran a roadside restaurant by the Trans-Canada Highway in Newfoundland.

One day the father overheard the son talking to a customer. The father looked outside and saw that the man's car had Ontario plates.

Later he took the son aside and said, "I heard you ask that man where he was from."

"Yes," said the son. "He said he was from Ontario."

"Well," said the father, "you could have seen that from the plates on his car. Son, if a man's not from Newfoundland, there's no need to embarrass him."

Proper Pronunciation

First off, here's the ways not to pronounce Newfoundland:

New-fin-lund
New-Found-Lund
New-fin-Lind.

Now, here's the way you *do* pronounce Newfoundland:

New-FUN-Land.

Newfies in Business

Two Newfies decide to go in business together on a 50-50 basis.

They agree to buy a truck and drive to Prince Edward Island. There they buy potatoes for $3.50 a barrel and drive back to Newfoundland and sell them for $3.50 a barrel.

After one or two trips, the one boy turns to the other boy and says, "B'y, we got to give this up. We're not makin' any money at this."

The other boy explodes, "Yeah, I told ya we shouda bought a bigger truck!"

Flight from St. John's

The control tower of Toronto Pearson International Airport gets an urgent message.

"This is the flight from Newfoundland. Our pilot and co-pilot have both collapsed and are unconscious. This is one of the passengers speaking. What should I do?"

Control tower: Okay. Don't panic. What is your present position?

Passenger: I'm sittin' right up front.

Your Pilot Speaking

On a transatlantic flight aboard a four-engined plane, the following announcement is made.

Pilot: Ladies and gentlemen, this is your pilot speaking. I'm very sorry, but one of our engines has malfunctioned. Nothing to worry about. It just means we'll arrive at our destination an hour late.

Later:

Pilot: Ladies and gentlemen, I'm afraid we've lost another engine. Don't worry; we'll just be landing two hours late.

Later:

Pilot: Sorry, folks, but we've lost our third engine. No cause for panic. We'll be arriving at our destination three hours late.

Newfie on board: Lord t'underin'! I hope that last engine don't quit. We'll be up here all day.

The Flying Newfie

A Newfie businessman goes to the St. John's airport and boards an Air Canada 747 bound for Europe. He is nervous for two reasons. He has never flown before and this is a long flight. The other reason for his nervousness is that he is landing in Paris, he has never before visited a French-speaking country, and he speaks not a word of French. So he is surprised and relieved when the plane takes off smoothly and he hears the soothing words of the flight attendant as she makes the following announcement:

"As a special service to our Paris-bound passengers, we offer a short course in conversational French. If you wish to learn some basic sentences, useful to every business traveller, put on your earphones, switch to Channel 7, and relax. The course in French lasts the six remaining hours of our flight. Feel free to fall asleep. The learning is subliminal. When you wake up, we will be landing. You will find that you have acquired basic French."

The Newfie puts on his earphones but switches by mistake to Channel 8. Before he knows it, he has fallen fast asleep. He sleeps through the entire flight. In the morning, as the plane lands, he wakes up, fully refreshed. He is secretly pleased that he now has the French language under his belt. He deplanes, and in the Charles de Gaulle Airport he faces his first Frenchman—a security officer.

"*Bonjour,*" says the security officer.

"Sssssssss," says the Newfie, recalling and reproducing the sound of six hours of static on Channel 8.

Plane Trip

Two Newfies are on a plane on a flight from Toronto to St. John's. They're sitting in first class, although their tickets are for coach. They begin to get rowdy, and the flight attendant politely asks them to move to their proper seats.

They respond, "No! We were here first, and we paid for our tickets, so these are our seats."

The stewardess starts to get frustrated so she goes to the cockpit and says to the captain, "Those two Newfies won't move to their proper seats."

The captain says, "Don't worry, I'll take care of it."

He leaves the cockpit, then comes back a minute later and says, "They're quiet now."

The stewardess says, "How'd you do that? I didn't hear anything."

The captain replies, "I just told them that that part of the plane wasn't going to Newfoundland."

Newfie Air

A rookie flight crew for Air Newfoundland is making its first approach to Toronto's Pearson International Airport.

"I have the runway in sight, give me quarter flaps," says the pilot.

"Quarter flaps," acknowledges the co-pilot.

"We're coming in pretty fast," says the pilot, "better give me half flaps and reduce power."

"Half flaps," says the co-pilot.

"This is going to be close! Three-quarter flaps!"

"Three-quarter flaps, sir!"

The wheels touch the end of the runway.

"Full flaps! Reverse thrust all engines!"

The plane comes to a screeching halt just before leaving the runway.

The pilot stares horror-struck out the front window. "That is the shortest damn runway I've ever seen in my life!"

The co-pilot looks out the left window and then the right. "Yeah, and the widest too."

The Contest

A Newfie and a Mainlander are sitting next to each other on a long flight from Halifax to Vancouver.

The Mainlander leans over to the Newfie and asks if he would like to play a fun game. The Newfie just wants to take a nap, so he declines and rolls over to the window to catch a few winks.

The Mainlander persists and explains that the game is real easy and a lot of fun. He explains, "I ask you a question, and if you don't know the answer, you pay me $5. Then you ask me a question, and if I don't know the answer, I'll pay you $5."

Again, the Newfie politely declines and tries to get to sleep. The Mainlander, now somewhat agitated, says, "Okay, if you don't know the answer, you pay me $5, and if I don't know the answer, I'll pay you $50!"

This catches the Newfie's attention, and he sees no end to this torment unless he plays, so he agrees to the game.

The Mainlander asks the first question. "What's the distance from the earth to the moon?"

The Newfie doesn't say a word, but reaches into his wallet, pulls out a $5 bill, and hands it to the Mainlander.

Now it's the Newfie's turn. He asks him, "What goes up a hill with three legs, and comes down on four?"

The Mainlander looks up at him with a puzzled look. Not wanting to lose the money, he thinks for a long time about the question while the Newfie goes back to sleep.

After about an hour, he wakes the Newfie and hands him $50. The Newfie politely takes the $50 and turns away to try to get back to sleep.

The Mainlander, more than a little miffed, shakes the Newfie and asks, "Well, so what's the answer?"

Without a word, the Newfie reaches into his wallet, hands the Mainlander $5, and turns away to get back to sleep.

Newfie Two-seater Outhouse

Instead of placing the holes side by side, they are placed one above the other.

Newfie Swing (Standard Model)

The ropes of the swing are secured to two branches, one on either side of the trunk of the tree, so that whoever uses the swing will slam right into the tree.

Newfie Swing
(as Redesigned by a Cape Breton Engineer)

The swing is still suspended from the same branches, but the middle section of the tree trunk has been cut away, so the entire upper part of the tree is held up by wooden supports propped under the branches. Brilliant!

Lost Dog

A Newfie came home and said to his wife, "Our dog is lost."
   The wife said, "We should put a notice in the newspaper."
   "Why?" asked the Newfie. "He can't read."

Newfie Jedi Knight

You might be a Newfie Jedi Knight if . . .

1. You ever heard the phrase, "May the Force be witt ya, b'y."
2. Your Jedi robe is made of seal skin.
3. You have ever used your light sabre to quarter a moose.
4. Both wings of your X-Wing are done over with sheet metal and rivets and are covered with polybond.
5. You have ever eaten bottled Ewok.
6. You have ever used a land-speeder to get away from wildlife officers.
7. The best part of spending time on Dagobah is the great weather.
8. Even C-3PO cannot understand what you are saying.
9. You have used Jedi mind tricks to help you drag off from the Sundance.
10. You have ever used the Force to persuade a Human Resources Canada officer to give you employment insurance cheques.

11. Your father has ever said to you, "Come on b'y, son, come on over 'ere to the dark side, and have a Dominion wit' yer old man."

12. You have ever had your R2-D2 unit use its self-defence electro-shock thingy to scare off mosquitoes on the May 24th weekend.

13. You have ever used the *Millennium Falcon* to smuggle booze and cigarettes from St. Pierre.

14. You have a Newfoundland dog painted on the hood of your land-speeder.

15. You think Andy Wells and Brian Tobin are part of the Dark Side of the Force.

16. You have ever fantasized about Danielle House wearing her hair like Princess Leah.

17. You have a hitch on the back of your land-speeder for hauling your trailer to gravel pits.

18. Chewbacca is the lead of your dogsled team.

19. You suggested that they outfit the *Millennium Falcon* with snowmobile skis.

20. You were the only person drinking Newfie screech during the cantina scene.

21. If you hear, "Luke, I is your father . . . tell me what the hell is your mother getting on with, b'y!"

Newfoundland Computer Lingo

1. Log on: Make the wood stove hotter.

2. Log off: Don't add no more wood.

3. Monitor: Keep an eye on that wood stove.

4. Download: Get the firewood off the truck.

5. Floppy disk: What you get from trying to carry too much firewood.

6. Ram: The thing that splits the firewood.

7. Hard drive: Getting home in the winter.

8. Prompt: "Throw another log on the fire."

9. Window: What to shut when it's cold outside.

10. Screen: What to shut in fly season.

11. Byte: What flies do.

12. Bit: What the flies did.

13. Megabyte: What BIG flies do.

14. Chip: Munchies when monitoring.

15. Micro chip: What's left after you eat the chips.

16. Modem: What you did to the hayfields.

17. Dot matrix: Old Dan Matrix's wife.

18. Lap top: Where kitty sleeps.

19. Software: The dumb plastic knives and forks they give you at the Big R.

20. Hardware: Real stainless steel cutlery.

21. Mouse: What eats the grain in the barn.

22. Mainframe: What holds up the barn.

23. Enter: City talk for "Come on in, b'y."

24. Web: The things spiders makes.

25. Website: The barn or attic.

26. Cursor: Someone who swears a lot.

27. Search engine: What you do when the car dies.

28. Screen saver: A repair kit for the torn window screen.

29. Home page: A map you keep in your back pocket just in case you get lost when picking berries.

30. Upgrade: Driving up Barter's Hill.

31. Server: The Mrs. at Donovan's who brings the jigs' dinner.

32. Mail server: The guy at Big R with Grade 8 who brings fish.

33. MS-DOS: Some new disease they discovered.

34. Sound card: One of them technological birthday cards that plays music.

35. User: Buddy down your street who keeps coming over and borrowing stuff.

36. Browser: What they call you when your eyebrows grow together.

37. Network: When you have to repair your fishing net.

38. Internet: Where the fish get caught.

39. Netscape: When a fish gets away.

40. On-line: When you gets the laundry on the wash-line.

41. Off-line: When the clothespins let go and the laundry falls on the ground.

Screech

A Newfoundlander came out of a liquor store with a bottle of screech.

He didn't want it to be so obvious that he had a bottle, so he wrapped it in a newspaper.

On the bus a fellow passenger asked, "Anything interesting in the paper?"

He nonchalantly replied, "There is now."

Newfie Witch

The Newfie witch sprinkles everyone who visits her with Potion of Screech.

"What good does that do?"

"It will keep you safe from dragons."

"There are no dragons in Newfoundland."

"That's good, because this bottle of Potion of Screech is no damn good, either."

Newfoundland News

Immensely popular on the Great Island from the 1930s to the 1960s was "The Gerald S. Doyle News Bulletin." This radio program has been referred to as "the oldest continuously aired news bulletin in the history of Canada."

Its daily news items were written and delivered by veteran broadcaster Gerald S. Doyle. News was local, even personal, and of direct interest to families in isolated communities. Here are some characteristic "Doyleisms" as noted by Bren Walsh in *The Globe and Mail*, April 17, 1965:

- Here is a message to Sarah Greening at Muscle Cove from her husband James in St. John's: Glasses broken. Cow not giving milk. Lucy passed exams. Salt scarce. No sign of fish. Love.
- The patient is still under the doctor's car.
- Your mother seriously ill, not expected to recover. Don't worry.
- Had eye operation this morning. Hope to see you soon.
- Father and horse arrived by last night's train. Both are well.

Wedding

A Newfie wedding is being held in one of the outports, and the revelry extends into the wee hours of the morning. Host and guest alike down screech like water.

The groom looks around for the bride, but she is nowhere to be seen. The groom's brother has also disappeared. One guest remembers seeing them creep off somewhere. Another guest says they are upstairs, in bed together.

Instead of growing angry, the groom philosophically says, "Ah, me brother's so tipsy with drink he thinks he's I."

The Newfie and the Yankee

The Newfie opens a candy store in St. John's. The first customer to walk in the door is a Yankee.

"I'll take a bag of ju-jubes," says the Yankee.

The Newfie hands the bag over to the Yankee, but instead of paying him, the Yankee says, "Now I want to exchange them for the bag of jelly beans. They're the same price."

So the Newfie takes the bag of ju-jubes from the Yankee and hands him the bag of jelly beans.

With that the Yankee says, "Toodle-oo!" and makes for the door.

"Hey, Yankee!" yells the Newfie. "Pay me the money you owe me!"

"Why do I owe you money?" asks the Yankee.

"For the jelly beans."

"But those jelly beans I took instead of the ju-jubes."

"Okay," says the Newfie, "then pay me for the ju-jubes."

"But," replies the Yankee with a hurt tone, "I already returned the ju-jubes to you. I'm afraid you're very confused."

The Newfie scratches his head as the Yankee walks out the door.

Measuring a Flagpole

Two Newfies were trying to measure a flagpole. Each time one of them tried to climb up with a tape measure, he slid back down.

A third man came along and said, "You know, all you have to do is pull that flagpole out of the ground, lay it down, and then measure it."

One of the Newfies shook his head and said, "No, that's no good, b'y. We wants to find out how tall it is, not how long it is."

Insurance

A Newfie went into the office of an insurance company and said he wanted to collect on his wife, who had just died.

The insurance agent looked at the policy and said that it was not a life insurance policy, but fire insurance.

"Well that's okay," said the Newfie. "I had her cremated."

Newfie and Backpack

A Newfie carrying a heavy backpack was walking along a road.

A farmer driving a loaded wagon stopped and offered him a ride. The Newfie climbed up and took a seat, but kept his backpack on. After a few minutes the farmer asked, "Why don't you take off that pack and put it in the wagon?"

"Oh," the Newfie answered. "That poor horse is pulling such a heavy load, I don't want to add to it for him."

Local Pride

An Albertan, an Ontarian, and a Newfie were talking.

The Ontarian asked the Albertan, "If you weren't an Albertan, what would you be?"

The Albertan thought a moment and said, "Well, I guess I'd be an Ontarian."

The Ontarian turned to the Newfie and asked, "If you weren't a Newfoundlander, what would you be?"

Without hesitation the Newfie said, "Ashamed."

Three Dead Men

The bodies of three dead men were laid out in the morgue. There was a Frenchman, an Irishman, and a Newfie. Each face wore a big smile.

The Frenchman died while he was making love. That is why there was a big smile on his face.

The Irishman died just after he was informed that he had won the Irish Sweepstakes. He had bought a big load of Irish whiskey and then drank himself to death. That is why he was smiling.

The Newfie had been struck by lightning. Why was he smiling? He thought he was having his picture taken.

Poll

A government man was taking a poll in a poor neighbourhood of St. John's.

He knocked on one door, and a small boy answered.

"Hello, little boy. Is your mother home?"

"No. She's in the mental hospital."

"Oh, dear. Is your father home?"

"No. He's in jail."

"Goodness me! Do you have an older brother?"

"Yes. He's in reform school."

"Heavens! Do you have an older sister?"

"Yes. She's at university."

"University? No kidding? What's she studying?"

"She's not studying them. They's studying her."

Fishing Boat

A couple of Newfies were in their fishing boat, pulling in a lot of fish.

One of them said, "This is a pretty good spot. We should mark it so we can find it again tomorrow."

He took out a pencil and started to mark the top of the water.

His friend said, "Don't be so stupid, b'y. You can't mark the water. Mark the side of the boat."

Anecdote

"I don't know if you could use this as a joke, but it is a true story,"
wrote the novelist and journalist Ed Butts in August 2002.

Many years ago my dad took me with him on a business trip to Newfoundland.

While we were there CN—which operated the ferry—announced that it was going on strike. Of course, there was a big rush of people wanting to get off the island before the strike.

We were in a long line-up of cars at Port Aux Basques, and things were proceeding very slowly. A man in the car next to ours got out and began chewing out one of the ferry employees who was directing cars. We could hear him telling the guy, "You get people to come to this place and then they can't even get on the damn boat to get home again, blah blah blah."

The guy listened to the tirade and then said in a pleasant voice, "Ah buddy, it's just that we likes you so much we wants to keep you."

Poor Room Service

An American businessman was staying at a hotel in St. John's.

He had some guests in his room, and he called room service for some ice. When the ice didn't come quickly enough, he called down again, becoming abusive with the person on the other end.

"What kind of service do you call this, and blah blah blah!"

The man on the other end listened to it all, and then said calmly, "Ah, buddy, you see, what happened is, the old woman who used to make the ice died, and she took the recipe with her."

Bus Schedule

Two drunk Newfies were standing by the side of the highway. Not far away was a cop.

One of the Newfies whispered something to his friend, who then staggered over to the cop and said, "Excuse me, sir, but has the bus to St. John's gone yet?"

"Yes," said the cop. "The bus to St. John's has gone."

The Newfie went back to his friend, and the two of them mumbled to each other. Then the Newfie stumbled back to the cop and said, "Beggin' your pardon again, officer, but has the bus to Gander gone by?"

"Yes," said the cop, a little peevishly this time. "The bus to Gander has gone by."

The Newfie again went back to his friend, and again they had a little conference. Then the Newfie staggered back to the cop and said, "Pardon me again, constable, sir, but has the bus to Port Aux Basques gone by?"

"Yes!" said the cop, quite annoyed now. "The bus to Port Aux Basques has gone by. There will be no more buses going by here today!"

The Newfie went back to his friend and said, "It's all right, me ol' trout. We can cross the highway now."

Who Killed Kennedy?

A teacher asked a Newfie kid, "Who killed John F. Kennedy?"

The kid replied, "Well, I didn't do it."

The teacher said the kid was being a smart alec and sent him home from school.

When the boy arrived home in the middle of the day, his father wanted to know why he wasn't in school. The boy told him what had happened.

The father took the boy back to school, and asked the teacher, "Why did you send my son home?"

The teacher said, "I asked him who killed John F. Kennedy, and he said he didn't do it."

"So what's your problem?" the father asked. "If he says he didn't do it, he didn't do it."

Newfie in Toronto

"Did you hear about the Newfoundlander who moved to Toronto?"

"No."

"During a cold spell last year, he cut a big chunk out of Grenadier Pond and thought that was ice-fishing."

"Is that it?"

"No. That's not the finish. A Toronto fellow bought the ice and took it home and tried to fry it."

The Nile

A Torontonian was boasting to a Newfie about all the travelling he'd done.

"And how about you?" said the boor. "Have you ever been up the Nile?"

"Oh yes," replied the Newfie. "I went right to the top."

Ferry Ride

A Toronto couple was boarding the ferry to Newfoundland.

The woman approached the Newfie skipper and said, "My husband is afraid he'll be seasick. Can you tell him what he should do if an attack should happen?"

"No need to tell him, missus. He'll do it all by himself."

Quebec Separation

Two Newfies were talking about Quebec.

One of them said, "B'y, that'll be bad if Quebec separates from Canada, eh?"

The other one said, "No, buddy, that'll be good for us. With Quebec out of the way, we won't have so far to drive to Toronto."

Drive to Toronto

It took Newfie a whole week to drive to Toronto.

When someone asked him why it took so long, he said, "Well, I stopped at a gas station and when I got the key for the men's room, there was a sign that said 'Clean Washrooms.' So I did— at every gas station I stopped at."

Send Money Home

A Newfoundlander named Clancy left his wife and children at home while he went to Toronto to find work. He promised that once he found a job, he would send money home. It took him a while, but he finally landed a job in a factory.

He'd barely been on the job a week when he received a letter from his wife. Clancy couldn't read, so he took the letter to work and asked his foreman to read it to him. The foreman was a rather gruff, impatient, busy man, and he didn't like wasting his time reading some working stiff's letters, so when he read the letter to Clancy he did so in a very harsh manner. (Here the teller must read the way the foreman would.)

Clancy!
When are you goin' to send some money home! You said you would, you know! The children and I really need it. Send something right away!
Your Wife

Clancy thanked the foreman, folded up the letter, and put it in his jacket pocket.

That Sunday he went to church, and as he was leaving after Mass, the elderly priest met him at the door and asked him if he'd heard from his wife.

"Oh yes," Clancy said. "I heard from her, all right. Here, look at this."

He gave the letter to the priest, who read it in his own kindly tone of voice.

Dear Clancy:
   When are you going to send some money home? You said you would, you know. The children and I really need it. Please send some right away.
Your Loving Wife

The priest looked at Clancy and said, "Clancy? Haven't you been sending money home to your wife?"

"Well," Clancy replied, "I wasn't goin' to after the way she spoke to me the first time, but I will now that she's changed her tone."

Parade of Penguins

A Newfie was driving his truck along the 401, heading for Toronto, when he saw another truck stopped at the side of the road. He stopped to offer assistance.

The other driver told him he had a load of penguins he was taking to the Metro Zoo. He said he would give the Newfie $100 to take the penguins to the zoo for him. So the Newfie took the $100, and loaded the penguins into his truck.

A few hours later the truck driver had his vehicle running again and was driving in Toronto. He stopped for a light at an intersection, and what should he see in the lane next to him but the Newfie's truck with all the penguins in the back.

He yelled over, "Hey! I thought I gave you $100 to take those penguins to the zoo!"

"Yeah," said the Newfie. "And I did take 'em to the zoo. But we had some money left over, so now I'm taking them to a movie."

Escalator

A Newfie went into a department store in Toronto and, for the first time in his life, saw an escalator—the one going down.

He watched it for a minute, and then said, "B'y, they better stop that thing soon, or the basement is gonna be all full of stairs."

Monkeys

A Torontonian was in St. John's and decided he'd have a bit of fun at the expense of one of the locals.

He went up to a Newfie and said, "Did you see a truckload of monkeys go by here?"

The Newfie said, "Why? Did you fall off?"

On to Toronto

Did you hear about the Newfies who went to Toronto?

They saw a sign that read "Toronto Left."

So they turned around and went home.

Big Nickel

A family moved from Corner Brook to Toronto. The little boy in the family began attending the local school and was soon the butt of jokes for kids who picked on him for being a "goofy Newfie."

One boy would show him a nickel and a dime, and ask him if he wanted the BIG nickel, or the little dime. The little boy would always take the BIG nickel, to the mirth of the other kids. A teacher watched this happen a couple of times, and then, in exasperation, took the little boy aside. "Surely," she said, "you know the difference in value between a nickel and a dime. Why do you let them do that to you?"

"Sure I know the difference," the boy said. "But if I ever take that dime, they're going to stop giving me nickels."

Newfie's Revenge

Two men were at the rail of the ferry going from Newfoundland to Nova Scotia. One was a Newfoundlander, the other a Torontonian. The Torontonian decided to have some fun at the Newfie's expense. He began to brag about what a big city Toronto was—certainly bigger than any place in Newfoundland. He exaggerated the size of everything—buildings, highways, parks. By the time he was finished, the Newfie was shaking his head in astonishment.

"B'y," he said, "we got nothin' like that in Newfoundland. In fact, I guess the biggest thing we got is me brother George."

"Oh," said the Torontonian, "what's so big about your brother George?"

"Well buddy, George is seven feet tall. He's six feet across the shoulders. And when he gets a hard-on, fifteen seagulls can perch on it."

The Torontonian was quiet for a while. He finally decided that the Newfie was having him on, so he decided to confess to his exaggerations. He explained that even though Toronto was a big city, things weren't really as big as he had claimed.

The Newfie confessed that he, too, had been exaggerating. He admitted that George was only about five foot ten and no bigger across the shoulders than most other men. "And them fifteen seagulls I told you about? Well, the last one got to stand on one foot."

Knock, Knock

Two Newfies meet in St. John's.

First Newfie: I'm just back from Toronto where I learned to play a new game.

Second Newfie: What's it called?

First Newfie: It's called "Knock, Knock."

Second Newfie: Show me.

First Newfie: Okay. (He knocks twice.)
Second Newfie: Don't show me any more. I have to answer the door.

Tellin' It Like It Is

A bar in a rough area of Toronto had difficulty finding a bouncer tough enough to keep order. The owner resorted to getting a gorilla, which he trained to remove the rowdies. He chained the gorilla to a concrete pillar until it was needed.

One night a Newfoundlander came in and became embroiled in a fight. In about five minutes he'd beaten up four or five patrons and the gorilla was turned loose. The Newfoundlander and the gorilla lurched struggling out onto the sidewalk and the door slammed shut.

A couple of minutes went by, the door opened, and the Newfoundlander came back in. He shut the door, dusted himself off, and complained, "Dat's th' trouble wit' Mainlanders. Dey makes enough money to buy a fur coat an' dey t'inks dey owns the world."

George and Aggie

George and Aggie had just flown to Toronto and so went to the baggage claim to collect their luggage.

A porter comes over to George and says, "Can I carry your bag, sir?"

George glances at him, then at Aggie, and says, "Naw, that's okay, skipper. She's a big girl. Let her walk."

Torontonians and a Newfie

A couple of Torontonians have just closed down their store on busy Yonge Street and are standing in the middle of their empty shop when the first one says to the second one, "I'll bet you ten bucks that if we wait here a few minutes, some Newfie is going to come by, peer through the window, enter our empty store, and ask us what we're selling."

Sure enough, just as he finishes speaking, a Newfie presses his face to the window, looks at the empty shelves, and walks into the store. He says, "How's she goin', b'y? I was just wonderin' what you fellas was sellin'?"

One of the Torontonians grins at the other and replies, "We're selling idiots, sir."

To this the Newfie responds, "Well, ya must be doin' some good business 'cause dere's only two o' ya left."

Hero to Zero

While visiting St. John's, a man from Toronto came upon a dog attacking a small boy. He grabbed the animal and throttled it with his bare hands.

A reporter for the *Evening Telegraph* saw the incident, congratulated the man, and told him the headline the following day would read: "Local Man Saves Child by Killing Vicious Animal."

The hero, however, told the reporter that he wasn't from St. John's.

"Well, then," the journalist said, "the headline will probably read, 'Newfoundlander Saves Child by Killing Dog.'"

"Actually," the man said, "I'm from Toronto."

"In that case," the reporter said in a huff, "the headline will read, 'Mainlander Kills Family Pet.'"

Treatment for Hemorrhoids

A Newfie is suffering from hemorrhoids.

He goes to the doctor, who gives him a box of suppositories and tells him to call him back in a week.

A week later the Newfie phones and says his hemorrhoids are worse than ever.

"Didn't you use those suppositories I gave you?" the doctor asks.

"What? Them big pills? I took every one of 'em! And for all the good they done, I might as well have shoved 'em up me arse!"

Big Car

Two Newfies were sitting on the porch, just passing time.

One of them said, "I wish I could afford one of them big Cadillac cars."

"Now, b'y, what would you want to buy one of them big things for?"

"I never said I wanted to buy one. I just said I wish I could afford one."

Price of Beer

Every Saturday night a group of Newfies would drive to a town fifty miles from their own town to drink beer in a tavern.

One night the bartender asks them, "Why do you come here every Saturday night when you've got a nice tavern in your own town?"

"Because the beer here is five cents a glass cheaper."

"But what about what it costs you in gasoline?"

"No problem. We just drinks till we makes a profit."

Saving Money

A Newfie comes home from work, puffing and panting.

When his wife asks him what's wrong, he says, "Instead of taking the bus, I ran home behind it and saved fifty cents."

His wife says, "Next time run home behind a taxi and save twenty dollars."

Construction Site

Two Newfies are working at a construction site, digging ditches with picks and shovels.

One of them looks at the foreman, standing there giving orders, and says to his buddy, "How come we got to work so hard, and that fella gets to just stand around and tell other people what to do?"

"I don't know. Why don't you ask him?"

So the Newfie goes over to the foreman and asks.

"Well," says the foreman, "I have education."

"What's that?" asks the Newfie.

The foreman says, "I'll show you," and takes the Newfie over to a brick wall. He holds his hand in front of the wall and tells the Newfie, "Hit my hand, just as hard as you can."

The Newfie lets fly with a punch, and just as his fist is about to touch the foreman's hand, the foreman pulls his hand away, and the Newfie slams his fist right into the brick wall.

"That," says the foreman, "is education. Now get back to work."

So, nursing his throbbing hand, the Newfie heads back to his ditch. His friend says, "Did you find out?"

"Yeah. He's got education."

"What's that?"

The Newfie holds his hand up in front of his own face and says, "Hit my hand."

Prison Sentence

A young man convicted of a serious crime stood before a judge in a Newfoundland court to hear his sentence.

The judge looked at him and said, "Young fellow, have you ever been to prison before?"

"No, your honour," he said tearfully, "I never have."

"Aw now, don't be so upset," the judge said. "You're goin' now."

Job Applications

A Newfie was filling out a job application.

Where it said "Sex M or F," he wrote, "Well, I prefer F but I usually have to settle for M."

At the line which said, "In the event of accident or illness, whom should we notify?" he wrote, "Preferably a doctor."

Two Newfies

Two Newfies, George and Harry, win a trip to Europe. There is a little problem, though, because George has lost the use of both legs and must use a pair of crutches to get around. But Harry says he'll take good care of George.

Off they go to Europe. When they return, the press is waiting at the airport to hear all about the trip.

"Well," says Harry, "we went to London, you know, where the Spoiled Family lives, and we went to that there Tower of London. I went all the way up to the top of the castle walls. B'y, some nice view from up there."

"How did George like it?"

"Oh, buddy, George couldn't go up all them stairs. George is a cripple, you know. Well, then we went to Paris, and we went to that Awful Tower. I went right up to the top and looked out over the whole city."

"And how did George like that?"

"B'y, George couldn't go up all them steps. George is a cripple, you know. Well, then we went to Rome, and in Rome we went to the Vatican. We got to see the Pope hisself. When the Pope seen George, he put his right hand on George's left shoulder, and George threw away his left crutch. Then the Pope put his left hand on George's right shoulder, and George threw away his right crutch."

"You mean, there was a miracle?" gasped the reporter. "Did George walk?"

"No, b'y. He fell flat on his face. George is a cripple, you know."

Medical Dictionary of Newfoundland

Artery: The study of paintings.

Bacteria: The back door of a cafeteria.

Barium: What doctors do when patients die.

Bowel: A letter like A, E, I, O, U.

Caesarean section: A neighbourhood in Rome.

CAT scan: Searching for a kitty.

Colic: A sheep dog.

D & C: Where Washington is.

Dilate: To live long.

Enema: Not a friend.

Fester: Quicker.

G.I. series: A soldiers' ball game.

Hangnail: A coat hook.

Impotent: Distinguished; well known.

Labour pain: Getting hurt at work.

Medical staff: A doctor's cane.

Morbid: A higher offer.

Nitrates: Cheaper than day rates.

Node: Was aware of.

Outpatient: A person who fainted.

Pap smear: A fatherhood test.

Pelvis: A cousin of Elvis.

Post-operative: A letter carrier.

Recovery room: A place to do upholstery.

Rectum: Dang near killed 'em.

Seizure: A Roman emperor.

Tablet: A small table.

Terminal illness: Getting sick at the airport.

Tumour: More than one.

Urine: Opposite of "you're out!"

Varicose: Nearby.

Vein: Conceited.

What's Wrong Today?

A Newfie walks into a bar in a really sad mood and, half in tears, asks the bartender to serve him six double drinks.

The bartender gets the drinks and asks him, "What's wrong?"

He says, "I just found out that my brother is gay."

The next day he comes back into the bar and again orders six drinks.

The bartender asks, "What's wrong today?"

He says, "I just found out that my son is gay."

The next day he comes back into the bar and again orders six drinks.

The bartender looks at the Newfie and asks, "Is there anyone in your family that likes women?"

"Yes," he says. "My wife!"

Camping

One day two Newfies decided to go camping, so they packed up their equipment and started out. Since it was a long way to the campsite, they decided to drive.

But half way there, their car broke down. They decided to camp where they were for the night. But one of them wanted to camp in the middle of the road, and the other wanted to sleep in the ditch. After a long argument, they set up their tent in the middle of the road and then fell into deep sleep.

That night a transport truck coming down the road swerved to miss them and landed in the ditch. When they awoke, one of them looked out and gasped, "Look, b'y! Now, y' see if we'd slept in the ditch, we would've got hit by that truck!"

British Colony Again

Newfoundland, not seeing the wealth and riches that Confederation promised, decided to go back to the old ways of a

British colony. To ease its people into the British way of life, the powers that be decided to change things slowly. The first thing they decided was that cars should drive on the left-hand side of the road, as they do in England. It was thought that this would be a very British thing to do. It was then decided that they would give this plan a few weeks to take hold, and if it worked out all right, they would do the same for the trucks and buses.

Permanent Wave

A Mainlander driving down the highway ran over a rabbit. Wondering what had happened, he stops his car and gets out to look.

As he is standing there, looking at the dead rabbit, a Newfie drives by. The Newfie, wondering if he can help, stops and asks the Mainlander what's up.

The Mainlander says, "I'm here visiting your fair province and I seem to have killed one of your land rodents."

The Newfie looks down and sees the dead rabbit. "No problem, b'y. Hang 'er down a few."

The Newfie goes to his truck and returns with an aerosol spray can. He empties the spray over the rabbit. He then chucks the empty can into the ditch and says, "There ya go, me son. Enjoy yer stay." He gets in his truck and is gone.

The rabbit gets up, hops ten feet toward the woods, turns around and waves, hops ten feet, turns around and waves, hops ten feet, and then is gone, into the woods.

The Mainlander is astounded. Wondering what the Newfie did, he walks over to the ditch, picks up the can, and reads the label.

It says: "Hair spray. Guaranteed to bring dead hair back to life with a permanent wave."

Crash Landing

Did you hear about the two Newfie fishermen?

Two Newfies take a plane up to northern Québec to go fishing. They fly across a very small lake.

One Newfie says to the pilot, "That's the lake, b'y!"

"Can't be," says the pilot. "It's too small to land on."

"Oh, yes," says the second Newfie. "That's where the pilot put her down last week."

"Well, okay," says the pilot.

They try to land, and in the process tear the wings off the plane, almost crash, and come to a stop, stuck up against the shore.

"Yup!" say the two Newfies. "That's just what happened last week!"

Home in the Fall

An Englishman, a Frenchman, and a Newfoundlander all arrived at the gates of Heaven.

St. Peter addressed the Englishman and asked him his nationality. He was told to walk due north to the colony of Englishmen in Heaven.

The Frenchman was told to walk due south to the commune where the French people live in Heaven.

When St. Peter came to the Newfoundlander, he asked, "And what are you?"

"I'm a Newfoundlander," he replied.

St. Peter said, "My son, you better stay by the gate. You'll want to return home in the fall."

True Confessional

A Newfie steals 5,000 feet of lumber from a building supply store.

Soon after, he starts to feel guilty, so he goes to confession at the local church.

Priest: How can I help you?

Newfie: Forgive me, Father, for I have sinned.

Priest: What is your sin, my son?

Newfie: I stole 5,000 feet of lumber, Father. What's my penance?

Priest: Do you know how to make a novena, my son?

Newfie: No, but if you got the plans, I got the lumber.

Rabbits

A Newfie was driving a transport truck across Canada to British Columbia with a load of live rabbits. The rabbits were loose in the trailer, rather than in cages. While driving near Sudbury, the truck slipped on a patch of ice on the road and slid off the road into the ditch. The trailer's back doors flew open and the rabbits began scurrying everywhere.

A police officer happened to be passing and saw the truck in the ditch. He stopped to investigate the accident. When he walked around the back of the trailer, there was the Newfie, flat on his back in the snow bank, laughing to kill himself.

Police officer: Sir, what's so funny? Your rabbits are loose and they're running everywhere.

Newfie: Yeah, I know! But they don't know where they're going. I got the address here in my pocket.

"A Heartwarming Story"

This letter was forwarded to me by a teacher at a junior high school in Gander, Newfoundland. It had been sent to the principal's office after the school had sponsored a luncheon for the elderly. The story is a credit to all humankind. Read it, soak it in, and bask in the warm feeling that it leaves you with.

Dear Gander School:

God bless you for the beautiful radio I won at your recent senior citizens' luncheon. I am eighty-four years old and live at the county home for the aged. All my people are gone. It's nice to know that someone thinks of me. God bless you for your kindness to an old forgotten lady. My roommate is ninety-five and always had her own radio, but would never let me listen to it, no matter how often or sweetly I asked. The other day her radio fell and broke into a lot of pieces. It was awful. She was very upset. She then asked if she could listen to mine, and I said screw you.

Sincerely,
Edna Johnston

Vacation

A Newfie was looking for an exotic cruise vacation, but on the cheap.

Perusing the St. John's paper, he was surprised to see a list of destinations and prices: "France, $1,500," "Australia, $2,500," and—lo and behold!—"Greece, $5.95."

"Just the t'ing," he thinks, and heads to the agency. He goes in, ponies up the cash, and they pour him a drink. He knocks it back, and everything goes black.

When he wakes up, he's chained to a rowing bench in a galley, with a drum beating a steady rhythm, and a row master cracking a whip. He starts pulling his oar.

Fourteen days later, there is nothing but bread and water rations and twenty-hour days at the oar. The boat finally makes port in Greece and the captain tells the rowers they're free to go.

The Newfie turns to his benchmate and says, "Damn if that ain't the worst vacation I've ever had."

The benchmate says, "Aye, my love, and last year they charged only $4.95."

Sick Newfie

Newfie goes to see his doctor, complaining he is sore all over.

"Doc," he says, "I get my finger and press it on my knee and, boy, does it hurt. Then I get my finger and press it on my elbow and, ouch, it hurts. Then I take my finger and press it on my forehead, ouch again. What do you think is wrong with me?"

The doc says, "Your finger's broke."

Lobster Catch

One day, a Newfie is walking down at the pier, carrying a lobster under each arm.

All of a sudden, a Fisheries warden comes up to the Newfie and says to him, "You know, you could be in very serious trouble fishing lobster out of season," to which the Newfie replies, "Hey, b'y, I am not fishing these here lobsters. They are my pets."

Continuing to explain to the warden, the Newfie says, "Ev'ry day I comes down to the wharf and gives a whistle and me two pet lobsters jump from the water. Then I take them for a walk on the wharf."

"I find that very hard to believe," says the warden. "Prove this to me."

So the Newfie walks to the edge of the wharf and throws the two lobsters into the bay.

Eagerly awaiting the proof of the story he just heard, the warden tells the Newfie, "Whistle for your pet lobsters, and they better show up or you're going to have to face the judge."

The Newfie turns to the warden and says, "What lobsters?"

Proud Father

A Nova Scotia lobster fisherman pulled his boat alongside that of a fellow fisherman and yelled, "I'm a father. My wife had a baby boy last night."

The other man asked, "What did he weigh?"

"Four pounds," said the proud father.

"Four pounds!" exclaimed the other. "Some days you hardly get your bait back!"

Fisherman

A fisherman from British Columbia and a fisherman from Newfoundland were bragging about the size of the fish caught in their respective waters.

The Newfie said, "We throw back anything under ten inches."

"Ten inches?" laughed the man from B.C. "That's not very long."

"Who said 'long'?" replied the Newfie. "We measure them between the eyes."

Two Fishermen

A fisherman arrived back in port with nothing to show for his day's work but a string of six puny perch.

As he was tying up his boat, another fisherman pulled up alongside, his boat weighed down by a huge marlin.

The first fisherman looked at it and said, "Only caught one, eh?"

Newfie Rangers

Two members of the Newfie rangers are on the parade ground when their captain approaches them, points to the flag of Newfoundland, and asks, "What does that flag mean to you?"

The first ranger says, "That flag is like my mother."

"Very good," replies the captain. Then he asks the second ranger, "And what does it mean to you?"

The second ranger replies, "That flag is like my aunt."

"Why is it like your aunt?" the captain asks.

"Because this man in my cousin."

Two Newfies

Two Newfies are having a race to the top of Signal Hill.

"If I get to the top of the hill first," says one, "I'm going to write my name on the monument up there."

"If I get to the top first," the other says, "I'm going to rub it out."

"Smart Pills"

An Ontarian visiting St. John's meets a Newfie at a local bar and poses the following question: "How come you Newfies think you are so smart?"

The Newfie replies, "We eats lots of fish, b'y, lots of fish." He pauses. "Tell you what, give me $35 and I'll get my wife to cook up the best fish dish you have ever tasted. That'll make you smart!"

The Mainlander gives the Newfie the money, and the next day goes to the Newfie's house for the fish dinner.

Afterward he tries to make a point. "That was a great feed of fish, but isn't $35 a little expensive since I didn't eat at a restaurant?"

Without a moment's hesitation, the Newfie replies, "Right, b'y, see, you are getting smarter already!"

Downside of Oil Exploration

An oil company was drilling test pits on the west coast of Newfoundland. It never found anything, and instead of filling the holes up, it came up with the clever idea to cover the holes with outhouses.

About a week later, a Newfoundlander comes across one of these outhouses in the woods and decides to use it.

The next day another fella finds him dead on the toilet. An investigation is opened to try to find out what happened. His wife is asked if there was anything wrong with him or if he was acting strangely that day.

His wife replied, "My husband was in perfect shape. The only thing strange about him was that he held his breath until he heard a splash."

The Policeman

On a recent trip back home, we were heading back from a night "on the town." I was sitting between my buddy (George, driving, no seatbelt) and his better half (Aggie), when we were stopped by one of Newfoundland's finest and the following exchange ensued:

Policeman: No seatbelt tonight?

George (who by now had his seatbelt on): It's on.

Policeman: But I saw you pass by without it.

George: No way, sir.

Policeman: I think you just put it on.

George: No, sir, wear it all the time.

Policeman: Jack, I saw you put it on as you stopped!

Aggie: Sir, you may as well forget it. There's no point arguing with him when he's drunk.

Stephenville Sausages

One day a guy from Stephenville decides to do the weekly grocery shopping for his wife. Even though she had given him a shopping list, when it came to buying the fish, the guy decided to try something different, as he was getting tired of eating fish all the time. He picked up a package of tasty-looking sausages, thinking they would be nice to try.

When he returned home, he told his wife he'd like her to cook the sausages for dinner. She agreed. But when he sat down at the table for supper and looked at his plate, all he saw was a couple of crisp pieces, so tiny he could barely see them. "What's this?" he asked his wife. "Where's them sausages I asked you to cook?"

"That's them," she said. "I don't know why people bother to buy them. After you cut off the head and tail, and guts them, they's nothin' much left to cook up!"

The Fire

A Frenchman, an Englishman, and a Newfie are waiting patiently at the top of a ten-story building, which is burning up fast.

Finally the firefighters get there, only to find that the fire truck's ladder doesn't reach the building's rooftop. The firefighters decide to get the old blanket out so that the men can jump. They do so and signal for the three men to leap. The men look at each other, wondering who would go first.

The Frenchman decides to go, and as he jumps, he yells, *"Vive la France!"* Hearing this, the firefighters below let the blanket go slack, and the Frenchman hits the pavement hard. The firefighters pull the blanket back up and signal the two remaining men to jump.

The Englishman decides to jump next, and as he leaps, he yells, "God Save the Queen!" Hearing this, the firefighters again let the blanket go slack, and the Englishman hits the pavement. Finally, the firefighters pull the blanket back up again and signal the Newfie to leap.

The Newfie replies, "Are you kiddin' me? I saw what you guys did to my two friends. Gently spread the blanket on the ground and back up."

Montreal Gift

Two brothers from Cupids are visiting Montreal. One of the brothers says to the other, "Hey, we gotta get a gift for Mom!"

So they walk into Zellers and look around. Finally, they decide to check out the bathroom accessories. They spot a beautiful toilet set, the kind with a plushy toilet seat and a little carpet to wrap around the toilet. They choose a pink set with a rose in the centre. They mail it to their mother in Newfoundland, then continue their trip, finally heading back home.

When they arrive at their house, their mother is waiting for them with a big smile on her face.

"My dear boys," she says, "I got your lovely gift; thank you!"

"How do you like it?" says one of the brothers.

"Oh, just great!" answers the mother. "The cape is perfect, but the beret is a little too big for my head."

Definition of a Pontiac

P oor
O le
N ewfie
T hinks
I t's
A
C adillac

World Travellers

George and Aggie won the 6/49 lottery and decided to take a trip.

"Spain is nice," the travel agent said.

"But Aggie and I don't speak any Spanish," George replied.

"That's okay, just speak in English very slowly, and you will be fine," promised the agent.

Things were grand. George and Aggie went to Spain, and the first night there decided to have a drink at the hotel bar.

George said to the waiter, "Bring . . . me . . . a . . . beer . . . please."

"Right . . . away . . . sir," came the reply.

"Where . . . are . . . you . . . from?" asked George.

"Clarenville . . . Newfoundland . . . Canada," replied the waiter.

"Isn't . . . this . . . grand!" Aggie said. "Here . . . you . . . are . . . two . . . fellas . . . from . . . Newfoundland . . . speaking . . . Spanish."

Drive-in

"Did you hear about the couple that drove in from Newfoundland and were found frozen to death in their car at the drive-in movie?"

"No. What happened to them?"

"They went to see *Closed for the Winter.*"

Pizza

A Newfie ordered a pizza. The clerk asked if he should cut it into six or twelve pieces.

"Six, please. I could never eat twelve pieces," replied the Newfie.

Question

Q. Why was the Newfie general sent to see a psychiatrist?

A. It seems he had to be treated for delusions of grandeur. He thought he was a lieutenant in the Canadian Armed Forces.

Auto Accidents

Q. Why did the Newfie motorist keep moving from one house to another?

A. Apparently he learned somewhere that most auto accidents take place within two miles of home.

Shorties

Q. What is written on the bottoms of coke bottles in Newfoundland?

A. Open other end.

Q. Why did the Newfie scale the chain-link fence?

A. To see what was on the other side.

Q. Why did the Newfie keep a coat hanger on the back seat?

A. In case he locked the keys in the car.

Q. Why did the Newfie get so excited after he finished a jigsaw puzzle in only six months?

A. Because the box said, "From two to four years."

Q. Why did the Newfie wear condoms on his ears?

A. So he wouldn't need hearing aids.

Q. Why should Newfies not be given coffee breaks?

A. It takes too long to retrain them.

Q. What did the Newfie name his pet zebra?

A. Spot.

Q. What goes vroom, screech, vroom, screech, vroom, screech?

A. A Newfie going through a flashing red light.

Q. How did the skeleton get in the closet?

A. It was a Newfie who won a game of hide and seek.

Q. Why isn't there a Newfie pope?

A. Because there aren't any Newfie cardinals.

Q. What do they call *Sesame Street* in Newfoundland?

A. University of the Air.

Q. Did you hear about the Newfie who stayed up all night wondering where the sun went?

A. It finally dawned on him.

Q. What was so unusual about the Newfie lesbian?

A. She fell in love with a man.

Q. Why did they shut down Newfie Air?

A. It seems the provincial airline ran out of coal.

Q. What's smarter than one Newfie?

A. Two Newfies.

Q. Why does a Newfie dictionary cost so little?

A. Because the words in it are not arranged in alphabetical order.

Q. Why does the new Newfie navy have boats with glass bottoms?

A. So they can see the old Newfie navy.

Q. Did you know there's a man in St. John's who uses only one-quarter of his brain?

A. So what does he do with the other quarter?

Q. Why didn't the Newfie get any ducks when he went duck hunting?

A. He couldn't throw the dog high enough.

Q. Why does the Newfie father go to school every day with his ten-year-old son?

A. They're in the same grade.

Q. How do you tell if a Newfie has been using the computer?

A. There is whiteout on the screen.

Q. How can you tell if a different Newfie has been using the computer?

A. There is printing on the whiteout.

Q. What did the Newfie think of the new computer?

A. He didn't like it because he couldn't tune in to Global TV.

Q. How do you drive a Newfie crazy?

A. You put him in a round room and make him count the corners.

Q. What did the Newfie say when he looked into a box of Cheerios?

A. "Oh, look! Donut seeds!"

Q. How do you get a Newfie out of a tree?

A. Wave.

Hitchhikers

Two Ontarians were driving their pickup truck in the hills of Quebec when they saw two Newfies hitchhiking. Knowing that they, too, were visitors to the province, the Ontarians decided to help them out and pick them up.

A few hours later, while the Newfies were sitting in the back, the driver lost control of the truck and drove into a lake. The Ontarians swam to shore and sat for a while, until they realized that the Newfies were nowhere to be seen.

The Ontarians went back into the water to find the Newfies. To their amazement, the Newfies were still in the back of the truck. Once back on shore, the Ontarians asked why they hadn't swum to shore in the first place. The Newfies replied, "We couldn't get the tailgate down!"

Fusion Cuisine

Not all Newfies approve of the modish "fusion cuisine."

Younger chefs "from away" are placing it on the menus of the trendy restaurants that are opening up these days in St. John's.

"Not only does the food taste godawful," one diner from an outport who preferred the traditional dishes complained, "but the portions are too small."

Genie at Sea

Two Newfies were adrift in a lifeboat after a dramatic escape from a burning vessel. While rummaging through the boat's provisions, one of the men stumbled across an old lamp. Secretly hoping that a genie would appear, he rubbed the lamp vigorously. To the amazement of the castaways, a genie did appear. This particular genie, however, stated that she could deliver only one wish, not the standard three.

Without giving much thought to the matter, the man blurted out, "Turn the entire ocean into beer."

Immediately the genie clapped her hands with a deafening crash, and the entire sea turned to the finest brew ever sampled by mortals. Simultaneously, the genie vanished to her freedom.

Only the gentle lapping of beer on the hull broke the sudden stillness as the two men considered their circumstances.

The other man looked disgustedly at the one whose wish had been granted. After a long, tension-filled moment, he spoke: "Nice going. Now we're going to have to pee in the boat."

Royal Conversation

While Her Majesty the Queen was in St. John's for the John Cabot celebrations held in 1998, she made a visit to the Purity Factory, the local, well-known bakery.

As she toured it, she stopped to ask a few questions. "What are you making?" she asked one of the workers.

He answered, "$13.85 an hour, Your Highness."

Bill 101

A Newfie, a Quebecer, and an Albertan were in a bar having a drink when it was announced on the TV news that Bill 101 had been voted in.

The Quebecer cheered. The Albertan cursed. And the Newfie thought there was a new Pope.

Get to Toronto?

"How did the first Newfie get to Toronto?"

"A bunch of them were playing hockey on the frozen-over Gulf of the St. Lawrence, and one guy got a breakaway."

School Lesson

A teacher said to a Newfie student, "Do you know that you are wearing one green sock and one brown sock?"

"Yes. So what?"

"Well, don't you think there's anything wrong with that?"

"Why should I? Me brother has a pair just like it."

Family Problems

Two Newfies from outports meet in a bar and strike up a conversation.

One of them complains about his family situation. The other listens for a while and then grumbles about his lot in life: "You think you have family problems! Listen to my situation.

"A few years ago I met a young widow with a grown-up daughter, and we got married. Later, my father married my stepdaughter. That made my stepdaughter my stepmother, and my father became my stepson. Also, my wife became the mother-in-law of her father-in-law.

"Then the daughter of my wife, my stepmother, had a son. This boy was my half-brother because he was my father's son, but he was also the son of my wife's daughter, which made him my wife's grandson. That made me the grandfather of my half-brother.

"This was nothing until my wife and I had a son. Now the sister of my son, my mother-in-law, is also the grandmother. This makes my father the brother-in-law of my child, whose stepsister is my father's wife.

"I am my stepmother's brother-in-law, my wife is her own child's aunt, my son is my father's nephew, and I am my own grandfather.

"And you think you have family problems!"

Newfies and the Sack

Two Newfies meet at the edge of the woods. One Newfie is going to hunt and carries an empty sack. The other Newfie is returning from the hunt and carries a bulging sack.

"What have you got in that sack?" asks the first Newfie.

"Grouse," replies the other Newfie.

"How many grouse?"

"Guess."

"I can't guess."

"If you can guess I'll give you both of them."

"Five?" asks the Newfie.

Newfie Fine

A Newfie is charged in court with parking his car in a restricted area. The judge asks him if he has anything to say in his defence.

"They should not post such misleading notices," he says.

"What do you mean?" asks the judge.
"The notice read, 'Fine for Parking Here.'"

Newfie Skydivers

A group of Newfies is having its first lesson in skydiving.
"What if the parachute doesn't open?" asks one Newfie meekly.
The instructor replies, "That's what we call jumping to a conclusion."

St. John's Robbery

The following item appeared recently in the *St. John's Herald:*
"Thieves broke into the Water Street Bank last night and escaped with over half a million dollars in currency. Police are baffled trying to figure out the motive for the crime."

Newfie in Bookstore

A Newfie enters a bookstore in St. John's.
He asks the clerk, "Can I have a book by Shakespeare?"
The clerk says, "Of course, sir. Which one?"
The fellow says, "William."

Newfie Reading

Q. Have you read any of Shakespeare's plays?
A. Only two of them.
Q. Which ones?
A. *Romeo* and *Juliet.*

Magic Ride

An Englishman, an Irishman, and a Newfie are enjoying themselves at the circus.

They are about to step onto the giant roller coaster when an old crone steps in front of them. "I warn you," she says. "This is a magic ride. You will land in whatever you shout out on the way down."

"I'm game for this!" says the Englishman. He goes on the ride and at the top is heard to shout, "Gold!"

Sure enough, when he reaches the bottom, he finds himself surrounded by heaps of golden coins.

The Irishman goes next and at the top is heard to shout, "Silver!"

At the bottom he lands in mounds of silver coins, more than he could ever carry at once.

The Newfie goes last and on the way down shouts, "Weeeeeee!"

Green on Top

A woman has just had a contractor build a new house for her, and now she is giving him instructions for the interior decoration.

In the living room, she tells him, "I'd like the walls in here to be green, but not a forest green, something more like a mossy green."

The contractor nods and then goes to the window, sticks his head out, and yells, "Green on top!"

The woman is baffled, but she leads him into the kitchen, where she says, "I'd like the kitchen to be yellow, but not lemon yellow, more a sunflower yellow."

The contractor nods and then goes to the window, sticks his head out, and yells, "Green on top!"

The woman is getting irritated with this routine, but nevertheless she leads him upstairs and into the nursery. "I'd like this room to be blue, but not a sky blue, more like a robin's egg blue."

Once again, the contractor nods and then goes to the window, sticks his head out, and yells, "Green on top!"

The woman can take it no more. "Now listen here," she says, "I'm giving you some complicated instructions, and are you paying attention? No! All you're doing is yelling out the window, 'Green on top!'"

"Oh, I'm sorry about that," says the contractor. "It's just that I've got some Newfies out there laying sod!"

Granny

The Newfie child asks, "Why have you gone on the pill, Granny?"

The Newfie granny replies, "I don't want to have any more grandchildren."

Newfie Patient

A Newfie goes to see a Newfie doctor.

"Doctor," he complains, "I am suffering from a strange disease. When I walk, my one foot is always ahead of my other foot."

The doctor thinks about this and then hands him two pills. "Take one pill after you have gone to sleep, the other before you wake up."

Dang Porsches!

A Newfie and his wife won the lottery, and after spending a lot of time thinking about what they should do with the money, they decided that the first thing they would buy was a nice car. So they made a trip to the Porsche dealership in Toronto.

The salesman let them take one of the cars for a test drive, but when the couple returned, the husband said to the dealer, "Man, your cars are pieces of junk! There I am, just driving along, and BANG!, it just quits!"

The salesman said to the husband, "Well, that can't be! Here's another one; I'm sure you'll change your mind."

So the couple took the second car out for a spin and then came back to the dealer, saying: "Man! Your cars are pieces of junk! I swear, there I am just driving along, and BANG!, it just quits!"

The salesman, knowing that the cars he was selling were some of the best ever made, offered the husband another car.

The couple peeled out of the lot and came back a short while later with the same complaint: "BANG!, it just quits!"

Finally, the dealer decided to find out just what was up with the cars. He took one for a drive while the couple waited at the lot, and everything seemed to be running smoothly. He brought the car back and told the couple, "Try this one; it seems to be running just fine."

Once again, the couple took the car out. Fifteen minutes later they were back, complaining that the car just—BANG!—quit on them again.

The salesman looked at the wife, as if to say, "Is this true?"

She nodded and told him, "I swear, it just stopped working right there in the middle of the road!"

So the salesman asked the husband, who had been driving, to tell him everything that happened while he was on the road with the car. The husband told him, "I didn't do anything different in any of the cars. I started her up, pulled her into first, and she's just purring like a kitten. So I move up into second, and she's startin' to speed up. In third she's goin' great, and in fourth startin' to pass a hundred clicks. So I put her into fifth, get her up to about 120, and then decide to see how this baby can really perform, so I jam it hard into 'R' for really fast, and the dang transmission falls out!"

Newfie Bank Robber

A Newfie approaches the teller of a bank in St. John's and says, "This is a robbery. Nobody'll get hurt if you give me what I want. I want all your 10s, 20s, and 30s in a bag."

Newfie Learner

A Newfie phones Memorial University and tells the operator that he wants to speak to the registrar of the Correspondence Department. He is put through.

"Registrar speaking. How can I help you?"

"I want to register for the course in Driver's Training," the Newfie says.

Newfie Algebra Lesson

Teacher: How much is 5q plus 5q?
Student: I don't know.
Teacher: 10q.
Student: You're welcome.

Newfie Traveller

A Newfie traveller was boasting to a stranger about the number of cities he had visited.

"I have been to St. John's, Saint John, Boston, Montreal, Toronto, and Fort McMurry."

"You must know Geography quite well," the stranger replied.

"Oh, very well," replied the Newfie traveller. "I spent four days in Geography."

Another Traveller

The Newfie travels throughout the province of Quebec and returns to St. John's, where he is quizzed by his friends about the Quebecers he met.

"They are a very gifted people," he replies. "Why, even a two-year-old child can speak perfect French!"

Newfie Lottery

Q. Have you heard about the new Newfie lottery?
A. The grand prize is $1 a week for 10,000 weeks.

Three Wise Men

One Christmas Eve, three Newfies died and approached the Pearly Gates.

St. Peter met them and told them to go away and come back the next day, as he was too busy with Christmas Eve to attend to them right then. They pleaded that they had no place to go and for St. Peter to let them in.

St. Peter said, "Okay, but only if each of you can come up with something related to Christmas. Then I'll let you in."

The first Newfie took out his car keys and shook them. St. Peter asked, "What do they have to do with Christmas?"

The Newfie said, "They represent the Bells of Christmas."

St. Peter let him in.

The second Newfie took out his car keys. The key chain had a little light, which he turned on.

St. Peter asked, "What does it have to do with Christmas?"

The Newfie said, "It represents the Star of Bethlehem."

St. Peter let him in.

The third Newfie reached into his pocket and pulled out a pair of women's panties and waved them about.

St. Peter asked, "What is that all about?"

The Newfie said, "They're Carol's!"

Murphy and the "Newfie Queen"

Here is a lively Maritime verse, the authorship of which is not imme-diately apparent. I have been assured that "the ballad has entertained three generations of Canadians."

Murphy, the Newfoundland fisherman,
Made an oath by the Moon and the Sun
That he'd go out on the Gulf and catch
The biggest fish in the sea, me son.

"They'll sing about me in Twillingate,
In Harbour Grace and St. John's, too;
From St. Anthony down to Port Aux Basques,
And Toronto, if it makes CBC News."

He set out in the *Newfie Queen*,
With his jiggin' gear and nets,
Some potatoes, baloney, and a bottle of screech,
To keep out the cold and the wet.

First, he chased off the Spanish trawlers,
The Norwegians and Frenchmen, too;
He said, "There ain't enough room out there
For both me and the likes of you."

He sailed the *Queen* o'er the watery graves
Of Newfoundland ships long gone,
And as the Gulf swelled and heaved all around him,
He roared out those Newfoundland songs.

Before he reached Cape Breton,
He hauled in a shark, a great white,
But, he threw it back as too small;
It didn't put up enough of a fight.

Murphy cruised up and down the foaming brine,
He cast his nets far and wide;
But every sea creature winched into the *Queen*
He dropped back over the side.

"Lord t'underin', but I wants the biggest," he cried,
"That ever by man was seen,
Compared to what I wants to catch, me b'y,
Moby Dick was just a sardine!"

Then as he sailed in the teeth of a gale,
The nets of the *Queen* found a prize;
The engine clanged to reverse; Murphy bellowed a curse,
"Lord Jaysus! That fish is some size!"

The waters churned 'neath the *Newfie Queen's* hull,
The net lines went taut with a scream;
Murphy fought the wheel as the tempest arose,
And the *Queen* nearly went on her beam.

And all through the long, dark, harrowing night,
Murphy sweated and worked mighty hard;
He swigged screech, ate his taters and 'loncy,
And dragged his catch yard by yard.

The wild wind wailed all around him;
Of the stars, there wasn't a spark;
He just couldn't see what he had in his nets
Out there in the Stygian dark.

Pre-dawn found him raising the beacon of home;
Poor Murphy was worn out, near dead;
He dropped anchor just inside the sheltering harbour,
Then fell down exhausted in bed.

Next morning found the whole bloody town
At dockside of Murphy's home port;
The Canadian Coast Guard was hailing the *Queen*,
Their Skipper was right out of sorts.

Armed Forces choppers were circling above,
Their racket jarred Murphy awake;
He hurried topside and his eyes opened wide
And he stammered out, "For Jaysus sake!"

There in the chill of a Newfoundland morn,
Under the blue of a Newfoundland sky,
Murphy saw what he had in the *Newfie Queen*'s nets;
Murphy had bagged P.E.I.

True Scary Tale

This occurred in a little town on the north coast of Newfoundland, and even though it sounds like an Alfred Hitchcock tale, it's true.

A man was on the side of the road hitchhiking on a dark night during a terrible storm. The night was rolling on and no cars were on the road. The storm was so strong that he could see only a foot or two in front of him. Suddenly, a car come toward him and stopped. The man, without thinking about it, got into the car and closed the door. Only then did he realize that there was nobody behind the wheel!

The car started to move away very slowly. The man looked at the road and saw a sharp curve ahead. Petrified, he started to pray under his breath, begging for his life. He had not yet come out of shock when, before the car hit the curve, a hand appeared through the window and at the last second turned the wheel. The man, now paralyzed with terror, watched the hand magically appear each time the car approached an obstacle.

Finally, although terrified, he managed to open the door and jump out of the car. Without looking back, he ran hard through the storm to the nearest town. Soaking wet, exhausted and in a state of shock, pale, and visibly shaken, he walked into the nearest bar and asked for two shots of screech. Still trembling with fright, he told everybody in the bar about his horrible experience with the spooky driverless car and the mysterious hand that kept appearing. The bar patrons listened intently, becoming frightened as they listened to this eerie story. Hair stood on end as they realized the man was telling the truth—he was crying and definitely not drunk.

About half an hour had gone by when two men walked into the same bar. One said to the other, "Look, me son, there's the very same arsehole who got into that car we was pushing!"

Touch the Stars

A Torontonian was boasting to a Newfie about the height of the CN Tower.

"It's the tallest free-standing structure in the world," he said. "When you're up on the tower, you can practically reach out and touch the stars."

The Newfie was getting tired of hearing about this tower being tallest, so he said, "Well, we've nothing quite that tall in St. John's. But if you stand on the roof of any church there, you can tickle the feet of the angels as they pass by."

With Rifle
and Fishing Rod

Canada is the country *par excellence* of the great outdoors, and it is esteemed as such by sportsmen and sportswomen, who come from far and wide to hunt and fish our wildlife and admire the beauty of our fauna and flora, land, water, and sky. Too bad the Australians had already coined the evocative term "the outback." We could have used it to refer to what a century or more ago was called the Great Northwest—the wilderness area north and west of the great cities that lie to the south.

Provision yourself with some jokes for your trek into the wilds for the adventures ahead.

Deer Story

According to folklorist Helen Creighton, the following story was wildly popular in Mahone Bay, N.S.

During one particular season, a person could shoot only one deer in and around Louisburg. One day a man went into the woods and saw another man coming out with a beautiful deer. He stopped and said, "That's a beautiful deer you have. Do they grow many here as fine as that?"

The man nodded, "Yes, it's a nice deer, all right. But you should see the one I got last week at Catalone."

The man looked at him. "Do you realize who I am? No? Well, I'm an inspector of the Mounted Police."

"Well," came the prompt rejoinder. "Do you realize who I am? I'm the biggest liar in Catalone."

Hunting Lodge

Above the fireplace of the hunting lodge hangs a moose head.

"Dad and I went hunting and I bagged that moose."

"What's it stuffed with?"

"Dad."

Hunting Trip

A group of Englishmen, on their first hunting trip in Canada, were camped on the shore of a northern lake.

They were greatly aggravated by the swarms of mosquitoes. They thought that if they put out their campfire, the pests would be unable to find them. So they doused the fire, but then, in the pitch black, they were able to make out the flashes of fireflies.

"It's no use," one of the Brits lamented. "The blighters have their own torches."

Hunters

A group of city slickers went on a hunting trip, setting up camp in the woods.

As evening drew on, one of the hunters walked into camp and asked, "Is everybody here?"

Someone said, "Yes."

Then the hunter asked, "Is anybody hurt?"

Someone said, "No."

"Great," the hunter said. "That means I just shot a deer."

Excellent Woodsman

A tour guide is explaining to the passengers on his tour bus that the Indians make excellent woodsmen: "An Indian can track a man or an animal over land, through the air, even under water."

No sooner has he said this than the tour bus rounds a bend in the highway and there, in the middle of the road, lies an Indian. He has one ear pressed to the white line. His left leg is held high in the air. The tour bus stops and the guide and passengers gather around the prostrate Indian.

"What are you tracking? What are you listening for?"

The Indian replies, "Down the road, about twenty-five miles, is a 1982 Ford pickup. It's red. The left front tire is bald. The front end is out of whack, and it has dents in every panel. There are Indians in the back, all drinking Molson's. There are two dogs on the front seat."

The tour guide nods, and the passengers marvel at this precise and detailed information.

"My God, man, how do you know all of this?"

The Indian replies, "I fell out of the bloody thing about half an hour ago."

The Condor

A trapper was living with his wife and two children in an isolated cabin in the Rocky Mountains.

One winter they got socked right in with snow and were isolated from the rest of the world for months on end. Their food ran out, and they were in danger of starving. The father went out hunting every day, but he never saw anything he could shoot. Finally, he spotted a giant condor. He knew the bird was protected, but he shot it anyhow so he could feed his family. The meat from the condor saved the lives of his wife and children.

Later, after the snow had melted, a game warden came on his tour of inspection. Looking around, he found the bones of the condor behind the cabin. He arrested the trapper and took him to jail.

When the trapper went before a judge, he tearfully explained the situation. The judge was sympathetic and released the man. As the man was about to leave the courtroom, the judge asked him, "By the way, just how did the condor taste?"

The man replied, "Oh, somewhere between whooping crane and golden eagle."

Hunters

A group of men went into the woods on a hunting trip.

Nobody wanted the job of being camp cook, so they drew straws for it. The man with the short straw got the job, with the condition that the first man to complain about the cooking had to take over the chore. The man who got the job hated it, and he did everything he could to try to make someone complain. He burned the food, he undercooked it, he loaded it with salt; but nothing worked. The men grumbled under their breath, but nobody outright complained.

Then one day the man found a moose turd in the woods, and got an idea. He took the turd back to camp, and cooked it in a pie. When the other men came back from their day's hunting, he served up moose turd pie.

One man started to eat a forkful, then gagged and yelled, "Hey! This is moose turd pie . . . but good!"

Canadian Trapper

An engineer, a psychologist, and a theologian were hunting in the wilderness of northern Canada. Suddenly, the temperature dropped and a furious snowstorm was upon them. They came across an isolated cabin, far removed from any town. The hunters had heard that the locals in the area were quite hospitable, so they knocked on the door to ask permission to rest.

No one answered their knocks, but they discovered the cabin was unlocked, and so they entered. It was a simple place; two rooms with a minimum of furniture and household equipment.

Nothing was unusual about the cabin except the stove. It was large, pot-bellied, and made of cast iron. What was strange about it was its location. It was suspended in mid-air by wires attached to the ceiling beams.

"Fascinating," said the psychologist. "It is obvious that this lonely trapper, isolated from humanity, has elevated this stove so that he can curl up under it and vicariously experience a return to the womb."

"Nonsense!" replied the engineer. "The man is practising the laws of thermodynamics. By elevating his stove, he has discovered a way to distribute heat more evenly throughout the cabin."

"With all due respect," interrupted the theologian, "I'm sure that hanging his stove from the ceiling has religious meaning. Fire lifted up has been a religious symbol for centuries."

The three debated the point for several hours without resolving the issue.

When the trapper finally returned, they immediately asked him why he had hung his heavy pot-bellied stove from the ceiling.

His answer was succinct. "Had plenty of wire, not much stove pipe."

Hunter and Bear

A Canadian hunter had been hunting all day. He fell asleep and was awakened late in the night by a large grizzly bear. The bear ripped the front of the tent and stood on its hind legs. The hunter had only one idea. He dropped to his knees, closed his eyes, and prayed, "Lord, please let this be a Christian bear."

When the hunter opened his eyes, he saw that the bear had dropped to its knees and was praying, "Lord, thank you for this meal which I am about to receive . . ."

Bear Advisory

The British Columbia department of parks sent out an advisory warning people going into the woods to be wary of black bears and grizzlies. The advisory told hikers and campers to wear little bells that would alert bears to their presence, and to carry pepper spray for self-defence.

The warning also advised people to watch for "bear sign." "The droppings of black bears," the notice said, "is smaller, and contains berries and sometimes the fur of small animals like squirrels and raccoons. The droppings of grizzly bears contains little bells and smells like pepper spray."

Lost in the Woods

A pair of hunters got lost in the woods.

"No problem," said one. "All we have to do is fire into the air three times, and someone will come to our rescue."

So he fired into the air three times. Time passed, and no one came.

The other man took a turn and fired three times into the air. Still no rescue.

One of them said, "Well, I'll try firing into the air three times once more, but it had better work this time, because these are our last three arrows."

The Hunting Trip

An Irishman, an Englishman, and a Newfie on a hunting trip were staying in a cabin in the woods. They decide to go hunting singly; one would go hunting while the other two stayed to guard the cabin.

The Irishman goes out first and comes back with a fox. He says, very simply, "I see tracks, I follow tracks, I catch fox."

Then the Englishman goes out and comes back with a rabbit. He says, "I see tracks, I follow tracks, I catch rabbit."

Then it was the Newfie's turn. He goes out and comes back limping and badly battered and bruised. He says, "I see tracks, I follow tracks, I get hit by train."

The Moose Hunt

Saturday

1:00 a.m. Alarm clock rings.

2:00 a.m. Hunting partners arrive, drag you out of bed.

2:30 a.m. Throw everything except the kitchen sink into the pick-up.

3:00 a.m. Leave for the deep woods.

3:15 a.m. Drive back home to pick up gun.

3:30 a.m. Drive like hell to get to the woods before daylight.

4:00 a.m. Set up camp. Forgot the damn tent.

4:30 a.m. Head for the woods.

6:05 a.m. See two moose.

6:06 a.m. Take aim and squeeze trigger.

6:07 a.m. Click.

6:08 a.m. Load gun while watching moose go over hill.

8:00 a.m. Head back to camp.

9:00 a.m. Still looking for camp.

10:00 a.m. Realize you don't know where camp is.

Noon. Fire your gun for help, eat wild berries.

2:15 p.m. Run out of bullets.

2:20 p.m. Strange feeling in stomach.

2:30 p.m. Realize you have eaten poisonous berries.

2:45 p.m. Rescued.

2:55 p.m. Rushed to hospital to have stomach pumped.

3:25 p.m. Arrive back at camp.

3:30 p.m. Leave camp to kill moose.

4:00 p.m. Return to camp for bullets.

4:01 p.m. Load gun, leave camp again.

5:00 p.m. Empty gun at squirrel that is bugging you.

6:00 p.m. Arrive at camp, see moose grazing in camp.

6:01 p.m. Load gun.

6:02 p.m. Fire gun.

6:03 p.m. Dead battery in pick-up truck.

6:05 p.m. Hunting partner arrives in camp, dragging moose.

6:06 p.m. Repress desire to shoot hunting partner.

6:07 p.m. Fall into fire.

6:10 p.m. Change clothes.

6:15 p.m. Take pick-up. Leave hunting partner and his moose in camp.

6:25 p.m. Pick-up engine boils over, hole shot in block.

6:25 p.m. Start walking.

6:30 p.m. Stumble and fall. Drop gun in mud.

6:35 p.m. Meet bear.

6:36 p.m. Take aim.

6:37 p.m. Fire gun. Blow up barrel, plugged with mud.

6:38 p.m. Mess pants.

6:39 p.m. Climb tree.

9:00 p.m. Bear leaves.

9:05 p.m. Wrap stupid gun around tree.

Midnight. Home at last.

Sunday

Watch football game on TV, slowly tearing hunting licence into small pieces, place in envelope and mail to Game Department with detailed instructions on where to place it.

Cowboy and Preacher

A cowboy bought a horse from a preacher. The clergyman told him that to make the horse go, he just had to say, "Praise the Lord." To make the horse stop, he had to say "Amen."

The cowboy climbed into the saddle, said, "Praise the Lord," and the horse took off like a shot. The cowboy yelled, "Whoa, whoa!" but the horse kept galloping along. They were almost at the brink of a deep canyon before the cowboy remembered the right word to use. He yelled "Amen!" and the horse stopped, just inches from the edge. Looking down at the rocks hundreds of feet below, the cowboy wiped the sweat from his brow and said, "Praise the Lord."

Letter Carrier

A letter carrier went to the doctor complaining of sore feet.

"You need a holiday," said the doctor. "Go some place where you can soak your feet in seawater. That will be the best thing for them."

So the letter carrier took a vacation in New Brunswick, on the shore of the Bay of Fundy. This was new scenery to him, as he had lived all his life in Baden, Ont. The only water he knew was the so-called Grand River.

He bought two buckets in a store, then walked out on a wharf and asked a local fisherman, "How much for two buckets of seawater?"

The fisherman thought to himself, "They're biting on land today," but with a perfectly straight face, said, "A dollar a bucket."

The letter carrier paid him $2 and went back to his hotel room with two buckets of seawater. He sat most of the day with his feet in the buckets, and his feet felt so good that he decided he needed more seawater.

Back he went to the wharf, where the same fisherman was still working on some gear. This time the tide was out. The letter carrier asked for two more buckets of seawater.

"You're lucky today," the fisherman said to him. "I'm almost sold out."

Great Outdoors

A city slicker who had never been in the woods decided to see the great outdoors.

He hired an Indian guide to take him through Whiteshell Provincial Park in Manitoba. As they camped on their first night, the city man said, "I did a lot of reading about this stuff to prepare myself. For example, it's true, isn't it, that I'll be safe from a bear attack if I carry a torch?"

The Indian replied, "Depends on how fast you carry the torch."

Fishing Trip

A man from Toronto went on a fishing trip to Newfoundland.

He caught one fish. He said to the fishing guide, "All in all, that trout cost me over a thousand dollars."

The guide replied, "Good thing you didn't catch two."

Fishing Trip

Four men liked to go to the woods on fishing trips. The problem was that one of them, Frank, snored so loudly that no one could sleep with him. So, to avoid embarrassing Frank by telling him the reason, the other men always insisted on each man having his own cabin.

One year they ran into a booking problem and found themselves with only two cabins. They didn't want to embarrass Frank by telling him to have a cabin to himself while the three of them took the other cabin.

The first night Jack shared the cabin with Frank. He emerged bleary eyed and exhausted. He hadn't slept a wink.

The second night John shared the cabin with Frank. He, too, did not get a moment of shut-eye.

The third night it was Bob's turn. He came out the next morning bright-eyed and bushy-tailed, while it was Frank who looked like he hadn't slept at all.

"How did you do it?" the others asked Bob when they had the chance.

"Simple," said Bob. "Before I turned in I went over to his bed and kissed him goodnight. He sat up all night watching me."

Tourist and Dog

A tourist from Toronto was strolling along a dock in Saint John, N.B., looking to buy some fresh seafood. He had his dog with him.

As he stopped to look over a display of fish, the dog stuck his snout into a tub full of live lobsters. One of the lobsters grabbed the dog by the nose with its claw. Howling, the dog ran off, with the lobster attached.

The owner of the lobsters began to yell at the tourist, "Call back your dog! Call back your dog!"

The tourist replied, "Why don't you call back your lobster?"

Fishermen

Two old fishermen got into an argument one day about arithmetic. Each one was sure he knew more about arithmetic than the other. The argument got so hot that the captain of the fishing boat decided to take a hand in it. He gave them a problem to work out: A fishing crew catches 500 pounds of cod and brings their catch to port. They sell it for 8 cents a pound. How much do they get for the fish?

The two fishermen went to work, but neither of them seemed to be having any luck with the problem. At last, one of them turned to the captain and asked him to repeat the problem. The captain agreed.

"A fishing crew catches 500 pounds of cod—"

"Did you say they caught cod?" asks the fisherman.

"Sure," said the captain.

"Well," said the fisherman, "no wonder I didn't get the answer. Here I've been figuring on salmon all the time."

Two Fishermen

Two fishermen met on the shore of the Saskatchewan River to indulge in their favourite pastime. One of the fishermen was supposed to bring the bait, the other fisherman the beer. But the fisherman who was supposed to bring the bait forgot and brought beer instead. So they had beer but no bait.

They were sitting on the shore drinking beer, wondering what to do for bait, when they spotted a western rattlesnake. It rattled its tail and had a frog in its mouth. They poured some beer on the snake's head, and as its forked tongue reached out to lick it, they grabbed the frog. Bits of the frog made great bait and they caught a couple of white fish.

The trouble was that they soon needed another frog. Then the two fishermen felt a tap on their shoulders. There was the snake, rattling its tail, with another frog in its mouth.

Ice Fishing

A man named Willard, from way down south, has never seen snow. But he has a cousin who lives up north in Canada, and so he decides to visit him.

He decides to visit in winter. Once there, Willard can't believe his eyes. All the snow! His cousin suggests that he try ice fishing.

"Ice fishing? Well, why the heck not?" he says.

So Willard borrows a fishing rod and a hatchet to chop a hole in the ice and sets out to go ice fishing. He walks out onto the ice, finds a spot, and starts chopping.

Suddenly, he hears a voice boom: "There are no fish here!"

Willard looks up and about but can't figure out who is yelling at him. But he concludes that maybe the voice is right and that there are no fish there. So he walks a little farther out onto the ice, and starts chopping again. Immediately he hears the voice booming again: "There are no fish here!"

Willard looks up and about to see who is talking to him. But it sounds to him as if the voice is booming down from the heavens.

"Well," he figures, "whoever is yelling at me is saying that there's no fish here, so I'll move on."

Once more, Willard finds a spot, and once more he starts chopping. As soon as his hatchet hits the ice, he hears the voice boom: "There are no fish here!"

Willard jumps to his feet. He yells back, "Who are you? God?"

"No, you idiot, I'm the arena manager."

Fishing and Boxing

Q. What do fishing and boxing have in common?
A. They both involve placing a hook to a jaw.

Bragging

A fisherman was always bragging about a big fish he'd caught. Every time he told the story, he'd spread his arms wide to show how big the fish was.

His friends got so sick of hearing about it, they decided that the next time he joined them for a drink, they were going to tie his hands together so he couldn't use them to demonstrate the size of his fish. And so they did. Nevertheless, after a couple of beers, the fisherman started into his fish story.

When he came to the part of the story at which he would usually spread his arms, he held up his bound hands in front of him, balled his hands into a pair of fists, and said, "Its eyes were this big!"

Fisherman

A man is fishing from a riverbank. In the tackle box beside him is some of the most expensive fishing gear money can buy—all the best lures and spinners, each one "guaranteed" to catch fish. But the man is catching nothing. He tries one lure after another, with no luck at all.

A short way down the river, a little boy is fishing. He is using worms for bait and is pulling in fish after fish—big ones, too.

The man can't help but see this, so the next day he shows up at the riverbank with a carton of worms purchased at a bait shop. He starts fishing, and again catches nothing.

Downstream, the little boy, with his worms for bait, continues to reel in the big ones. Finally the man walks over to him and says, "Kid, what is your secret? I'm using worms, just like you are, and I'm not catching a thing. What are you doing that I'm not?"

The kid opened the palm of his hand and spat out six worms he had in his mouth. "You gotta keep 'em warm," he said.

7

What We Drink, What We Eat

Jan Morris has travelled widely and written about the countries she has visited with warmth and a sense of wonder. Everyone should read her book on this country titled *City to City* (1990).

I volunteered to show her some of Toronto's most interesting sites, including Casa Loma, Queen's Park, and the Beaches. Approaching lunchtime, I asked her, "What would you like to eat? Chinese, Italian, Thai?"

She replied, "How about Canadian?"

"That will be a problem," I said, trying to think beyond Tim Hortons. We never did find a restaurant that prided itself on its "Canadian cuisine."

Nonetheless, Canadian cuisine does have distinctive ingredients besides fiddleheads and Arctic char. And we have distinctive drinks other than Molson's beer and Seagram's whiskey.

What we drink and what we eat go together. Yet our attitudes to potables (especially beverages that are distilled, brewed, and fermented) are often laughable, hardly laudable. Prohibitionists and teetotallers have given way to dieters and slenderizers. As for the food we eat, you may judge from the following lore the degree of seriousness with which we take our breakfasts, lunches, dinners, and snacks.

Food and Drink

Notices

Please don't butt your cigarettes on our plates,
otherwise we shall be forced to serve your eggs in the ashtrays.

—*Sign, motel breakfast room, Clappison's Corners, Ont., 1970s*

In Case of Atomic Attack
Keep calm, pay your bill
& get the hell out of here!

—*Sign, restaurant near North Bay, Ont., 1950s*

Menus

Common Feed $1.00
Square Meal $2.00
Belt Buster $3.00
Moral Gorge $4.00

—*Menu, Dawson City, 1898, noted by Grant MacEwan in* Pat Burns: Cattle King *(1979)*

Free Ketchup!

—*"The Sanitary Café came to have a sign in its window surely unique in the annals of the restaurant trade," explained Andrew Allan in* A Self-Portrait *(1974). He is referring to a dining spot in Peterborough, Ont., in the 1920s.*

What foods these mortals be!

—*Line in a menu, Toronto, 1947*

Potatoes au gratin with cheese
—*Menu item, Scarborough, Ont., 1960s*

Northern Fried Chicken
—*Menu specialty, restaurant on Highway 11, south of Huntsville, Ont., 1974*

Battered Fish & Chips ... $1.45
—*Sign, Kresge's cafeteria, Toronto, 1975*

Cripes, English Style .85
Fruit Cripes, 2 in Order 1.10
—*Menu, pancake shop, Guelph, Ont., 1975*

Knish Lorraine
—*Menu item, restaurant catering to a Jewish clientele, Toronto, 1976*

Crêpes aux Pommes de Terre d'un brun doré
Golden Brown Potato Latkes
—*Bilingual sign, Ben's Delicatessen, Montreal, 1984*

Signs

Notre Dame de Grâce Kosher Meat Market
—*Name of a meat market, combining French, Jewish, and English words, near St. Urbain Street, Montreal, 1970, as recalled by Mordecai Richler*

CHIENS CHAUDS
—*Sign (literally "hot dogs"), Quebec restaurant near the Vermont border, 1955*

HOT D'OG
—*Sign, roadside restaurant, Trois-Rivières, 1960s*

Try Our Delicious Bland of Coffee!
—*Sign, stall, St. Lawrence Market, Toronto, 1979*

Due to Circumstances Beyond Our Control:
Our butler and maid have resigned.
Your cooperation in helping
to keep this place clean will be greatly appreciated.
—*Sign, restaurant kitchen, Shelbourne, Ont., 1979*

We Serve Rock & Roll
and Canadian Food
—*Sign, restaurant window, Toronto, 1980*

ON THIS SITE
IN 1897 NOTHING
HAPPENED
—*Door plaque, Mermaid Sea Food Restaurant, Toronto, 1980*

Eat like a Horse
for 50 cents.
To eat like a Man
will cost you $1.50
—*Sign, restaurant window, western Canada, 1940s*

Sandwiches $1.00
Sandwiches on a Plate $1.25
—*Sign, cafeteria counter, Marlane Hotel, Castlegar, B.C., 1977*

We are good for what ales you.
—*Sign, Wheat Sheaf Tavern, Toronto, 1978*

Marriage is Forever
—*Words written in icing on a wedding cake being sold in a bakery specializing in day-old baked goods, spotted by John Morgan of the Royal Canadian Air Farce, 1977*

Rabbit and Fox

A rabbit and a fox entered a restaurant and sat down.

A waiter came over and the rabbit ordered a salad.

When the waiter asked the fox what he wanted, the rabbit said, "If he were hungry, do you think I'd be here?"

Baby Seal

A baby seal waddles into a bar and sits on the barstool.

The bartender asks, "What'll you have?"

The seal replies, "Anything but a Canadian Club."

Traditional Eskimo Recipe for Rabbit Stew

First catch one rabbit.

Drinking

A fellow who liked to stay out all night drinking with the boys moved to the Yukon because he heard the nights were six months long.

Drink

Two brothers are talking. One is a tippler. The other is a teetotaller.

"We have a good relationship," says the tippler. "He prays for me while I drink to his health."

Badlands

A cowboy was dragging himself on hands and knees across the Badlands of Alberta. His horse was dead, and he had gone two days without water. He was almost finished.

What should he see, then, but another cowboy on a horse.

The cowboy saw the dying man, galloped over, jumped off his horse, and grabbed his canteen. He knelt beside the thirsty man and handed him the canteen of water. "Here, mister," he said, "drink this."

The man took the canteen and was about to drink from it. Suddenly he hesitated, looked at his rescuer, and asked, "Did you already drink out of this?"

Evils of Drink

In his sermon, a preacher thundered against the evils of drink.

"If I had my way," he roared, "every drop of intoxicating spirits would be dumped in the river." Then he said, "And now, our next hymn shall be . . ."

Someone in the congregation shouted, "'Shall We Gather by the River.'"

Evils of Alcohol

A minister was giving a sermon on the evils of alcohol.

"There are more than ten bars in this city, and I've never been in one of them," he said.

Someone in the congregation asked loudly, "Which one is that?"

Sir John A.

Sir John A. Macdonald, as everyone knows, was fond of the bottle.

The morning after a rough night of drinking, he was expected to make a speech. He had to wait while his political opponent spoke, and as the man went on talking, Sir John's uneasy stomach got the better of him and he belched and then vomited, right there in front of the audience.

Instead of being embarrassed, Sir John A. righted himself and declared, "What that man said just made me sick."

Sir John A. Again

It is wrong to say that Sir John A. Macdonald was addicted to the demon rum.

It was known that he drank on two days only—on the day that it rains, and on the day that it does not rain.

Two Alcoholics

Thomas D'Arcy McGee was as fond of the bottle as was Sir John A. Macdonald.

One day Sir John A. said to him, "McGee, this government cannot afford two alcoholics. You have got to stop."

Literary Drunk

A decrepit old gaffer in London, Ont., was arrested for public drunkenness.

This man was something of a literary scholar, so when he appeared before the judge and was asked if he had anything to say before his sentence was pronounced, he said, "How inhumane man is to his fellow man. I am not as besotted as Poe, as wicked as Byron, as ungracious as Keats, as drunken as Burns, as vulgar as Shakespeare . . ."

"That's enough," said the judge. "Lock this man up for seven days, and bring in those other no-goods he just fingered."

Tenth Trip to the Bar

A man and a woman were attending a reception.

When the man returned to their table from his tenth trip to the bar, the woman hissed at him, "This is your tenth trip to the bar! What will people think of you?"

The man replied, "Nothing. I told the bartender I was getting the drinks for you."

Settling an Argument

An American, a Canadian, and an Australian were sitting in a seedy bar enjoying a few beers.

The American grabbed his beer, knocked it back in one gulp, threw the glass into the air, and shot it with his handgun. As he set the handgun on the bar, he said to the Canadian and the Australian, "In the great U.S. of A., we have so much money, we never drink out of the same glass twice."

Next the Australian drank his beer, threw the glass into the air, and shot the glass with the American's gun. As he was setting the gun back on the bar, he proclaimed, "In Australia, we have so much sand that glass is cheap, and we too never drink out of the same glass twice."

Finally, the Canadian drank his beer, grabbed the gun off the bar, and shot the American. As he was setting the gun back on the bar, he told the Australian, "In Canada, we have so many Americans, we never have to drink with the same one twice."

Brewers

Brewers in P.E.I. have learned to make beer from potatoes.

Now the bartender can set 'em up and say, "This spud's for you."

First Mate and Captain

The first mate on board a ship received word that his wife had given birth to a son. That night, in celebration, he got drunk after getting off duty.

The next day he took a look at the ship's log and saw the captain's entry: "First mate was drunk last night."

He immediately protested to the captain. "Look, skipper, I never get drunk on board ship. Last night was an exception. I had a new son, and I was off duty. This looks bad on my record."

The captain was unsympathetic. "Facts are facts," he said. "And the fact remains that you were drunk last night."

The next day the captain looked in the ship's log and saw an entry made by the first mate: "The captain was sober last night."

Drinker

A man came home after an evening at the bar. His wife was waiting up for him. As soon as she smelled his breath, she said, "You've been drinking!"

"Of course, I have," he said, and pulled a half a bottle of whiskey out of his coat pocket. He handed it to her and said, "Take a drink of that!"

She took a sip and nearly gagged. "Blah!" she said. "That tastes awful!"

"There! And you thought I was enjoyin' myself!"

Big John

During the days of the opening of the West, an Easterner goes to a Prairie town and gets a job in a saloon. The owner tells him his various duties and then says, "One very important thing to remember if you ever hear that Big John is coming to town, drop whatever you're doing and run. Don't worry about the saloon, just run."

For a few weeks all goes well. Then one afternoon a cowboy rushes into the saloon and yells, "Run for your lives! Big John's comin' to town!" In an instant the saloon is empty. Even the toughest gunfighters clear out. The Mounties close their detachment and are nowhere to be seen. The Easterner, however, doesn't run away. He wants to see this Big John character whom everyone is so afraid of.

Soon a huge man comes into town. He's riding on a buffalo, and he has a mountain lion on a leash. He stops in front of the saloon, gets off the buffalo, and punches it right between the eyes. "You stay thar!" he bellows. Then he kicks the mountain lion in the balls and says, "That goes fer you too." He strides up to the saloon, kicks the door down, steps in, and roars, "Gimme a drink!"

The poor man at the bar is trembling with fear. With shaking hands he pours a shot of whiskey into a glass and hands it to the brute. The big guy swats it aside and hollers, "I said a drink!" The terrified man hands him the whole bottle. The big guy bites the neck off the bottle and pours a whole quart of ol' popskull liquor down his throat.

Now beside himself with terror, the man at the bar says, "W-w-w-would you l-l-l-like another drink, sir?"

"No time," the big man answers. "Gotta run. Big John's coming to town."

The Buffalo Theory

One afternoon at Hooters in Calgary, Cliff was explaining the Buffalo Theory to his buddy Norm. Here's how it goes.

"Well, ya see, Norm, it's like this . . . A herd of buffalo can move only as fast as the slowest buffalo. And when a herd is hunted, it is the slowest and weakest ones at the back that are killed first. This natural selection is good for the herd as a whole because the general speed and health of the group keeps improving by the regular killing of the weakest members."

Cliff paused and then continued, "In much the same way, the human brain can operate only as fast as the slowest brain cells. Excessive intake of alcohol, as we all know, kills brain cells, but naturally it attacks the slowest and weakest brain cells first. In this way, regular consumption of beer eliminates the weaker brain cells, making the brain a faster and more efficient machine."

Cliff paused again, before concluding, "And that, Norm, is why you always feel smarter after a few beers!"

Half Full or Half Empty?

Here are some definitions:

When an optimist sees a half glass, he says the glass is half full.

When a pessimist sees a half glass, he says the glass is half empty.

When a Canadian sees a half glass, he yells, "Waiter!"

Fast Friends

A man stumbles up to the only other patron in a bar and asks if he could buy him a drink.

"Why, of course," comes the reply.

The first man then asks, "Where are you from?"

"I'm from Newfoundland," replies the second man.

The first man responds, "You don't say. I'm from Newfoundland, too! Let's have another round to Newfoundland."

"Of course," replies the second man.

Curious, the first man then asks, "Where in Newfoundland are you from?"

"St. John's," comes the reply.

"I can't believe it," says the first man. "I'm from St. John's, too! Let's have another drink to Newfoundland."

"Of course," replies the second man.

Curiosity again strikes and the first man asks, "What school did you go to?"

"St. Mary's," replies the second man. "I graduated in '62."

"This is unbelievable!" the first man says. "I went to St. Mary's and I graduated in '62, too!"

Then in comes one of the regulars, who sits down at the bar. "What's been going on?" he asks the bartender.

"Nothing much," replies the bartender. "The O'Malley twins are drunk again."

Old Smoothie with the Hearty Flavour!

After the Great Canadian Beer Festival, the brewmasters all decide to go out for a beer.

The guy from Molson's sits down and says, "Bartender, I would like Canada's best beer. Give me a Molson Canadian."

The bartender dusts off a bottle from the shelf and gives it to him.

The guy from Moosehead says, "I'd like the best beer in the world. Give me a Moosehead."

The bartender gives him one.

The guy from Kokanee says, "I'd like the only beer made with glacier spring water. Give me a Kokanee."

The guy from Dominion Brewery sits down and says, "Give me a Coke."

The bartender is a little taken aback, but gives him what he ordered.

The other brewmasters look over at him and ask, "Why aren't you drinking a Dominion?"

The Newfie brewmaster replies, "Well, I figured if you guys aren't drinking beer, neither will I."

Metric

Q. How do you convert from imperial to metric?

A. Times two, add thirty. (That way, a carton of 24 Canadian is the equivalent of 78 American bottles of beer.)

J.C. & Dubya

Jean Chrétien and George W. Bush were sitting in the backyard of 24 Sussex Drive, having a barbecue.

Bush had brought along his own beer from the States. He promptly opened one can of his American beer and drank it down in one gulp. Chrétien opened a bottle of Canadian beer, took a sip, and then sat back in his chair.

Bush smirked at Chrétien, walked over to his cooler, and grabbed another can of American beer. He popped the top and finished the second can of beer in one gulp as well. Chrétien smiled and took another sip from the bottle of beer in his hand.

Bush shook his head and said to Jean, "You'll never get drunk on so little beer! I've had two cans of American beer in the time it's taken you to have two sips of your Canadian beer!"

Chrétien smiled and replied, "Da beer in my hand is worth the two in you, Bush."

Chicken and Porcupine

A Newfie crossed a chicken with a porcupine so he could eat and pick his teeth at the same time.

Milk-drinking Newfie

"Did you hear the one about the Newfoundlander who died drinking milk?"

"No."

"The cow fell on him."

Chocolate Chip Cookies

An old, old man was lying in his deathbed. His most favourite food in the world was chocolate chip cookies. As he lay there, gasping for each breath, he was sure he could smell freshly baked chocolate chip cookies coming from downstairs.

He crawled out of bed and slowly limped down the stairs. Sure enough, on the table across the kitchen was a huge platter of chocolate chip cookies. The old man finally made it to the table and reached a shaking hand toward the cookies.

Suddenly, his wife slapped his hand sharply and yelled, "Don't touch those! They're for the funeral!"

My Wife's Cooking

Two men work side by side in a factory. One man is always tired and rundown, while his partner is always cheerful and energetic, even at the end of the day.

One day the tired man asks, "Why is it that you're always so full of energy? You take pills or something?"

"It's my wife's cooking," the man answers proudly. "Yes sir! My wife is the best cook in the world. Keeps me happy and as fit as a fiddle. Why don't you come home to dinner with me tomorrow? One meal of my wife's cooking, and you'll be a new man."

So the next day the tired man accompanies his peppy friend home. As they're going up the walk, the front door opens and out comes the man's dog. The dog is as frisky as can be, and the visitor notices that it has testicles the size of grapefruit.

"My God!" he exclaims. "Look at the size of the balls on that dog!"

"And just think," says his friend, "he only gets to lick the plate."

Upscale Restaurant

A woman was eating in a rather upscale but quite busy Toronto restaurant. She noticed that each of the waiters had a spoon in his shirt pocket.

When a waiter came near her table, she stopped him and said, "I can't help but notice that you all have spoons in your shirt pockets. Why is that?"

"My, but you are a very perceptive person," the waiter said. "You see, we are pretty busy here, so we had an efficiency expert come in to tell us how we might best utilize time. He noticed that the utensil a customer is most likely to drop is the spoon. Therefore, we carry clean spoons in our shirt pockets. If a customer drops a spoon, one of us can immediately replace it, and then on our next trip to the kitchen, drop off the dirty one and pick up a clean one. That saves an extra trip to the kitchen."

"I guess that makes sense," said the woman. "But since you've been standing there, I've noticed that you—and all the other waiters—have a black thread sticking out from the zipper of your pants. Why is that?"

"Goodness, but you are perceptive. Well, the efficiency expert even followed us into the men's room. He noticed that what really takes time in there is not using the urinal but washing the hands afterward. Therefore, he came up with the black thread. When I go for a pee, I just have to undo my zipper and use the thread to pull out my . . . you know . . . which means I don't have to actually touch it with my fingers. If I don't touch it, I don't have to wash my hands. That saves time."

The woman thinks for a moment, then says, "I can see how you'd use the thread to pull it out, but how do you push it back in if you can't touch it?"

The waiter replied, "Well, I don't know about the other guys, but I use my spoon."

False Facts Department

The first McDonald's franchise to open for business outside the United States was located in Calgary. Specials listed on its opening-day menu included McMoose Burgers and McBeaver Tails.

It was announced that, in a cost-saving move, the parliamentary restaurant on Parliament Hill would become the new jewel in the crown of a major fast-food chain: Sir John A.

There also would be a new name for the popular tourist ceremony on Parliament Hill: "The Changing of the Right Guard Anti-perspirant."

French Dressing

A fellow walks into a restaurant in Montreal and says, "I would like a salad with French dressing."

He is surprised to be served a plate of lettuce with a slice of tomato, grated cheese, and a photograph of Céline Dion putting on her jacket.

Barbecue

It takes years of practice before a wife can consider herself a really good cook.

For the Canadian husband, all it takes is a backyard, a barbecue, and an apron with funny sayings on it.

Lunch Time

Jean Chrétien and Joe Clark had lunch together at a restaurant in Hull that specialized in French-Canadian cuisine.

Chrétien looked at the menu and said, "I'll have the tortière."

Clark looked at the menu and said to the waitress, "I'd like a quickie."

The waitress blushed crimson. Chrétien looked at the menu and said, "Joe, that's quiche."

Joe Clark, Cook

Joe Clark finally calls it quits. To the relief of many, he ups and leaves public life for good.

This act delights many, but it alarms his wife, Maureen McTeer. "Whatever will Joe do to occupy himself?" she asks herself. Then the answer occurs to her: "He can learn to cook."

She buys him a cookbook, a simple one, one that will take him through a week of recipes for beginning cooks.

Here are Joe's thoughts on the matter:

Monday It's fun to cook for Maureen. Today I made angel's food cake. The recipe said, "Beat twelve eggs separately." Our High River neighbours were nice enough to lend me some extra bowls.

Tuesday Maureen asked for fruit salad for supper. The recipe said, "Serve without dressing." So I didn't dress. What a surprise when Maureen brought a girlfriend home for supper!

Wednesday A good day for rice. The recipe said, "Wash thoroughly before steaming the rice." It seemed kind of silly, but I took a bath. I can't say it improved the rice any.

Thursday Today Maureen asked for salad again. I tried a new recipe. It said, "Prepare ingredients; then toss on a bed of lettuce one hour before serving." I did this, but it led to Maureen asking me what I was doing rolling around in the garden.

Friday I found an easy recipe for cookies. It said, "Put all ingredients in bowl and beat them." There must have been something wrong with this recipe. When I got back, everything was the same as when I had left.

Saturday   Maureen did the shopping today and brought home a chicken. She said, "Dress it for Sunday." Oh boy! For some reason Maureen keeps counting to ten.

Sunday   Maureen's folks came to dinner. I wanted to serve roast. All I could find in the fridge was hamburger. Suddenly I had a flash of genius. I put the hamburger in the oven and set the controls to "Roast." It still came out hamburger, much to my disappointment.

Good Night, Dear Diary   This has been a very exciting week. I am eager for tomorrow to come so I can try out a new recipe on Maureen. If we could just get a bigger oven, I would like to surprise her with Chocolate Moose.

Love and Marriage

The lyrics of the popular song assure us that "love and marriage go together like a horse and carriage." While that may be true, in theory, love's path is a wayward one. Few marriages are "made in heaven," as our light humour assures us. Attraction and passion are fraught with problems and possibilities, as these jokes show.

The humour in this chapter has an orientation that is at once romantic and familial (unlike the jokes that appear elsewhere, which are devoted to more than passion).

Farmer's Daughter

"Did you hear the one about the Canadian and the farmer's daughter?

"They got married."

Dogsled

A man was trying to impress a young woman in a bar in Dawson City.

He said, "I came all the way here from Whitehorse by dogsled just to see you."

She said, "That sounds like a lot of mush to me."

Wanted

Wanted: A refined, educated healthy gentleman, age 65 to 70, by woman of same qualifications. Strictly platonic companionship. References thoroughly screened. If I have the guts to put this ad in and you are lonely, don't be chicken, answer it.

"Companions Wanted," *The Globe and Mail*, January 14, 1977.

Maiden's Prayer

"The Maiden's Prayer to the Virgin" was quoted in a private letter from Hugh John Macdonald to James Coyne, December 15, 1871, as noted by P.B. Waite in Macdonald: His Life and World *(1975).*

Mary Mother, we believe
   That without sin you did conceive;
   Teach, we pray thee, believing,
   How to sin without conceiving.

Contraceptives

A fellow went into Kmart to buy some condoms, but the pharmacist apologized and said they were sold out.

"Why don't you try Boots," the pharmacist suggested.

"Because I want to slip in, not march in," the fellow replied.

Marital Advice

A couple remained childless after several years of marriage. They had tried everything under the sun to have a baby.

Finally they went to a doctor, who told them, "There is no medical reason why you two should not conceive a child. It's all a matter of stress. Forget about the fertility pills, the cycle methods, and all the mumbo-jumbo. Just relax. The next time you're in the mood to make love, just do it, and let fertilization take care of itself."

A month later the doctor examined the wife and told her she was pregnant.

"We did just as you said, Doctor," she told him. "We were sitting down to coffee, and I dropped my serviette, and we both reached to pick it up. Our fingers touched, and all of a sudden we were in the mood to make love, so we did. The only problem is, we are no longer allowed in Tim Hortons."

Labour Pains

A man excitedly called the hospital to say that his wife had started having labour pains.

The person on the phone asked, "Is this her first child?"

"No," came the reply. "This is her husband."

Maternity Ward

Here is a snippet of conversation heard in a maternity ward:

"I told you those pills were aspirin."

Christening

A Dartmouth shipyard worker was at his wife's bedside, looking at their newborn baby.

The wife said, "You're going to have to call the church about having him christened."

"Like hell!" the man said. "Nobody's hitting my son with a bottle!"

Xaviera Hollander

Xaviera Hollander was the New York madam and the author of record who wrote *The Happy Hooker* and its best-selling sequels. As unlikely as it might seem, she lived and worked in Toronto in the early 1970s.

She was a landed immigrant, she was lively. She was also quite quotable. She once told an interviewer, "What Oshawa needs is a good brothel!"

"I love Canada," she said. "It's the most stable country in the world. But some old ladies here think I'm always trying to steal their husbands."

She fought a series of deportation orders all the way to the Supreme Court of Canada. When she lost that appeal in April 1976, she explained her predicament in a casual way.

"So far," she said, "I've lost every appeal except my sex appeal."

Last heard, she is living and working in Holland.

Niagara Falls

Eleven tightrope walkers—ten men and one woman—were clinging to a rope that stretched from one cliff of the Niagara gorge to the other. Their ropewalk had gone disastrously wrong. The rope was beginning to fray, so they immediately agreed that one of them would have to let go, or else the rope would snap and everyone would plunge to their death in the whirlpool below.

But they could not decide who should let go. Finally the woman who was clinging to the rope gave a touching speech. Yelling to be heard by the others above the roar of the whirlpool, she offered to give up her life to save the others because women were used to giving up things for the sake of their husbands and children, because they were used to giving in to the vanity of men, and because, after all, men were the superior sex and it was only right that they be saved.

When she finished speaking, all the men clapped.

Getting a Divorce

It's early October, and an elderly man in Toronto calls his son in Ottawa. "I hate to ruin your day, but I have to tell you that your mother and I are divorcing; forty-five years of misery is enough," he says.

"Pop, what are you talking about?" the son screams.

"We can't stand the sight of each other any longer," the old man says. "We're sick of each other, and I'm sick of talking about this, so you call your sister in Calgary and tell her." Then he hangs up.

Frantic, the son calls his sister, who explodes on the phone. "They're not getting divorced, not if I have anything to do with it," she shouts. "I'll take care of this."

She calls to Toronto immediately and screams at the old man, "You are not getting divorced. Don't do a single thing until I get there. I'm calling my brother back, and we'll both be there tomorrow. Until then, don't do a thing, do you hear me?" Then she hangs up.

The old man hangs up the phone and turns to his wife. "Well," he says, "they're coming for Thanksgiving and paying their own fares . . . Now what do we tell them for Christmas?"

Marriage Counsellor

A husband and wife were sitting in the office of a marriage counsellor.

The husband had a sour look on his face. The counsellor asked, "Mr. Smith, did you wake up grouchy this morning?"

"No. I let her sleep."

Wedding Reception

A Torontonian was talking to a friend.

"Those Cape Bretoners aren't so tough," he said. "Last weekend I was at a wedding, and at the reception, a Cape Bretoner and one of my cousins got into an argument. Well, my cousin, my uncle, my father, two of my brothers, and I almost threw him out."

Twins

Clancy the Newfoundlander had just become the father of triplets.

As he was walking out of church on Sunday, the priest said to him, "Well, Clancy, it seems God has smiled upon you."

"Smiled?" said Clancy. "He laughed out loud!"

Wildflower

A little boy came into the house with a wildflower for his mother.

"Oh my," she said. "You picked that for me all by yourself?"

"Yes," he replied. "And the whole world was holding on to the other end."

Three Babies

A Cape Bretoner was in the father's waiting room while his wife was in the delivery room.

Presently a smiling nurse came out with three babies. The man looked them over for a few seconds, then said, "I'll take the one in the middle."

Triplets

Two Cape Breton women met at Kmart. One of them was beaming with happiness.

"The doctor tells me I'm pregnant," she said. "And not only that, but I'm going to have triplets. You know, he said triplets happen only once in every three million times."

"My God," said the other, "when do you ever get time to do the housework?"

The Baby Man

The Smiths, who lived in Fredericton, N.B., had no children and decided to use a proxy father to start their family.

On the day the proxy father was to arrive, Mr. Smith kissed his wife goodbye and said, "I'm off. The man should be here soon."

Half an hour later, just by chance, a door-to-door baby photographer rang the doorbell, hoping to make a sale.

"Good morning, madam," he said. "You don't know me but—"

"Oh, no need to explain," Mrs. Smith cut in. "I've been expecting you."

"Really?" the man said. "Well, good. I've made a specialty of babies."

"That's what my husband and I had hoped. Please come in and have a seat. Just where do we start?" Mrs. Smith asked, blushing.

"Leave everything to me. I usually try two in the bathtub, one on the couch, and perhaps a couple on the bed. Sometimes the living-room floor is fun, too. You can really spread out."

"Bathtub? Living-room floor?" Mrs. Smith said, amazed. "No wonder it didn't work for Harry and me."

"Well, madam, none of us can guarantee a good one every time. But if we try several positions and I shoot from six or seven angles, I'm sure you'll be pleased with the results."

"I hope we can get this over with quickly," gasped Mrs. Smith.

"Madam, in my line of work, a man must take his time. I'd love to be in and out in five minutes, but you'd be disappointed with that, I'm sure."

"Don't I know!" Mrs. Smith exclaimed.

The photographer then opened his briefcase and pulled out a portfolio of his baby pictures. "This one was done on the top of a bus in the main street downtown."

"Oh, my God!" Mrs. Smith exclaimed.

"And these twins turned out exceptionally well when you consider that their mother was so difficult to work with."

"Difficult?"

"Yes. I finally had to take her to the exhibition grounds to get the job done right. People were crowding around four and five deep, pushing to get a look."

"Four and five deep?" Mrs. Smith asked, eyes wide with amazement.

"Yes. And for more than three hours. The mother was constantly squealing and yelling. I could hardly concentrate. Then darkness approached and I began to rush my shots. I finally packed it all in when the squirrels began nibbling at my equipment."

"They actually chewed on your . . . um . . . equipment?"

"That's right. Well, madam, if you're ready, I'll set up my tripod so we can get to work."

"Tripod!" Mrs. Smith looked extremely worried now.

"Oh yes. I have to use a tripod to rest my Canon on. It's much too big for me to hold while I'm getting ready for action. Madam? Good Lord! She's fainted!"

Engagement

Girl to a friend: "I've gotten engaged to a man from Ireland."

"Oh, really?"

"No, O'Riley."

Flight Attendant

A man is sitting at an airport bar and notices a beautiful woman sitting next to him. He thinks to himself, "Wow, she is so gorgeous, she must be a flight attendant." So he decides to scoot toward her and try to pick her up.

But he can't think of a pick-up line. After pondering for a while, he turns toward her and says, "Love to fly and it shows?"

She gives him a blank, confused stare, and he immediately thinks to himself, "Oh crap, she must not fly for Delta."

So he thinks of something else, and he says, "Something special in the air?"

She gives him the same confused look. He thinks, "Damn! She must not fly for American."

So next he says, "I would really love to fly your friendly skies."

Suddenly, the woman, irritated beyond belief with this guy, barks out, "Man, what the hell do you want?"

The man in a relieved voice says, "Ah, Air Canada."

Subject: Mathematics and Life

I received this piece of urban lore via e-mail from a noted Toronto-based commentator on September 2, 2002. To the best of my knowledge, it is of Canadian origin and it originated with a woman. It ended with the following recommendation: "Send this to a smart woman who needs a laugh and to the guys you think can handle it!"

Office Arithmetic

Smart boss + smart employee = profit
Smart boss + dumb employee = production
Dumb boss + smart employee = promotion
Dumb boss + dumb employee = overtime

Shopping Math

A man will pay $2 for a $1 item he needs.
A woman will pay $1 for a $2 item that she doesn't need.

Romance Mathematics

Smart man + smart woman = romance
Smart man + dumb woman = affair
Dumb man + smart woman = marriage
Dumb man + dumb woman = pregnancy

General Equations and Statistics

A woman worries about the future until she gets a husband.
A man never worries about the future until he gets a wife.
A successful man is one who makes more money than his wife can spend.
A successful woman is one who can find such a man.

Happiness

To be happy with a man, you must understand him a lot and love him a little.
To be happy with a woman, you must love her a lot and not try to understand her at all.

Longevity

Married men live longer than single men, but married men are a lot more willing to die.

Propensity to Change

A woman marries a man expecting he will change, but he doesn't.
A man marries a woman expecting that she won't change, and she does.

Discussion Technique

A woman has the last word in any argument.
Anything a man says after that is the beginning of a new argument.

How to Stop People from Bugging You about Getting Married

Old aunts used to come up to me at weddings, poking me in the ribs and cackling, telling me, "You're next."
They stopped after I started doing the same thing to them at funerals.

Pamela Anderson Lee

Pamela Anderson Lee, Junoesque model and ebullient film personality, is the pride of Vancouver Island. She now lives in Malibu, California. She once told an interviewer that she plans to be married only twice in her life. This is how she expressed it:

"I plan to be married for the first time and for the last time."

Honeymoon

A couple visits Niagara Falls for their honeymoon.

On the first morning, the bride wants to see the falls, so the bridegroom pulls up the shade, sees that it's raining, and goes back to bed.

This happens the second morning and again the third morning.

On the fourth morning, the groom goes to the window, takes hold of the cord, and goes up with the shade.

Honeymoon Capital of the World

The following remarks were overheard at a large tourist hotel in Niagara Falls.

- "After the honeymoon, I felt like a new man. The trouble was, so did she."
- "When they came down to breakfast on the first morning, they asked for separate bills."

Newfie Couple

A Newfie couple is parked on a country road at night.

He says, "Do you want to go in the back seat?"

She says, "No, I want to stay up front with you."

Mountie's Wife

Did you hear the one about the Mountie's wife who is in bed with her lover when she hears her husband gallop into the yard?

She hides her lover in the bedroom closet. The Mountie comes into the bedroom, looks around, but notices nothing amiss.

Later on, the Mountie goes back to work and the lover escapes.

Family Court

A judge in family court in Corner Brook is interviewing a woman about her proposed divorce.

The judge asks, "What are the grounds?"

The woman replies, "About four acres with a nice little house in the middle. Oh, yes, and a stream running by."

"No," he says, "I meant what was the foundation of this case?"

"Concrete. And the house itself is frame."

The judge is becoming exasperated. "That's not what I mean. What are your relations like?"

"I've an aunt and uncle living near Corner Brook, and so do my husband's parents."

The judge says, "But do you have a real grudge?"

"No," she replies. "We just have a two-car carport. But it's fine for the Volkswagen and the Ford pick-up."

"Please," he tries again. "Is there any infidelity in your marriage?"

"Yes, both my son and daughter have stereo sets. We don't necessarily like the music, but when they're playing rock-n-roll, they'll sometimes wear headsets."

"Madam, does your husband ever beat you up?"

"Yes, about twice a week he gets up much earlier than I do to go to the mill."

Exploding in rage, the judge says, "But why do you want a divorce?"

"Oh, I don't want a divorce," she said. "I've never wanted a divorce. My husband does. He says he can't communicate with me."

Astronauts in Orbit

Astronaut Marc Garneau took a fancy to fellow astronaut Judy Payette.

He made small talk and then asked her outright if she was interested in him.

Mark: How about a date tonight?

Judy: Sure! Your space or mine?

aMONG tHE BeLievers

Religion has an important role to play in the lives of Canadians.

Sociologists are always measuring the allegiance of members of the general public to the leading affiliations, beliefs, cabals, churches, cliques, congregations, conventions, covens, creeds, cults, denominations, faiths, persuasions, rites, schisms, sects, and so on.

Religious matters were meaningful to the majority of Canadians in the past, continue to be meaningful in the present, and will presumably remain meaningful in the future. In the meantime, here are some jokes about Canadians and their churches, synagogues, covens, prayer halls, and temples.

Church Signs

Closed on Sunday
See you in Church

—*Sign on the gate of Jack Miner's Bird Sanctuary, Kingsville, Ont., 1940s*

Jesus Said, Behold, I Come Quickly
—*Message on the marquee of the Gospel Temple, Ottawa, 1963*

Thou Shalt Not
Commit Adultery
For Whoremongers
and Adulterers
God Will Judge
—*Billboard on the Prairies, 1966*

Ladies' Hats and Men's Coats
Not Necessary
But Collection Is
—*Notice for a service, Knox Church, Macdonald's Corners, Dalhousie Lake, Ont., 1970*

Drive Carefully
Your Car May Not Be the Only Thing
Recalled by Its Maker
—*Baptist church, Fonthill, Ont., 1970*

Many a Love Nest
Is Upset by a Lark
—*United church, Aurora, Ont., 1970*

Our God is Alive and Well
Sorry to Hear about Yours
—*United church, Vancouver, 1971*

Seven Days without Church
Makes One Weak
—*Protestant church, Toronto, 1974*

Please Come to My Birthday Party
Love, Jesus
—*Anglican church, London, Ont., Christmas 1974*

Love Is Something You Do
—*Timothy Eaton Memorial Church, Toronto, 1975*

Litany Candles?
—*Pun said to be seen in a Montreal church by pun-collector John S. Crosbie*

Heaven and Hell

There are many ways in which Heaven and Hell are different. Here are just a few ways in which they are known to differ.

In the heavenly pastures, the police are Canadian; the bankers are Swiss; the dancers are Brazilian; the chefs are French; the merchants are German; the lovers are Italian; and the organizers of Heaven are the British.

Hell is different, for in the infernal fields the police are German; the bankers are Brazilian; the dancers are Swiss; the chefs are British; the lovers are Canadian; the mechanics are French; and the organizers of Hell are the Italians.

Heaven

A missionary was trying, without much success, to convert the chief of the Micmacs to the missionary's particular form of Protestantism.

He pleaded with the chief, asking, "When you die, don't you want to go to Heaven?"

"No," said the chief. "If Heaven was any good, you English would have already grabbed it."

Good Thief

A priest carrying a satchel filled with money from the church collection was on his way to the bank when he saw a known "tough crook" of the neighbourhood standing on the corner he was approaching.

The priest was so nervous that, as he passed by the thug, he tripped over the curb and the moneybag went flying from his hand. The hood picked up the satchel, then helped the priest to his feet and handed it back to him.

"Oh my!" said the surprised Father. "I was always given to believe that you were not an honest character."

"Maybe I ain't all the time," said the tough guy, "but I am always honest to goodness."

Bishop of Ottawa

His Lordship the Bishop of Ottawa had grown weary of attending parliamentary functions as well as the national days of all the various embassies.

At one of the latter, he arrived on his last legs and collapsed into the nearest chair. The hostess approached him and asked him coyly, "A pot of tea, My Lord?"

"No tea," said the bishop.

"A cup of coffee, My Lord?"

"No coffee," said the bishop.

An understanding hostess, she leaned over and whispered in his ear, "Shall I serve you Scotch and water?"

"No water," said the bishop, brightening.

Pearly Gates

St. Peter is surprised to see someone approach the Pearly Gates. He was not expecting his first visitor to Heaven for another hour.

St. Peter: How did you get up here?

New arrival: Flu.

Scriptural Injunctions

A priest was driving along a country road in an English Catholic district of Quebec when he saw a nun by the side of the road. He stopped and offered her a lift, which she accepted. She got in and crossed her legs, forcing the habit to open and reveal the side of her shapely leg. The priest, looking, nearly ran off the road. He changed gear and let his hand slide up her leg. She immediately says, "Father, remember Psalm 129."

The priest apologized profusely and removed his hand. But he was unable to avoid glancing from time to time at her leg.

Farther on, he again changed gear and, staring at her leg for the umpteenth time, he let his hand slide up her leg again. The nun once again said, "Father, remember Psalm 129." Once again the priest apologized, "Sorry, Sister, but you know the flesh is weak."

Arriving at the convent, the nun got out and the priest drove on to his church. When he reached it, he rushed to the Bible and looked up Psalm 129. It said: "Go forth and seek, further up you will find glory."

Moral of the story: You should always be well informed in your job or you might miss a great opportunity.

Absolute Silence

The Trappists have a monastery in Oka, Que., where the rule of silence is strictly respected.

A man joins the monastery and is warned about the rule of absolute silence. "Once every five years," the abbot explains to him, "you may come to my office and speak to me. But other than that, no talking is allowed."

The man accepts this, becomes a monk, and for five years not a word comes from his lips. On the day he is allowed to speak to the abbot, the abbot says, "Well, do you have anything to say?"

"Yes," the man replies. "My cell is quite cold at night."

"I will look into it," says the abbot.

The man doesn't say another word for five more years. Once again he is in the abbot's office, and the abbot asks him if he has anything to say. "Yes," says the man. "The food is not very good."

"I will look into it," says the abbot.

Another five years of silence go by, and the man is again in the abbot's office. This time he says, "The coarse clothing we have to wear tends to irritate the skin."

The abbot says he will look into it.

Another five years pass, and the man is in the abbot's office yet again. This time he says that he doesn't want to be a monk anymore. He wants to leave the monastery. "Well, that doesn't surprise me," says the abbot. "You've done nothing but complain since you got here."

Promised Land

It is known that Moses, who led the Israelites out of Egypt toward the Promised Land, suffered a stammer.

He wanted to order his people to "Go forth to Canaan." What he actually said was, "Go forth to Canada."

Old Bible

Joe lived in the same old house in Toronto that his great-grandparents had lived in when they first emigrated from Europe.

He decided to clean out the attic one day. He later told a friend, "You wouldn't believe the old junk I found up there. I threw out a dusty old Bible that was printed by Guten-something or other."

"Gutenberg!" cried his friend. "You threw out a Gutenberg Bible!"

"Well sure," said Joe. "Somebody named Luther scribbled all over it."

The Nature of Jesus

There are three good arguments that Jesus was black:
1. He called everyone "brother."
2. He liked gospel.
3. He couldn't get a fair trial.

There are three equally good arguments that Jesus was Jewish:
1. He went into his father's business.
2. He lived at home until he was thirty-three.
3. He was sure his mother was a virgin and his mother was sure he was God.

There are three equally good arguments that Jesus was Italian:
1. He talked with his hands.
2. He had wine with every meal.
3. He used olive oil.

There are three equally good arguments that Jesus was Californian:
1. He never cut his hair.
2. He walked around barefoot all the time.
3. He started a new religion.

There are three equally good arguments that Jesus was Irish:
1. He never got married.
2. He was always telling stories.
3. He loved green pastures.

There are three equally good arguments that Jesus was a woman:
1. He fed a crowd at a moment's notice when there was hardly any food at hand.
2. He kept repeating his message to a bunch of men who just would not understand.
3. Even when he was dead, he had to get up because there was more work for him to do.

Finally, there are three equally good arguments that Jesus was Canadian:

1.. He fed the hungry and healed the poor.
2. He said the peacemakers shall inherit the earth.
3. He never learned to speak French.

Herd of Swine

A Sunday school teacher asked a pupil, "What happened when the evil spirits went into the herd of swine?"

The pupil replied, "It was the world's first devilled ham."

Suffering of Job

A Sunday school teacher asked a little girl a difficult question: "Why did God allow Job to suffer?"

The girl said, "God allowed Job to suffer because Job said bad words, even when he was a baby."

The teacher asked the girl, "Why do you say that?"

The girl replied, "It tells us in the Bible, 'Job cursed the day he was born.'"

Forgiveness

A minister was lecturing on forgiving one's enemies.

He told everyone in the congregation who had an enemy he or she hadn't forgiven to stand up. All did except for one old man, who was in fact the oldest man in town.

"Come now, Mr. Jones," the minister said. "A man of your long years must certainly have made some enemies."

"Lots of 'em," the old man replied.

"And have you forgiven them all?" the reverend asked.

"No need to," the old man said, "because I've outlived every one of the bastards."

Cross

Q. What do you get if you cross an atheist with a Jehovah's Witness?

A. Someone who rings your doorbell for no reason.

Q. What do you get if you cross an existentialist with a Jehovah's Witness?

A. Someone who rings your doorbell and asks, "What am I doing here?"

Sermons

A preacher at a church in Moose Jaw, Sask., always began his sermons by thanking the Lord for whatever the day's weather was. Rain, sunshine, cool weather, warm weather—he thanked the Lord for them all.

One Sunday morning it was so cold and blowing such a blizzard that only a small number of the congregation made it to church. The members sat there as the preacher mounted his pulpit and wondered how he would ever thank the Lord for that day's weather.

The preacher said, "Lord, we thank Thee that Thou dost send us so few Sundays like today."

Beach Holiday

Two old orthodox Jews who had immigrated to Canada from the Old Country went to Wasaga Beach for the first time.

They looked out across the water, and what should they see but a bikini-clad girl water-skiing behind a motorboat.

"Have you ever seen anything like that?" asked one.

"No, I never have," said the other.

After watching for about ten minutes, one of them said, "Well, I guess we can go now. There's nothing else to see here. It's obvious she isn't going to catch him."

The Atheist and the Bear

One day an atheist was walking through the woods in the interior of British Columbia, admiring all that evolution had created.

"What majestic trees! What a powerful river! What beautiful animals!" he said to himself.

As he was walking alongside the river, he heard a rustling in the bushes behind him. Turning to look, he saw an eight-foot grizzly bear beginning to charge toward him. He ran as fast as he could down the path. He looked over his shoulder and saw that the bear was rapidly closing on him. Somehow, he ran even faster, so scared that tears came to his eyes.

He looked again, and the bear was even closer. His heart was pounding in his chest, and he tried to run faster yet. But alas, he tripped and fell to the ground. As he rolled over to pick himself up, the bear was right over him.

"Oh, my God . . . !"

Time stopped. The bear froze. The forest was silent. Even the river stopped moving.

As a brilliant light shone upon the man, a thunderous voice came from all around.

"You deny my existence for all these years, teaching others that I don't exist. And even credit creation to some cosmic accident. Do you expect me to help you out of this predicament? Am I to count you as a believer?"

Difficult as it was, the atheist looked directly into the light and said, "It would be hypocritical to ask to be a Christian after all these years, but perhaps you could make the bear a Christian?"

"Very well," said the thunderous voice.

The light went out. The river ran. The sounds of the forest resumed, and the bear dropped down on his knees, brought both paws together, bowed his head, and spoke, "Lord, thank you for this food which I am about to receive."

Nun and Vampire

A nun and a laywoman were walking down a street in Winnipeg one night when a vampire jumped out at them and said, "I am a vampire, and I'm going to drink your blood!"

The laywoman quickly said to the nun, "Hurry! Show him your cross!"

So the nun put on an angry look, shook her finger at the vampire, and said, "I want to tell you, you are in big, big trouble, mister . . ."

Church and Synagogue

In the Kensington area of Toronto there was a Catholic church across the street from a synagogue. Over the years the Catholic church grew bigger and more ornate, while the synagogue remained small and rather poor looking.

One day the rabbi said to one of his assistants, "On Sunday, go over there and sit in on one of their services and see what it is they're doing to be so prosperous." So on Sunday the assistant attended Mass.

When he returned to the synagogue, he said, "I think I know their secret. In the middle of their service, the priest sings, 'Do you want to play dominoes?' Then all the people sing, 'Yes, we want to play dominoes.' Then a guy passes around a basket to take side bets."

Typical Canadian Baby

A Canadian is drinking in a New York bar when he gets a call on his cell phone. He hangs up, grinning from ear to ear, and orders a round of drinks for everybody in the bar because, he announces, his wife has just produced a typical Canadian baby boy weighing twenty-five pounds.

Nobody can believe that any new baby can weigh in at twenty-five pounds, but the proud father just shrugs, "That's about average up north, folks. As I said, my boy's a typical Canadian baby boy."

Congratulations showered him from all around, and many exclamations of "Wow!" were heard. One woman actually fainted from sympathy pains.

Two weeks later the Canadian returns to the bar. The bartender recognizes him and says, "Say, you're the father of that typical Canadian baby who weighed twenty-five pounds at birth, aren't you? Everybody's been making bets about how big he'd be in two weeks' time. We were going to call you. So how much does he weigh now?"

The proud father answers, "Seventeen pounds."

The bartender is puzzled and concerned. "What happened? He weighed twenty-five pounds already the day he was born."

The still-proud father takes a slow swig from his Molson Canadian beer, wipes his lips on his shirt sleeve, leans in to the bartender, and proudly says, "Had him circumcised."

Maternity Wing

A Catholic priest is in the baby-viewing room of the maternity wing of St. Joseph's Hospital. Another man comes in and stands beside him to look through the window.

"Which one is yours?" the priest asks.

"That little boy there," the man says proudly.

"A fine-looking boy," the priest says. "What's his name?"

"Robert Joseph," says the man.

"A good Christian name," says the priest. "Is this your first?"

"No," says the man. "My wife and I have six other children."

"Well," says the priest, "we can't have too many little Catholics, now, can we?"

"Actually," says the man, "we're Presbyterians."

"Sex maniac," mutters the priest, and walks away.

Priest and Minister

A Catholic priest was driving up Yonge Street. He wasn't paying full attention to his driving and at an intersection bumped into the back of a car driven by a Protestant minister.

As the two clergymen were looking over the damage, a police officer came up to them, asked a couple of questions, and then said to the priest in his broad Irish brogue, "So tell me, Father, how fast do you think the Good Reverend was goin' when he backed into you?"

Funeral

Old man Dooley's dog had died, so he went to his priest, Father O'Reilly, and asked if he could arrange a funeral.

"Now Dooley," the priest said, "I'm sorry for you and all that, but I can't be using my church to have a funeral for a dog. Maybe you better go and ask the Protestants if they can do something for you."

"Okay, Father," Dooley said. "Do you think it will help if I offer them $500?"

"Saints preserve us!" the priest exclaimed. "You didn't tell me the dog was a Catholic!"

Loonie

I'm a loonie. I buy next to nothing at the grocery store. I'm sneered at as a cheap tip in a restaurant. Kids regard me the way their parents once regarded a nickel. I don't even get an hour at a parking meter anymore. So why is it such a big deal when I'm dropped into a church collection basket?

St. Peter at the Pearly Gates

No sooner was the loonie minted than one died and appeared before St. Peter at the Pearly Gates.

St. Peter glared at the loonie and said, "I don't think I can admit you. But let me check the Big Book to see if you are mentioned anywhere in its pages."

St. Peter riffled through the book's pages, looked up, smiled, and said, "Yes, you're here. I can admit you."

So that's how the loonie entered Heaven.

No sooner was the twoonie minted than one died and appeared before St. Peter at the Pearly Gates.

St. Peter glared at the twoonie and said, "I don't think I can admit you. But let me check the Big Book to see if you are mentioned anywhere in its pages."

St. Peter riffled through the book's pages, looked up, smiled, and said, "Yes, you're here. I can admit you."

And that's how the twoonie entered Heaven.

Soon thereafter a $10 bill died and appeared before St. Peter at the Pearly Gates.

St. Peter glared at the $10 bill and said, "I don't think I can admit you. But let me check the Big Book to see if you are mentioned anywhere in its pages."

St. Peter riffled through the book's pages, looked up, frowned, and said, "You're not here. I'm sorry I can't admit you to Heaven."

"Why not?" pleaded the $10 bill. "You admitted first the loonie and then the twoonie. I've been around a lot longer than those two newcomers."

"Yes, that is true," said St. Peter sorrowfully. "But I checked the Big Book, and there is no reference to you appearing on a collection plate in church."

Both Wishes Granted

Two Canadians met St. Peter at the Pearly Gates.

St. Peter told them that Heaven was a bit behind in its paperwork, and they would have to go back to earth for a week. He asked them how they would like to spend their extra week on earth.

The first man said, "I'd like to be an eagle, soaring over the Rocky Mountains."

The other man said, without embarrassment, "I want to be a stud."

St. Peter immediately said, "Both wishes granted."

He snapped his fingers and the two Canadians disappeared.

A week later the paperwork was all ready, and St. Peter told Archangel Gabriel to fetch the two men.

"Where will I find them?" the archangel asked.

St. Peter said, "One of them is an eagle, soaring over the Rocky Mountains. The other one is in a snow tire in northern Ontario."

Cheaters in Heaven

Three men have died and are standing at the Pearly Gates, waiting to get into Heaven. St. Peter explains to them that the type of eternity they will experience in Heaven will be based on what they did while they lived on earth.

He asks the first man, "How many times did you cheat on your wife?"

The man thinks about it for a few moments and then, with downcast eyes, replies, "Seventeen times."

St. Peter tells him, "I admire your honesty, but that is a high number. You will be given a Volvo to drive in Heaven and a small, one-bedroom apartment."

The man thanks St. Peter and enters Heaven.

The next man is asked the same question, "How many times did you cheat on your wife?"

He thinks about it for only two or three seconds and then says, "Four times!"

St. Peter is impressed and gives the man a comfortable sports car to drive in Heaven and a bungalow in which to pass eternity.

The last man is asked how many times he cheated on his wife. He does not even hesitate for a second. "Never!" he exclaims, with obvious pride.

St. Peter, very impressed, gives the man a limousine with chauffeur to drive in Heaven and a beautiful Georgian mansion in which to reside.

A few weeks later, the first two men meet on a busy heavenly street and begin talking. Then they see the third man pull up in his limo, bawling his eyes out.

"What could possibly be wrong?" they ask the crying man. "You lived a faithful life, and now you've got a limo, a mansion, and more respect in Heaven than anyone else. You shouldn't be crying!"

"No, you don't understand!" he replies. "I just saw my wife go by—on a skateboard!"

At the Pearly Gates

Here is a traditional verse that appears in collections of folklore. This version comes from Robert Shelley's The Great Canadian Joke Book *(1976).*

A farmer stood at the Pearly Gates,
His face all ruddy and old.
"What have you done," St. Peter said,
"To gain admittance to the fold?"

"I've been an Albertan farmer, sir;
I've farmed for many a year."
He slowly raised his hand to his cheek
And brushed away a tear.

The Pearly Gates swung open wide;
St. Peter rang the bell.
"Come in, old man, you're welcome here;
You've already been through hell."

St. James' Cathedral

Prime Minister Pierre Elliott Trudeau was observed entering St. James' Cathedral in Montreal.

"I wonder what he's going to do there," one observer said to another.

"I suppose he's going to pray."

"Really? To whom?"

Nathan Phillips

Newspaperman Michael Hanlon told the following story in his Toronto Star *column, January 9, 1976.*

When Nathan Phillips was mayor of Toronto, he attended a big Roman Catholic lunch at the King Edward Hotel, bringing greetings from the city.

He looked at James Cardinal McGuigan, archbishop of Toronto, and said, "You know, Your Eminence, I was thinking only the other day that if you and I had been switched in our cradles, today you would be mayor of all the people and I would be the cardinal."

There were nervous titters from the priests and nuns present, until the cardinal stood up, put an arm around Nate's shoulders, and said, "If we had been switched in our cradles, Your Worship, I would be mayor, but you would be Pope."

Catholic and Marxist

Archbishop Léger, the leading Catholic prelate in Canada, and Tim Buck, the leader of the Canadian Communist Party, enjoyed a brief conversation during a chance encounter in an airport lounge. The conversation went something like this:

"I have always wondered about an historical irregularity," Buck admitted to Léger. "How come the Church grows richer while the people grow poorer? What Communism wants is for the people to grow richer and the Church to grow poorer."

"The reason is simple," Léger said. "We promise them Heaven; you deliver Hell."

Lucien Bouchard

Quebec premier Lucien Bouchard may have been a lukewarm separatist but he was a good Catholic.

He went to his favourite father confessor and made his confession. "Father, I am guilty of the sin of vanity."

"What makes you think so?" asked the old priest.

"Every morning, when I look into the mirror as I shave, I think, 'What a wonderful and important person I am.'"

"Never fear, my dear premier, that is not a sin. It is only a mistake."

Pope of the Far North

Allan Fotheringham, columnist, essayist, and purveyor of scuttlebutt, likes to tell the story of the 1984 visit of Pope John Paul II to the Northwest Territories. It was to be the first papal visit to the Far North, and Fort Simpson was selected to be its single stop. Northerners who lived in the town were delighted. Northerners who lived elsewhere were miffed.

"Legend has it that an irate Yellowknife city councillor, citing this as an insult to the major centre, moved that the Northwest Territories cancel the visit.

"Another councillor stood up. 'Don't worry,' he said. 'If he kisses the ground when he gets off the plane, he may be here all winter.'"

Heaven

An architectural historian—not Witold Rybczynski, but an American of his calibre—was commissioned to write a book about famous churches around the world.

For his first chapter he decided to write about Canadian churches. So he bought a plane ticket and took a trip to British Columbia, thinking that he would work his way across the country from west to east.

On his first day in Victoria, he was inside a church taking photographs when he noticed a golden telephone mounted on the wall with a sign that read "$10,000 per call." The American, being intrigued, asked a priest who was strolling by what the telephone was used for.

The priest replied that it was a direct line to Heaven and that for $10,000 you could talk to God. The American thanked the priest and went along his way.

Next stop was in Vancouver. There, at a very large cathedral, he saw the same golden telephone, with a similar sign. He wondered if this was the same kind of telephone he saw in Victoria and so asked a nearby nun what its purpose was.

She told him that it was a direct line to Heaven and that for $10,000 he could talk to God. "Okay, thank you," said the American.

He then travelled to Edmonton, Calgary, Regina, Winnipeg, Toronto, Ottawa, Montreal, and Halifax. In every church he saw the same golden telephone with the same "$10,000 per call" sign under it.

Finally the American arrived in St. John's. Again, the same golden telephone, but this time the sign under it read: "10¢ per call." The American was intrigued, so he asked the priest, "Father, I've travelled all over Canada, and I've seen this same golden telephone in many churches. I'm told that it is a direct line to Heaven. But in all the other provinces the price per call was $10,000. Why is it so cheap here?"

The priest smiled and answered, "You're in Newfoundland now, son. It's a local call."

The Devil and the Little Old Man

One Sunday just as Mass was about to start, the Devil rushed through the church doors and screamed, "I'm the Devil!"

Everyone panicked and ran from the church in terror—all but one little old man who was sitting all by himself at the front of the church.

"Humph!" thought the Devil. "Who does he think he is?" Then he walked up to the little old man. "Do you know who I am?" the Devil demanded.

"I sure do," said the man.

"Then why aren't you afraid of me?" asked the Devil.

The old man looked up at the Devil and replied, "Why should I be? I've been married to your sister for forty years."

Creationism

And God populated the earth with broccoli and cauliflower and spinach, green and yellow vegetables of all kinds, so Man would live long and healthy lives. But Satan created McDonald's, and McDonald's brought forth the 99-cent double cheeseburger. And McDonald's said to Man, "You want fries with that?" And Man said, "Supersize them." And Man gained pounds.

And God said, "Try my crispy fresh salad." But Satan created ice cream. And Man gained pounds.

And God said, "I have sent thee heart-healthy vegetables and olive oil with which to cook them."

But Satan created chicken-fried steak so big it needs its own platter. And Man gained pounds, and his bad cholesterol went through the roof.

And God brought forth running shoes and Man resolved to lose those extra pounds. But Satan created cable TV with remote control so Man would not have to toil to change channels between ESPN and ESPN2. So Man watched others exercise and Man gained pounds.

And God brought forth the potato, a vegetable naturally low in fat and brimming with nutrition. But Satan created deep-fried potatoes, called potato chips, and sour cream dip. And Man clutched his remote control and ate the potato chips swaddled in cholesterol. It tasted good but Man went into cardiac arrest.

And God sighed and created quadruple bypass surgery. But Satan saw to it that Paul Martin, the Minister of Finance of the day, slashed federal-provincial transfer payments, thereby jeopardizing Canada's medicare system . . .

teacher's dirty Looks

School children used to sing a song about the approach of the summer holidays—when there would be "no more teacher's dirty looks."

On the 24th of May, when school kids set off fireworks, one piece they love to ignite is affectionately known as the Burning Schoolhouse—the cardboard model of a red-brick school building with a Roman candle for a chimney. It's 100 percent Canadian!

This chapter offers a steely look at training, instruction, and education. There are jokes here that range from kiddy fun (elementary school stuff) to semi-adult humour (secondary school and collegiate) to community college and university wit (tough stuff).

Marshall McLuhan used to say, "Ignorance is learned." Here are some jokes about such matters.

Community College Howlers

Howlers are student blunders. Here are some printed in Fighting Words, *the faculty bulletin of Centennial College, Scarborough, Ont., Fall 1983.*

- His anger outbursted into an outrage.
- The car started to sputter, slowed down, and died to a halt.
- After fastening up our seatbelts, the plane headed toward the runway.
- Whether living together is the ideal arrangement over marriage is a highly personnel question.
- The married couple today take vows of marriage, which means 'til death do us apart.
- I met this student in one of my classes named Laura.
- So to conclude my essay on "Don't Judge a Book by its Cover" it would be said that, unless you DO know something about the book, if the cover is bad the story is good and vice-versa. The reason for this, good writters can not draw.
- Violent events have existed throughout history and have been increasing ever since.
- It [Paganism] was the predominant religion before the year 10,000 when the first Crusaders came in and made everyone catch on to the idea of Christianity quick.
- Later in the novel he killed Carter only because he thought he was going to kill him.
- No, I don't think Wormold is an evil man. Wormold is a vacuum cleaner sales man.
- Discriminating people must learn to deal with all individuals, regardless of their colour, religion, or sexual aptitude.
- Another problem elderly people have to cope with is their degenerate characteristics.
- The condom gives the male the responsibility of birth control, reducing the failure to about 5 percent.
- I feel that upon hiring myself that both parties would benefit.
- To top it off, a young man took off his clothes and ran up and down the isles.

- Below is a list of the problems which will allow for a safer and speedier evacuation in the future if eliminated.
- Can it be in today's modern technological society, where men have gone on the moon and where huge computers are capable of handling millions of pieces of information, that we cannot produce blue Smarties?
- Braziers and panty hose must be worn at all times.
- Adult pornography has been around for a long time. The photos are very exposed.
- To many old people, an institution is an unavoidable last resort.
- In 1971, Trudeau married Margaret Sinclair, a woman half his age, who fathered three boys.

American-Eye View

For over twenty years, Bob Williams taught primary school in St. Louis, Missouri. Canadian studies was one of the subjects he taught his nine-year-old Grade 4 pupils. He had them write about this country, and they did so with reckless abandon. Five columns of their boners appeared as "Kangaroos Are Peculiar to Canada," Canadian Weekend, November 10, 1979.

- Compared with Lake Winnipeg, people have been living in Canada for only a drop in the bucket.
- The first explorers came to Canada in yesuls vessils vesles botes.
- John Cabot discovered Labrador in 1497, but I forget whether this was in A.C. or D.C. times.
- Canada has many imports. One of its best of all imports is tourists.
- There are many animals peculiar to Canada. Just for one, it would be peculiar to see a kangaroo there.

- While most cows can only give milk, some Canadian cows have been taught how to give dairy products.
- Their water scientists have figured out how to change their river current into electric current.
- They call their falling water a natural resource. Here, we call it rain.
- Their forests are found mostly in woodsy places.
- Much of Canada's lumber supply is used in the making of forests.
- Now that the dinosaurs are dead, we can safely call them clumsy and stupid.
- Nova Scotia has few industries. Their main product is history.
- Edward was a prince in England when he was not an island in Canada.
- Montreal is in Quebec in case I ever want to know.
- Ottawa is for living in or passing through, depending on whether you are people or Highway 17.
- If the shoreline of Hudson Bay was ever straightened out, it would reach much farther.
- Lake Winnipeg is in Manitoba at the present time.
- Fortunately, Alberta and Saskatchewan fit snugly together.
- One of the larger suburbs of Edmonton is Alberta.
- Many natural resources are found in the outer skirts of Vancouver.
- Mountains hump their way all up and down Canada.
- Trying to walk across the Yukon Territory in the winter is a very exciting way of getting frozen to death.
- Legend has it that some terrible monsters live in many Canadian caves. These monsters are called Spelunkers.
- West of Vancouver Island it has been found that railroad travel is faster by boat.

- How Canada can keep both its natural beauty and its civilization should be part of everybody's spare-time thinking.
- I remember everything about Canada's Prime Minister except who his name is.
- From now on I will put both gladness and wonder in my same thought about Canada.

Newfoundland's Grade 12 Equivalency Test

Grade 12 Equivalency Test

FINAL MARK:_____

NAME:_____

Time limit: 3 weeks

Value/Question

15/ 1. What language is spoken by French Canadians?

10/ 2. Give the important characteristics of the ancient Babylonian Empire with particular emphasis on their architecture, literature, and law; OR, Give the first names of Bob Dylan, Bob Hope, and Uncle Bob.

10/ 3. What religion is the Pope? Jewish, Catholic, Hindu, or Muslim.

10/ 4. What is a silver dollar made of?

15/ 5. What time is it when the big hand is on the 1 and the little hand is on the 5?

10/ 6. How many commandments was Moses given (approximately)?

25/ 7. What team did Wayne Gretzky play for?

10/ 8. What do you call the people living in Canada's North: Southerners, Westerners, Northerners, or Easterners?

25/ 9. Spell the following words: Quarter, unemployment, welfare.

15/ 10. Six kings of England were named George, the last one was George VI. Name the other five.

20/ 11. Who won the Second World War? Who came second?

10/ 12. Where does rain come from: Supermarkets, Eaton's, U.S.A., or the sky?

10/ 13. Can you explain Einstein's Theory of Relativity? Yes/No

25/ 14. What is Newfoundland famous for: Newfies, fish, dories, or all of the above?

15/ 15. The song "O Canada" is the national anthem for what country?

10/ 16. Explain Economics in detail; OR, spell your name in block letters.

10/ 17. What holiday falls on Easter Monday: Christmas, Hallowe'en, Easter, or New Year's?

15/ 18. What are coat hangers used for?

15/ 19. Where would the basement be located in a three-storey house?

25/ 20. Did you print your name on the top of this test? Yes/No
_____

300

Some Ridiculous Riddles

Q. Where did Noah sail his ark?
A. To the Ark-tic.

Q. Why are there so many ophthalmologists in Niagara Falls?
A. Because of the cataracts.

Q. Why is Canada like a rooming house?
A. Because of its American borders.

Q. When can you carry water in a sieve?
A. When it's frozen.

Q. When is a man like frozen rain?
A. When he is hale.

Q. Why is a cloud like Santa Claus?
A. Because it holds the rain, dear.

Q. Why was the CPR especially patriotic?
A. Because it has bound the country together with the strongest ties.

Q. What does the steamer *Empress of Canada* weigh just before leaving Halifax harbour?
A. She weighs anchor.

Q. When did Chicoutimi begin with a C and end with an E?
A. Chicoutimi always began with a C and END always began with an E.

Q. Why is the letter C like Ottawa?
A. Because it is the capital of Canada.

Q. Why do they say Sir John A. Macdonald was an orphan?
A. Because he was the foundling Father of Confederation.

Q. What is ploughed but never planted?
A. Snow.

Q. What kind of Indians does Dracula like?
A. Full-blooded Indians.

Q. Why are you sure that Indians were the first people in North America?
A. Because they had reservations.

Q. What is the name of the arithmetically minded bugs of Winnipeg?
A. Mosquitoes. They add to misery, subtract from pleasure, divide your attention, and multiply quickly.

Q. What was the longest river in Canada before the Mackenzie River was discovered?
A. The Mackenzie River.

Q. What do you say to a nosey moose?
A. Vamoose!

The Period

A kindergarten class had a homework assignment to find out about something exciting and relate it to the class the next day.

The first little boy who was called upon walked up to the front of the class. With a piece of chalk, he made a small white dot on the blackboard, then sat back down.

Puzzled, the teacher asked him just what it was. "It's a period," said the little boy.

"Well, I can see that," she said. "But what is so exciting about a period?"

"Damned if I know," said the little boy. "But this morning my sister was missing one, Dad had a heart attack, Mom fainted, and the man next door shot himself."

Instruction

A first-grade teacher was going through the alphabet with her class.
She asked one little boy, "What comes after g?"
The pupil said, "Whiz."

Little Johnny's Reply

One day the teacher came into class and asked little Johnny to come up with a sentence containing the words "defence," "defeat," and "detail."

Little Johnny thought for a while and then answered, "The horse jumped over 'defence,' 'defeat' before 'detail.'"

Fatal Accident

"Did you hear old Jake had a fatal accident? He fell down a well."
"Really? Kicked the bucket, eh?"

Three Seasons

A teacher asked her class how many seasons there are.
One little boy said, "Three—baseball, football, and hockey."

General Brock

A teacher asked her class, "In which of his battles was General Brock killed?"

A little boy said, "His last."

Brock's Monument

A tour guide in the Niagara area was showing Brock's Monument to a group of American visitors.

He said, "This is where General Brock fell."

One of the tourists looked up and said, "That's quite a drop. Must have killed him."

Greatest Canadians

A teacher told her class to make a list of the people they considered to be the greatest Canadians. After about ten minutes, every student except little Johnny had turned in the list.

The teacher asked him, "Can't you finish your list, Johnny?"

He replied, "I just can't decide who to put in jail."

Derivations

A teacher was telling his class about the origins of the word "manuscript."

He said, "It comes from the Latin words 'manu' and 'scriptus,' and so means 'written by hand.' But when you think of it, what other kind of writing could there have been in those days?"

One student said, "Footnotes?"

Wad of Gum

A teacher saw a wad of gum on the floor by a student's desk.

"Is that yours?" he asked the boy.

"Oh no, sir," the kid replied. "You saw it first."

New Twins

A teacher was speaking to a little girl in her class.

She said, "I hear you have new twins at your house."

"Yes," said the little girl. "Daddy says that God sent them to us, and that He knows where we're going to get the money."

Kitty-cat

A little girl was sitting on the curb in front of her house, crying.

A lady came by and asked her what was wrong.

The little girl sniffed, "My kitty-cat died."

The woman said, "Oh, that's a shame. But now your kitty is with Jesus."

The little girl looked up and said, "Are you nuts? What would Jesus want with a dead cat?"

Six Apples

An elementary school teacher said to her class, "A mother has seven children, and six apples. She wants to divide the apples equally among the children. How can she make sure that each child gets the same share?"

One of the pupils says, "Make applesauce."

Animal in Class

A teacher asked her class to name an animal that has eyes but cannot see, that has legs but cannot run, and that can jump as high as the CN Tower.

The kids thought about it but could not come up with an answer.

Finally, the teacher said, "A wooden horse. It has eyes but cannot see, and legs but cannot run."

One of the kids said, "But a wooden horse can't jump."

The teacher replied, "Neither can the CN Tower."

Summertime Reading

A Grade 1 teacher was welcoming her students back to school after their summer vacation.

She said, "Now, before we begin work, would anyone like to share with the class anything interesting you may have done on your summer holidays?"

Nobody volunteered, so she said, "How about you, Mary?"

Mary said, "Well, Miss, it was my birthday in July, and for my birthday I received a bow-wow."

The teacher said, "Now, Mary, you are no longer in kindergarten. You are a big girl now. You don't say 'bow-wow,' you can say 'dog.'"

So Mary said, "It was my birthday in July, and for my birthday I received a dog."

The teacher then said, "How about you, David?"

David said, "Miss, I went to visit a farm in August, and at the farm I saw a moo-moo."

The teacher said, "Now, David, you are no longer in kindergarten. You are a big boy now. So you don't say 'moo-moo,' you say 'cow.'"

So David said, "Okay, Miss, I went to visit a farm in August, and I saw a cow."

Johnny was waving his hand in anxious anticipation, crying out, "Miss, Miss!"

The teacher said, "Yes, Johnny? Would you like to share something with us?"

Johnny said, "Yes, Miss. I read a really good book over the summer."

The teacher said, "Good! What was the name of the book?"

Johnny said, *"Winnie the Dump."*

Grammar

A grammar teacher asked a student to give him two pronouns.

The student replied, "Who, me?"

Grammar Again

A grammar teacher was in her kitchen making dinner when her little girl ran in and cried, "Mommy, Mommy! Daddy has fell off the roof."

The mother quickly responded, "Daddy has *fallen* off the roof! Quick, hand me the phone so I can call an ambulance."

Prose and Poetry

A teacher asked her class the difference between prose and poetry.

A student said, "A boy named Rick went into water up to his knees. That's prose. If he went a bit deeper it would be poetry."

Spelling

A teacher asked a little boy to spell the word "straight."

He did so.

Then she asked, "What does it mean?"

He said, "Without ginger ale."

Commandments

A Sunday school teacher was discussing the Ten Commandments with her five- and six-year-olds.

After explaining the commandment to honour thy father and thy mother, she asked, "Is there a commandment that teaches us how to treat our brothers and sisters?"

Without missing a beat, one little boy—the oldest child in a family—answered, "Thou shall not kill."

Little Boy

A woman in a farmhouse heard a racket out front and dashed outside to see what was happening. There she saw a hay wagon overturned in the dirt lane, and a little boy sitting at the side of the lane, covered in mud.

"My goodness!" she said. "Come inside, young man, and let me clean you up!"

The boy said, "I don't know, ma'am. I don't think Pa would like it."

"Nonsense," she said. "Now, come along."

She took him inside, stripped his clothes off, scrubbed him from head to toe in the tub, and washed and dried his clothes. After dressing him again, she said, "Now, you sit down at the table and I'll give you a nice hot piece of pie and a cold glass of milk."

The boy said, "I don't know, ma'am. I don't think Pa would like it."

"Don't be silly," she said, and she served him the pie and milk. After he had finished she said, "Now, I'm going to call my husband and son in from the barn, and get them to set that hay wagon of yours upright."

The boy said, "Oh, thank you, ma'am. Pa would like that."

The woman said, "I'm sure he would. But, just where is your father?"

"Under the wagon."

Girl Oyster

A girl oyster had a date with a boy lobster. When she got home from her evening out, all the other oysters in her family wanted to know what it was like.

"Oh, he was so charming," she said. "He led me out to the dance floor, he put his arm around me, and . . . oh, no! My pearls are gone!"

Rescue on Ice

An Englishman taking a walk in a park on a cold winter day heard a cry for help coming from the direction of the pond. He ran to it and saw that a boy had fallen through the ice and was clinging to the edge.

Crawling on his belly, the man made his way to the hole, pulled the boy out, and dragged him to safety. When they were on solid ground, he asked the boy, "How did you come to fall in?"

The boy answered, "I didn't come to fall in. I came to skate."

Pearls of Wisdom

The teacher had not quite finished addressing his class of students about some important matters when the school bell rang. The students immediately started to get up to go, without waiting to be dismissed.

"Stay seated, please," the teacher said. "I have a few more pearls to cast."

Flat Tire

It was a beautiful spring morning, so four teenage boys on their way to school in the car one of them owned decided to go for a little drive in the country. When they arrived at school at lunchtime, they told the teacher that they'd had a flat tire, and that's why they were late.

"Well, that's perfectly understandable," said the teacher. "But you missed a test this morning, so you'll have to take it now."

She sat each of them down at a separate desk, gave each a blank piece of paper, and said, "Now I want each of you to write . . . which tire was flat."

What Words?

A teenage girl came home from a movie, and her mother asked her how it was.

"Really neat," said the girl. "It had neat special effects and the actors did a neat job, although I thought one guy was lousy.

There was lots of neat action and some of the funny lines were neat. But I thought the music was lousy; it sounded like that lousy classical stuff. And also the popcorn they served was lousy. But I had a pretty neat evening."

The mother said, "You are beginning to sound like a trendy California Valley girl, not like what you are: a genteel young woman who attends the Upper Canadian Academy. So there are two words you have to stop using. They are 'neat' and 'lousy.'"

"Okay," said the girl. "What words are they?"

The Man and the Mule

The following story was a favourite of NDP leader T. C. (Tommy) Douglas.

A man owned a mule that would not lead, drink, feed, harness, or be ridden. The man's neighbour said he was a mule specialist and told the man to put the mule on a truck and bring him over.

The first thing the neighbour did once the mule arrived was hit it between the eyes with a club. The mule's knees buckled.

The mule's owner said, "I did not bring him over for that kind of cruelty."

The neighbour said, "If you are going to teach a mule anything, the first thing you have to do is get his attention."

French Language Instruction

A language instructor was explaining to her French class that in French, nouns, unlike their English counterparts, are grammatically designated as masculine or feminine.

One puzzled student asked, "What gender is the word 'computer'?"

The teacher did not know, or wasn't telling, so for fun, she split the class into two groups, appropriately enough by gender, and asked the two groups to decide whether "computer" should be a masculine or feminine noun. Both groups were required to give a number of reasons for their recommendation.

The men's group decided that computers should definitely be of the feminine gender for the following reasons:

1. No one but their creator understands their internal logic.
2. The native language they use to communicate with other computers is incomprehensible to everyone else.
3. Even the smallest mistakes are stored in long-term memory for possible later retrieval.
4. As soon as you make a commitment to one, you find yourself spending half your paycheque on accessories for it.
5. If you push the wrong button, she shuts down and won't tell you what's wrong.
6. You always have to do things her way!
7. She uses way more paper than you do.

The women's group, however, concluded that computers should be masculine for the following reasons:

1. In order to get their attention, you have to turn them on.
2. They have a lot of data but they are still clueless.
3. They are supposed to help you solve problems, but half of the time they are the problem.
4. As soon as you commit to one, you realize that if you'd waited a little longer, you could have gotten a better model.

Chemical Factory

Members of a school group on a day excursion were being escorted around the laboratory of a large chemical plant in Sarnia, Ont.

One kid asked the chemist who was their guide what experiment the lab was working on.

"Well," the scientist said, "we're trying to develop a universal solvent."

"What's that?"

"A liquid that will dissolve anything."

"Oh? Then watcha gonna keep it in?"

Short Story Assignment

In a creative writing class at the University of British Columbia, the instructor informed the students about the ingredients of a good short story.

"It has to employ one or more of these essentials: religion, emotion, sex, mystery, surprise, or royalty."

The instructor then assigned the students to write a story that employs all these ingredients.

One student's submission was but one sentence long. It went like this:

"My God!" wept the beauty-contest queen. "I'm pregnant! Who can the father be?"

Indigent Student

A young man attending the University of British Columbia sent the following note to his father in Penticton:

"No mun, no fun, your son."

The father sent the following reply: "So sad, too bad, your dad."

Nepotism

A Quebec senator phones one of the vice-presidents of Bombardier with a request: "Next month my son graduates from the Faculty of Engineering at Laval University. I would like him to work at Bombardier. I would like you to hire him as your assistant."

There is no response from the vice-president, so he continues, "Mind you, I don't want you to show him any special favours. No favouritism toward him, of course. Just treat him as you would treat any of my sons."

Adult Education

Q. What is the definition of adult education?
A. Contradicting the boss.

Significant Signs

Two doctors opened an office in a small town and put up a sign reading, "Dr. Smith and Dr. Jones: Psychiatry and Proctology."

The town council was not too happy with that sign, so the doctors changed it to "Hysterias and Posteriors."

This was not acceptable either, so in an effort to satisfy the council, the doctors changed the sign to "Schizoids and Hemorrhoids." No go.

Next they tried, "Catatonics and High Colonics." Thumbs down again.

Then came, "Manic-depressives and Anal-retentives." Still no good.

So they tried, "Minds and Behinds." Unacceptable again.

So they tried, "Lost Souls and Assholes." That did not wash.

Nor did "Analysis and Anal Cysts," "Nuts and Butts," "Freaks and Cheeks," or "Loons and Moons."

Almost at their wits' ends, the doctors finally came up with a business slogan acceptable to the town council.

"Dr. Smith and Dr. Jones: Odds and Ends."

McMaster Admissions

A mature student was completing an application form for admission to the innovative M.D. program of the Faculty of Health Sciences at McMaster University in Hamilton, Ont.

It included a questionnaire. He paused before answering the question, "Do you consider yourself a leader or a follower?"

He thought about it for some time and then wrote, "Although I have every confidence in myself and my abilities, I am also aware of my limitations, and so must say that I am a follower."

He mailed off the application form.

A few weeks later he received a letter from the Faculty of Health Sciences. It began, "Congratulations on your successful application and on your honesty. This year there were 400 applicants and only 150 were successful. Be forewarned, however, that you are going to be the only follower among 149 leaders."

Aims of Education

For centuries, philosophers and educators have attempted to define the aims of education.

Way back in 1965 I heard a definition that strikes me as amusing and reasonable. I was listening to an Ontario-wide talk show on CBC Radio. A listener called in and offered to share his definition. He said he had heard it at least forty years earlier in the Old Country (England) and had remembered it all those years.

So the following definition of the aims of education is now at least eighty years old.

"An education should prepare you to do three things. These are to entertain yourself, to entertain a friend, and to entertain an idea."

Hockey ðaze
iN Canaða

The origins of ice hockey are a matter of conjecture and argument. All that is certain is that the game was first played by Canadians on Canadian ice. Sports historians suggest it originated in the nineteenth century, its place of birth being Saint John, Montreal, Windsor, or Kingston. Even Fort Franklin, N.W.T., has a claim. No matter, it is the country's most popular game, bar none—"the Canadian specific," poet Al Purdy declared.

Whether it's about a sport or a spectacle, a contest or a business, here are some hockey stories. (Jokes about sportsmanship in general appear in the next chapter, "Really Good Sports.")

Hockey

Was it H.L. Mencken or Eric Nicol or someone else who described ice hockey in the following terms?

"Ice hockey is a violent game. You take a stick and hit a puck, or anyone who has recently hit a puck."

Winnie the Wonderful

Sir Winston Churchill was attending the championship game at Wembley Stadium between the Lethbridge Maple Leafs and the ranking British team, the Liverpool Scullions.

At stake was the Winston Churchill Cup, which was taken by the Lethbridge team, despite that the Canadians were one man short and playing defensively.

Not quite understanding the psychology of playing with four men plus a goalie, rather than with five men plus a goalie, Winston complained, "Why don't they attack?"

Gump and Jacques

This story is told of Lorne "Gump" Worsley and Jacques Plante, famous hockey players.

When the New York Rangers announced that the club had traded Worsley to the Montreal Canadiens for Plante, a television producer phoned both men in turn to invite them to appear on a sports show to discuss the controversial deal.

Plante asked how much he would be paid.

"We don't usually pay guests," the producer explained, "but we are prepared to make a payment to you and to Worsley of $50 each."

Plante then phoned Worsley. "Are they paying you $100, too?" he asked suspiciously.

"Yeah," said Worsley.

Plante then phoned the producer again. "Why are you paying Worsley a hundred bucks and me only 50?" he asked.

The producer protested that he was not, and managed to convince Plante that each man was receiving only $50.

Plante showed up for the telecast, Worsley did not.

Plante then got in touch with Worsley to ask him why he had not appeared.

"Why should I?" asked Worsley. "They were paying you $100 and me only $50."

Toronto Maple Leafs

I've started watching Toronto Maple Leaf games. My doctor says I should avoid any excitement.

Toronto Maple Leafs Again

Snow White returned home one evening to find that the lovely cottage she shared with the Seven Dwarfs had been destroyed by fire.

She was doubly worried because when she had left in the morning, all seven of the dwarfs were still asleep in their bedrooms.

As she scrambled among the wreckage, frantically calling out their names, she heard a loud cry for help: "Go Leafs Go!"

"Thank goodness," sobbed Snow White. "At least Dopey's still alive!"

Hockey Game

Don Cherry is talking to a sports columnist.

"Do you know the real reason why the Toronto Maple Leafs lost last night's game to the Montreal Canadiens?"

The sports columnist says, "No, why?"

"It was part of an interprovincial agreement between Premier Eves of Ontario and Premier Landry of Quebec."

Hockey Fans

Jim and Dave were both big hockey fans.

They made an agreement that whichever one of them died first would try to come back from the dead and tell the other whether or not hockey was played in Heaven.

Well, Dave passed away first, and Jim began going to mediums, trying to get in touch with his old pal. Finally, about two years after Dave's death, Jim found a powerful medium, who reached Dave's spirit.

Dave said, "I've got good news and bad news for you. The good news is, yes, we play great hockey in Heaven. The bad news is, you're starting in goal next week."

Maple Leafs

A sportswriter wrote the following description of a once-promising player who became a hockey has-been:

"He decided to give up first-class hockey. But he'll still be playing for the Toronto Maple Leafs."

Hockey Fans

Four hockey fans are mountain climbing.

Each climber happens to be a rabid fan of a different team in the National Hockey League. As they climb higher and higher, they argue more and more about which of them is the most loyal to their particular team.

Finally, as they reach the summit, the climber from Vancouver takes a running leap and throws himself off the mountain, yelling, "This is for the Vancouver Canucks."

Not wanting to be outdone, the climber from Calgary throws himself off the mountain, shouting, "This is for the Calgary Flames."

Seeing this, the Toronto climber walks to the edge of the precipice and yells, "This is for the Toronto Maple Leafs," and pushes the guy from Montreal off the cliff.

The Rocket and the Gordie

When hockey broadcaster Foster Hewitt was asked to name the three most valuable players in the National Hockey League, he replied, "Rocket Richard, Rocket Richard, Rocket Richard!"

Maurice (Rocket) Richard was the leading star of the star-studded Montreal Canadiens. He established a record by scoring fifty goals in fifty games. He had no rival for honours among Quebecers. His chief rival for honours outside Quebec was Gordie Howe, who played for the Detroit Red Wings. Gordie scored 869 NHL goals—and amassed 2,419 minutes in penalties!

Upon his retirement, the Rocket appeared on *Hockey Night in Canada,* serving as one of the CBC's "colour commentators." He had covered a Detroit-Montreal game when the popular announcer Danny Gallivan asked him to pick the three stars of the night's game.

"Well, for the first star, I would have to choose my brother, 'the Pocket Rocket.' Tonight he skated like the wind, and he scored the first goal that put us in front."

Gallivan agreed that this was a good choice. "How about the second star?"

"For the second star, I would have to say Jean Beliveau. He is such a good player. He set up two of the goals that we scored tonight."

Gallivan agreed. "No one could question Beliveau's value to the team. Now, how about the third star?"

"The third star, I pick Jacques Lapierre. He is such a fine defenceman. If it wasn't for Jacques, you would never know how many goals those guys with Detroit might have made."

"Well," said Gallivan, "those are all very worthy choices. But let me ask you if you would have an honourable mention?"

"An honourable mention?" asked the Rocket. "Oh, sure. I suppose so. For the honourable mention, I would say that big guy, you know, Gordie Howe, that scored the four goals that beat us."

All-Star Hockey Broadcast

In the past, all-star games featured the season's champion hockey team (usually the Montreal Canadiens) in play against a team composed of the best players selected from the rest of the teams in the National Hockey League.

Here is a partial transcript of the action at one all-star game played in Montreal in the 1950s, featuring Danny Gallivan, with his partner Dick Irvin calling the play.

"And here comes Delvecchio, with a pass to Mosienko, then it's to Mikita, over to Pavelich, and on to Nesterenko, and then to Mahovlich, on Sawchuk, and it's retrieved by Litzenberger, and here comes Armstrong . . . Armstrong? What a ridiculous name for a hockey player!"

Chrétien's Favourite

A reporter interviewing Jean Chrétien asked him if he had a favourite hockey player.

"*Mais, oui,*" replied the prime minister.

"May I ask who he is?" asked the reporter.

"*Mais, oui.*"

"Well, who is he?"

"Jacques Plante," replied the prime minister.

"Jacques Plante? He's an interesting choice. Certainly a valuable player and a fine goalkeeper. Might I ask why Jacques Plante appeals so much to you?"

"*Mais, oui.*"

"Why?"

"Because he never made the first move."

Hockey Team

Q. Why couldn't the Cape Breton hockey team make it to the championships in Toronto?

A. Nobody was willing to pick up twenty-two hitchhikers.

Seats to the Finals

It's Game 7 of the Stanley Cup Final, and a man makes his way to his seat right at centre ice. He sits down, noticing that the seat next to him is empty. He leans over and asks his neighbour if someone will be sitting there.

"No," says the neighbour. "The seat is empty."

"This is incredible," said the man. "Who in their right mind would have a seat like this for the Stanley Cup and not use it?"

The neighbour says, "Well, actually, the seat belongs to me. I was supposed to come with my wife, but she passed away. This is the first Stanley Cup we haven't been to together since we got married in 1967."

"Oh, I'm sorry to hear that. That's terrible. But couldn't you find someone else, a friend or relative, or even a neighbour, to take the seat?"

The man shakes his head. "No, they're all at the funeral."

Press Story

This sham news story (at least I think it's a hoax!) was conceived with a will, composed with a deft wit, and written with a sharp eye for both local and national colour (probably by a Westerner).

OTTAWA AWARDS STANLEY CUP TO QUEBEC

OTTAWA—The federal government today announced it would award the Stanley Cup to Quebec, even though Alberta's Calgary Flames won the competition.

The cup will go, instead, to Quebec's Montreal Canadiens, who were defeated by the Flames four games to two in the best-of-seven series.

Prime Minister Brian Mulroney said the hockey series was "only a guideline," and non-binding. He conceded that Calgary might have been the best hockey team, "but we have to look at what's best for Canada."

"We have to support Canada's hockey industry, which is centred in Montreal," said the prime minister. "Montreal is in the best position to take full advantage of the Stanley Cup."

He said the decision to overrule the playoff results was "difficult and painful," but that national interests had to prevail over petty "regional considerations."

Loss of the coveted trophy left most of Alberta seething with rage. "It's another example of Quebec getting the goodies and the West getting the shaft," said Ted Byfield, editor of the stridently regionalized news magazine *Western Report*.

Western Tory M.P.s were not so hostile. They shuffled their feet, clenched their buttocks, pursed their lips, and said nothing at all. Neither did Alberta premier Don Getty, who was golfing and unavailable for comment.

However, reliable sources indicated he seemed "quite upset" and was "way off his game."

Indignant Quebec M.P.s who lobbied long and hard for the Stanley Cup vehemently denied that the decision had anything to do with politics.

"It's not as if the West isn't getting its fair share of federal support," sniffed Benoît Bouchard, the Tories' senior Quebec cabinet minister. "We've announced the Lloydminster upgrader eight or nine times. The West received the very lucrative contract for air in the CF-18 deal. And let's not forget about all that rain for western farmers this spring."

Quebec Industry Minister Pierre Johnson dismissed western complaints as "anti-French hysteria from Alberta dinosaurs."

"Quebec absolutely deserves this," he said. "The

Montreal Canadiens have extensive experience as Stanley Cup champions, while the Calgary Flames have none at all. Sure Calgary won this particular series with a couple of fluke goals and lucky saves, but the Canadiens have proven themselves over the long haul.

"If we're denied the Stanley Cup now, it could only rejuvenate Quebec separatism and threaten the integrity of all of Canada."

"Ottawa has done plenty for the West," said Saskatchewan premier Grant Devine. "Just look at the Dundurn army base. They could have shut it down, and they didn't. They let Swift Current keep the Memorial Cup. And there's a darn good chance we'll get to keep our Via Rail service too."

Quebec premier Robert Bourassa was delighted to see the cup go to Montreal. He said the trophy will be re-engraved with its new name—"La Coupe Stanley" to comply with Quebec sign laws.

ReaLLy Good Sports

The Canadian people are considered by everyone everywhere in the world to be "good sports." (It may be argued that we show an excess of goodness in our peacekeeping and foreign policy initiatives and a mildness in our general lack of initiative in fields that require excellence and endeavour. As I mentioned in the Preface, our policies have a church-basement feel to them, and this embraces our inclination to sermonize and missionize.)

But when it comes to sports, we Canadians are "good sportsmen" and "good sportswomen" in the best sense of these words. We have a wilderness around us that encourages undertakings that require physical endurance.

This chapter features jokes and lore about feats of sportsmanship. The careful reader will note that all references to hockey have been hived off. They appear in the previous chapter, "Hockey Daze in Canada."

Brooms

For the curlers among us.

Two brooms were hanging in the closet; after a while they got to know each other so well they decided to get married.

One broom was, of course, the bride broom. The other the groom broom.

The bride broom looked very beautiful in her white dress. The groom broom was handsome and suave in his tuxedo.

The wedding was lovely. After the wedding, at the wedding dinner, the bride broom leaned over and said to the groom broom, "I think I am going to have a little whisk broom!"

"Impossible!" said the groom broom. "We haven't even swept together."

Pearson and Baseball

I am indebted to retired diplomat Sidney Freifeld for the following story about Lester B. Pearson. It appears in his lively book of reminiscences, Undiplomatic Notes: Tales from the Canadian Foreign Service *(1990).*

Back in 1961, after Pearson had left public service and was leading the Liberal Party, he visited his riding of Algoma East. After fielding political questions during a conference with the press, a reporter asked him—Pearson was an avid baseball fan—which team he thought would win the World Series, about to commence between the Cincinnati Reds and the New York Yankees.

Unhesitatingly he picked New York, and the reporter asked him why.

"Can you imagine the headlines if I picked that Cincinnati would win?" Mr. Pearson responded. "PEARSON FAVOURS REDS OVER YANKEES."

Toronto Argonauts

Torontonians love lost causes . . . like the Maple Leafs hockey team and the Argonauts football team. Here are some Argo jokes taken from "Grey Cup '82," Toronto Star, November 24, 1982.

What has 68 legs and lives in the cellar?
The Toronto Argonauts.

Why did the Argo quarterback never bother to have a phone installed in his home?
Because he'd never be able to find the receiver.

How does an opposing coach get his players to behave?
If they don't, he won't let them play against the Argos.

Did you know there are really three Argo teams?
One on the field, one at the arrival level, and one at the departure gate.

What do opposing teams use to prepare to play the Argonauts?
Laughing gas.

An oil-rich Sheik asked his son what he wanted for his birthday.
The boy asked for a Mickey Mouse outfit, so . . . his dad bought him the Toronto Argonauts.

Highway 401
Argos 0

Argos

While watching an Argos game, Bill fell asleep on the couch.
His wife left him there overnight, then shook him awake in the morning.

"Wake up, Bill," she said. "It's twenty to seven."

Bill opened his eyes and said, "For whom?"

SkyDome

Montreal's Olympic Stadium has a retractable roof. It is known as "the Big O" because of its ovular shape and as "the Big Owe" because of its excessive cost.

Sports figures in Toronto decided that the Ontario city needed its own dome, one with a roof that is really retractable (not like Montreal's and sometimes retractable).

Toronto's dome was named the SkyDome following a contest sponsored by the *Toronto Star* newspaper. But to this day there are Torontonians who argue that it should have been named after the father of sports personality Stafford Smythe—sportsman Conn Smythe.

Then it would have been known as the Conn Dome.

Scots Joke

I have this joke from bibliophile David Skene-Melvin, who adds the following annotation: "Links, i.e., a golf course in British speak = lynx."

A Scotsman arrives at an isolated post of the Hudson's Bay Company to take up the position of factor.

He arrives with a set of golf clubs in his baggage.

"What on earth are these for?" inquires one of the employees, eyeing the golf clubs. "You won't be needing them here. There are no golf clubs."

"Och, aye," replied the Scot, "wasn' a' I told that the country is full of links."

Golf Again

An arrogant Toronto businessman is playing a round with a business client at the Glen Eden Club and continually abuses his caddy. At the sixth hole—170 metres over water—he demands of the caddy, "What club do I use here?"

The caddy replies, "Well, when Prime Minister Chrétien played here with Prime Minister Blair, they both used a six iron."

As rude as ever, the businessman grabs the six iron and hits the ball. It lands in the middle of the pond. "Hey, you bastard! You gave me a six iron and it obviously wasn't enough. I went right into the water!"

The caddy replies, "That's what the prime ministers did, too."

George Chuvalo

One of the greatest boxers of his time, George Chuvalo held the Canadian and Commonwealth heavyweight titles. He fought most of the great heavyweights and was never knocked down.

That was what he was like in his mature years. As a youngster he was somewhat less formidable but still very professional.

It seems he was taking a stroll along the Beaches area of Toronto when he was set upon by a dozen street kids, who beat him black and blue and took away his wallet. He arrived home with two black eyes, puffed cheeks, and a torn shirt.

"What happened?" his mother asked him.

Young George told her about the attack by the street kids.

"Why didn't you hit back? Surely you could have knocked the hell out of those street kids!"

"Sure," replied young George. "But my fee at the local boxing club for flooring a champion is $50. I don't fight for free."

Recent Study

A report recently released by the Sports Canada Study Group makes fascinating reading. It examines people's recreational preferences.

Highlights of the report appear here. They will be of special interest to employment specialists and sports enthusiasts.

202 the Penguin Book of MORE Canadian Jokes

1. Increasingly, the sport of choice for the unemployed or the incarcerated is basketball.

2. The sport of choice for maintenance-level employees is football.

3. The sport of choice for frontline workers is bowling.

4. The sport of choice for supervisors is baseball.

5. The sport of choice for middle management is tennis.

6. The sport of choice for corporate officers is golf.

The report concludes: The higher you are in the corporate structure, the smaller your balls.

Tennis Stars

When Carling Bassett finally retired from competitive tennis, she had a record of 0-17 against the game's reigning star, Martina Navratilova.

When asked what she had learned from playing with Navratilova, Bassett replied, "How to shake hands."

Sports Putdown

Here is a piece of lore that comes from the United States. I am not sure of its provenance, but it was sent to me from a friend in New York City on June 5, 2002, as an instance of "anti-Canadian humour" then current in the United States.

Canadians are not a protected class; everyone agrees they were created by God simply to be abused. For example, on *Baseball Tonight* on May 7, 2002, ESPN's Peter Gammons responded to reporter Karl Ravech's comment that only 2,000 fans showed up for Montreal's game against the Rockies by saying: "Sure, but that's 3,780 Canadian."

Ferguson Jenkins

Ferguson Jenkins was the first Canadian player to be inducted into the U.S. Baseball Hall of Fame. Fergy was a great guy, both as a pitcher and as a gentleman.

The story is told that one winter, when Fergy was a youngster, a neighbour knocked at the door of his house and upbraided his father.

"I want you to know that your son threw a snowball at me as I was passing your house just now."

"Did he hit you?" the father asked.

"No, he just missed."

"Well, then," the father replied, "it wasn't my son."

Scots Immigrant

A Scotsman who had recently immigrated attended his first baseball game in his new country, and after a base hit, he heard the fans roaring, "Run . . . run!"

The next batter connected heavily with the ball and the Scotsman stood up and roared with the crowd in his thick accent, "R-r-run ya bahstard, r-run will ya!"

A third batter slammed a hit and again the Scotsman, obviously pleased with his knowledge of the game, screamed, "R-r-run ya bahstard, r-r-run will ya!"

The next batter held his swing at three and two, and as the umpire called a walk, the Scotsman stood up yelling, "R-r-run ya bahstard, r-r-run!"

The surrounding fans giggled quietly, and he sat down confused.

A friendly fan, sensing the Scotsman's embarrassment, whispered, "He doesn't have to run, he's got four balls."

After this explanation, the Scotsman stood up in disbelief and screamed, "Walk with p-r-r-ride, man!"

Definition

Cross-country skiing: What Canadians do when they have bad brakes and bald tires.

Skydiving

A man decided to try skydiving. He jumped out of the plane and pulled the ripcord. Nothing happened. He tried it again and again. Nothing. Then he tried the cord for the emergency chute. Still nothing, and he was plummeting toward the ground.

As he looked down, he saw another man, coming up! As they passed each other, he yelled, "Hey, do you know anything about skydiving?"

"No," cried the other man. "Do you know anything about gas stoves?"

at peace and War

13

In this chapter you will find humour about peace and war, specifically about keeping the peace at home and waging wars abroad.

Historians like to assure us that our country is one of the few yet to wage an aggressive war abroad. Yet Canadians are courageous warriors who "fight the good fight"—but not without a grim chuckle or two. Here and there you will find a little "gallows humour."

The Mounties are charged with "keeping the peace" on the domestic front, so some jokes about the Royal Canadian Mounted Police appear here. Canadian soldiers have distinguished themselves in the two Great Wars and have since become dedicated peacekeepers, as well as peacemakers in the world's trouble spots. There is wit and wisdom in those undertakings as well.

Wolfe's Dying Words

There are various accounts that preserve the dying words of General James Wolfe, the leader of the English forces, who died during the battle on the Plains of Abraham, September 13, 1759. Here is a little-known version, as recalled by the English versifier and traveller Sir Edwin Arnold, who was often confused with the English poet Matthew Arnold, much to the latter's dismay.

"They say, as the surgeon drew the fatal musket ball from the wound of Wolfe, he exclaimed, 'Why, this is not the bullet of an enemy!' and that the gallant general answered with a faint smile on his dying face—gay even in extremity—'Well, Doctor, I don't think it could be the bullet of a friend!'"

Mosquitoes

The story is told about some British officers stationed at Fort George, Kingston, Upper Canada.

It was evening, and as they sat down to eat dinner in the officers' mess, they were tormented by hordes of mosquitoes.

Somebody said, "Shall I close the window?"

Someone else replied, "Yes. I think they're all in now."

War of 1812

The War of 1812 was a draw.

Canada won it on the battlefield, but Americans continue to win it on the screen.

Vincent Massey

Vincent Massey, in his memoirs *What's Past Is Prologue* (1963), frowned on the tendency of Canadians to wave the flag—the American flag—to attract tourists from south of the border. He was particularly hard on the willingness of Canadians to allow their patrimony of names to be squandered.

"In some cases," he wrote, "hotels bearing historic Canadian names have been rechristened by non-Canadian owners who have acquired them. The General Brock Hotel in Niagara Falls, Ontario, commemorated the career of Sir Isaac Brock, who because of his gallantry and brilliant campaigning in the War of 1812 is rightly called the 'Hero of Upper Canada.' Indeed, he more than anyone else was responsible for this great region's remaining under the British Crown.

"The hotel, under new ownership, was renamed without apparently any murmur of protest from the local community. I longed to make a deliberate mistake in some speech in the region of Niagara and speak in moving terms of that great soldier, Major-General Sir Sheraton Brock, to see what the reaction would be."

He never did. Probably no one would notice the difference.

Mounties

The young Englishman was so cross-eyed that he went southeast to join the North-West Mounted Police.

In the 1920s

In 1920 the Royal Canadian Mounted Police was formed. And with the force came a great tradition of law and order. The initials RCMP became known across the land.

To some people, the RCMP identified not the Mounties but the presence in the House of Commons of a fearful lobby group—the Roman Catholic Members of Parliament!

Gambling Pun

A member of the Force was an inveterate gambler. Time and again, his superiors warned him about the cost and the dangers of gambling, and for a while it seemed that the constable had reformed. Then one night, an opportunity arose that he could not refuse. He not only joined the poker game, but he drove there in a staff car.

As usual, he was losing. Pretty soon he ran out of cash. However, the other players were on a roll and in the mood to accept collateral to keep the constable in the game. He persuaded them to accept the new set of shock absorbers that had just been mounted on the car. Alas, he lost those too.

When he returned to the barracks, his superiors noted that the sedan was sagging. They questioned him. Tired and disgusted with himself, he could only grunt, "Gambling, that's what made the Mountie car low."

Snitch Detail

I first heard this joke in the 1960s, when an immigrant from Hungary told it to me. It was about life in his native land under the Communists. The joke resurfaced with a Canadian angle in the 1990s.

"Hello, is this the RCMP?"

"Yes. Snitch detail."

"I'm calling to report on my neighbour, Billy Bob Smith."

"What about him?"

"He's got some marijuana. He's hiding the cache inside his firewood."

"I want to ask you for his address and to thank you very much for your call, sir."

The next day, RCMP officers descend on Billy Bob's house. They search the woodshed and find the firewood. Wielding axes, they split apart every single log, but they find no cache of marijuana in the firewood. They apologize to Billy Bob and leave.

The phone rings at Billy Bob's house. "Hey, Billy Bob! Did the RCMP come?"

"Yeah!"

"Did they chop your firewood for ya?"

"Yep."

"Merry Christmas, buddy."

F.R. Scott

The constitutional-law specialist F.R. Scott went to see J.G.
McConnell, the crusty publisher of the *Montreal Star*. The year
was 1943 and the newspaper was refusing to carry advertisements
for public meetings of the CCF with which Scott was affiliated.

"Why do you refuse paid advertisements in the *Montreal Star*
for the CCF even when J.M. Coldwell is coming to speak, when
you carry ads all the time for the Communist Party?"

"Because the Communists aren't dangerous," replied McConnell.

Max the Bank Robber

Max the bank robber was sent to Kingston Pen: hard labour on
the rock pile.

There is a strict rule of silence for the convicts. First day on
the job, Max hears a man shout out, "Number seven."

All the convicts laugh, until the guards tell them to shut up.

A while later, another prisoner yells, "Number nineteen."

Again all the convicts laugh, until they are silenced by the
guards.

This happens several times during the day. When they are
back in their cells, Max asks his cellmate what it's all about.

The man explains, "We aren't allowed to talk while we're
working, see. So we memorized all of the jokes we know, and
gave each one a number. Then, to break the monotony out
there, a guy will yell out a number; we all think of the joke that
goes with the number, and we have a laugh."

Max thinks this is a good idea, and he wants to get in on it.
So the next day, about an hour into the work shift, he yells out,
"Number eight."

Nothing happens.

An hour later another man yells, "Number eight," and they all
crack up.

So Max tries it again. "Number twelve," he shouts.

No reaction.

Later, another man shouts, "Number twelve," and the prisoners all roar with laughter.

Back in the cell, Max says to his cellmate, "I don't get it. I say a number, and nobody laughs. Someone else says the same number, and everybody laughs."

His cellmate says, "Well, maybe you just don't know how to tell a joke."

Kingston Pen

A resident of Kingston, Ont., was convicted of armed robbery and sent to the Kingston Penitentiary for five years.

Three years into his sentence, he escaped. He made his way carefully by side streets to his home. When he went inside, his wife said, "So, where the hell have you been? You escaped six hours ago."

Ex-con

A burglar who had served five years in the Kingston Penitentiary was being released.

He was summoned to the warden's office, where the warden returned his personal belongings and gave him a stern lecture on going straight.

Finally the warden asked, "Is there anything else I can do for you?"

"Yes," said the man. "Give me back my tools."

Astrologer

A married man went to consult Swami Narayana, the fortune teller who called himself the "Superpsychic."

"Tell me my fortune," the man said.

Narayana cast the man's horoscope, then studied it intently. He frowned and explained, "I am afraid to tell you what I see."

"Tell me. I can take it."

"You will be a widower within the week."

"I know that already," the man protested. "What I came to you to find out is this—Will I get caught?"

Knowing the Law

A traffic officer flags down a motorist who is driving 100 km/h in a 60 km/h zone.

The officer asks the motorist for his driver's licence and his ownership licence.

"My name is Eddie Greenspan," says the motorist.

"Greenspan? Eddie Greenspan? Are you the lawyer?"

"Yes."

"The famous lawyer who handles difficult cases involving famous people and wins most of them?"

"Yes."

"The same lawyer who knows the law backwards and forwards?"

"Yes."

"The lawyer who ridicules the efforts of Toronto's chief of police?"

"Yes."

"Well," says the officer. "You won't be able to plead ignorance of the law, will you?"

The Cape Bretoner and the Drunk

A Cape Bretoner is sitting at a bar, having a drink and minding his own business. A man comes up behind him and knocks him to the floor. The bartender hears the noise, turns around, and sees the Cape Bretoner stretched out, the other guy standing over him.

"Wow!" the bartender says. "What did you hit him with?"

"Karate chop from Japan."

The Cape Bretoner comes to, gets back on his stool, and resumes sipping his drink. Suddenly the other man lays him out again.

"Wow!" the bartender exclaims again. "What did you hit him with that time?"

"Kung-fu kick from China."

Again the Cape Bretoner gets back up, only to be flattened a third time.

"Wow!" the bartender says again. "What did you hit him with now?"

"Tae kwon do punch from Korea."

The Cape Bretoner hauls himself to his feet and leaves the bar. About ten minutes later, the bartender hears a noise, turns around, and this time sees the other man out cold on the floor, and the Cape Bretoner standing over him.

"Wow!" he exclaims. "What did you hit him with?"

"Monkey wrench from Canadian Tire."

Hells Angels

A grizzled old man was eating in a truck stop in northern Ontario when three Hells Angels bikers walked in. The first biker walked up to the old man and butted his cigarette into the old man's pie, and then took a seat at the counter.

The second biker walked up to the old man and spit into the old man's glass of milk, and then he took a seat at the counter.

The third biker walked up to the old man and upset the old man's plate of meat and potatoes, and then he took a seat at the counter.

Without a word of protest, the old man quietly left the diner. Shortly thereafter, one of the bikers said to the waitress, "Humph, not much of a man, was he?"

The waitress replied, "He's not much of a truck driver either. He just backed his truck over three motorcycles."

Apprehension Rate

The federal government is trying to decide whether the RCMP, CSIS, or the National Security Directorate is the most effective agency for apprehending criminals. The issue is to be decided with a test.

A rabbit is let loose in the woods north of Ottawa and each organization has to apprehend it.

The RCMP goes in. They place animal informants throughout the forest. They question all plant and mineral witnesses. After three months of extensive investigation, they conclude that rabbits do not exist.

CSIS goes in. After two weeks with no leads, they burn down all the barns, killing everything in them, including the rabbit, and they make no apologies. It seems the rabbit had it coming.

The National Security Directorate goes in. Their agents emerge two hours later with a badly beaten bear. The bear is yelling, "Okay! Okay! I'm a rabbit! I'm a rabbit!"

Cops and Robbers

Three little boys decide to play cops and robbers.

One boy says, "I'll be the cop."

The second boy says, "I'll be the robber."

The third boy asks, "What can I be?"

One of the others tells him, "The commercial."

Spy Dog

A man in Ottawa hears a dog is for sale and so goes to the owner's house. He rings the bell, and the owner tells him the dog is in the backyard. The guy goes into the backyard and sees a mutt sitting there.

"You talk?" he asks.

"Yep," the mutt replies. "English, French, and some Ukrainian."

"So, what's your story?"

The mutt looks up and says, "Well, I discovered this gift pretty young, and I wanted to help the government, so I told the RCMP about my gift, and in no time they had me going from city to city, sitting in rooms with suspects and members of the smaller political parties. No one figured a dog would be eaves-dropping. I was one of their most valuable spies eight years running. The travelling and undercover work really tired me out, and I knew I wasn't getting any younger and I wanted to settle down. So I signed up for a job at Uplands Airport to do some plainclothes security work, mostly wandering near suspicious characters and listening in. I uncovered some incredible drug dealings there and was awarded a batch of medals. Had a wife, a mess of puppies, and now I'm just retired."

The guy is amazed. He goes back in and asks the owner how much he is asking for the dog.

The owner says, "Ten dollars."

Right away the guy says he'll buy him, but asks the owner, "This dog is amazing. Why on earth are you selling him?"

The owner replies, "Because he's such a damn liar."

Noteworthy Dates

Significant Events in Twentieth-century North American History:

1917: The year World War I begins.
1918: The year the United States wins World War I.
1941: The year World War II begins.
1945: The year the United States wins World War II.

American Hero

An American and a Canadian were sharing a drink.

The American began bragging about the heroes of American history. He said, "You Canadians don't have anyone like, say, Paul Revere."

The Canadian said, "Paul Revere? Wasn't he the guy who ran to get help?"

Mouth Organ

A Canadian soldier was about to go on a tour of duty in Europe. He promised his wife that he would be absolutely faithful to her. He said, "While the other guys are going out with French and Italian and Spanish girls, I will stay in and learn to play a musical instrument."

So, the next day, when she saw him off at the airport, she gave him a mouth organ.

Six months later, she was at the airport again to greet him upon his return. As he began to embrace her, she said, "Wait a minute! Before you do anything else, let me hear you play that mouth organ."

First Contingent

A Canadian soldier, billeted in England, did not appreciate the way the food was prepared at the local inn. He barely touched the food that was served him.

The proprietor was indignant. "Aren't you ashamed to be wasting food that way?" he chided. "Don't you know that food will win the war?"

"Could be," replied the soldier, "but who's going to get the enemy to eat here?"

Pigeon Corps

During the Great War, a young man from Toronto was being assessed by an officer to determine how best he could serve his country.

"Can you shoot a gun?" asked the officer.

"No, sir."

"Can you do clerical work?"

"Um, no, sir. Sorry, sir," replied the young man, who was starting to feel a little underskilled.

"Well, young man, what can you do?" barked the officer.

"I can take messages, sir!"

"Excellent. We will assign you to the Pigeon Corps. You will be in charge of vital messages being delivered from the front line using our pigeons."

The young man was then dispatched to intercept a carrier pigeon from the front lines.

He returned an hour later, covered in feathers.

"Well," asked the officer, "what's the message?"

"Well, sir, it was lot harder than I thought it was going to be, but here it is . . ."

The young man continued proudly, "Coo, coo."

Drill

A sergeant had finished drilling his men for the day.

"All right, you idiots," he barked. "Fall out!"

All but one man fell out and headed for the barracks.

"What the hell are you doing?" the sergeant asked.

"There certainly were a lot of them, weren't there, Sarge?"

Job Application

A veteran of the Great War was filling out a job application.

Where it said, "Last Employer," he wrote, "Canadian Army."

The next space asked, "Reason for leaving."

He wrote, "Armistice."

Cable

A cable was sent to British prime minister Neville Chamberlain in London at the time of the Munich Crisis. It was sent by an old gentleman who was living in retirement in Victoria, B.C.

It read enigmatically: EVENTS WILL FOLLOW

Wartime Censorship

During World War II, the press introduced self-censorship.

It became a routine to delete place names from wartime dispatches to confuse provocateurs and saboteurs.

A dispatch from Paris might begin, "From somewhere in Europe . . ."

Similarly, in a story set in Halifax, the city was regularly described as "an East Coast Canadian port."

The Canadian Press wire service, reporting on a speech in the British House of Commons by Lord Halifax, identified him, in a fit of mindlessness, as "Lord East Coast Canadian Port . . ."

Army Language

It was World War II, and Canadian troops were arriving in England.

A young British officer at a large military base decided to go over to the Canadian section and have a look at these colonials.

When he arrived, the soldiers were all at work, digging ditches, doing construction, and so on. He was appalled at the language he heard coming out of them, and he went back to the senior British commander of the base to complain about it.

"Now, lieutenant," said the elder Brit, "you must understand that these Canadian chaps have grown up on the very fringes of civilization, and they are a bit rough. So they tend to call a spade a spade."

"But they don't, sir!" the young man protested. "They call it a damn shovel."

Battle of Britain

A Canadian veteran of the Battle of Britain was giving a talk to a ladies' club, describing his exploits in his Spitfire fighter plane.

"So there I was in the thick of it over London. Fuckers to the left of me; fuckers to the right of me."

The ladies all gasped in shock, but the president of their club got up and said, "Now ladies, the captain is merely telling the kind of enemy fighters he was engaging: Fokkers."

"No, ma'am," the veteran said, "those buggers were Messerschmitts."

Paratroopers

A sergeant was training his men to be paratroopers.

He told them, "After you leave the aircraft, count to three and pull the ripcord. If your parachute fails to open, pull the emergency cord. There will be a truck waiting to pick you all up."

One soldier jumped and pulled the ripcord. Nothing happened. He pulled the emergency cord. Nothing happened. "Damn!" he said. "I bet that truck won't be there either."

Bomber Instructions

The rear-gunner of a World War II bomber was in trouble with the brass.

"What did you do," the captain yelled at him, "when you were told there was an enemy fighter at five o'clock?"

"I sat back and waited," he replied, "because it was only four-thirty."

World War II

Walter Kanitz, a well-known Toronto-based broadcaster, enjoyed telling this story.

The commanding officer of the Canadian forces in West Germany receives a letter from a young woman in Ottawa.

"I just read in the papers," the girl wrote, "that you have ordered your soldiers to fraternize with German girls. I am herewith lodging a protest, as I consider your order most unfair. I am a Canadian girl, and although already twenty-three years old, I have not been fraternized with as yet."

War Complaint

George Ignatieff, who served as Vincent Massey's private secretary in London, England, during World War II, recalled with relish one piece of correspondence that passed over his desk. Ignatieff tells the story in his memoirs, *The Making of a Peacemonger* (1985).

"I particularly remember a letter from a British housewife who explained that, because a Canadian soldier had spent his leave in her house, both she and her daughter were pregnant. To compound the felony, the visitor had taken off with her daughter's bicycle.

"'She needs same to go to work,' the letter concluded with apparent rancour. 'Please have it returned.'

"We did."

Newfie Soldier

It is World War II, and a Newfoundlander joins the Canadian Army.

The sergeant decides that it would be dangerous to give a gun to a Newfie, so he hands him a broomstick instead.

"What am I supposed to do with this?" the Newfie asks.

"You point it at the enemy," the sergeant says, "and you say, 'Bang, bang!'"

"What if I get into hand-to-hand combat?" the Newfie asks.

"Well, you pretend you've got a bayonet on the end, and you poke the enemy with it and say, 'Stab, stab!'"

The Newfie crosses "the pond" and sees action in France. The Germans are attacking his division, and he points his broomstick and says, "Bang, bang!" The Germans close with the Canadians, and the fighting is hand to hand. The Newfie uses his broomstick like a bayonet, saying, "Stab, stab!" as he knocks over German soldiers.

Then he is faced with a huge German soldier, who marches toward him relentlessly. The Newfie says, "Bang, bang!" but the German keeps coming. The Newfie hits him repeatedly with the end of the broomstick, saying, "Stab, stab!" but the German keeps coming. In fact, the big German bowls the Newfie over and walks right over him. As the German walks over him, the Newfie can hear the German say, "Tank . . . tank . . . tank!"

World War II

It was World War II, and a Canadian and a German were in an aerial dogfight over the North Sea.

Watching the fight were two sharks. The pilots shot each other down, so one of the sharks said, "You go and eat the German, and I'll go and eat the Canadian. We'll meet back here after lunch."

So off they swam.

An hour later they met, and one of the sharks said, "So, how was your lunch?"

"Oh, just great. Nice, tasty German. Very good. How was your Canadian?"

"I didn't eat him."

"Why not?"

"Well, as he was struggling to keep his head above the water, he started singing 'The Maple Leaf Forever,' and I couldn't swallow that crap."

French-Canadian Soldier

A French Canadian from Quebec City enlisted and served with the Canadian Army as it advanced through France in World War II. All around him he saw desolation: smashed towns, starving children, people in rags.

One of his fellow soldiers said, "Isn't it terrible, what these French people have been through?"

"Hmph!" grunted the French Canadian. "Don't feel sorry for dese French people. It is dere own fault. Dey should never 'ave left Quebec."

French Fact

Before members of the Canadian Corps landed on the beach at Normandy, the captain warned his troops.

"Remember," he said, "the French are patriotic and particular. If they say France is bigger than Ontario, agree with them."

Mess Hall

The soldiers in the mess hall of a Canadian Forces base were grumbling about the quality of the food. They were especially upset over the quality of the bread, which they refused to eat.

The officer in charge of the mess hall growled at them. "You're a bunch of spoiled wussies," he said. "If our boys in the trenches of the Great War had had that bread, they'd have eaten every scrap!"

"Yes, sir," said one man. "But it was still fresh then."

Going on Leave

A private stationed at a Canadian Forces base was about to go on a long-awaited, forty-eight-hour leave. He was really looking forward to doing a little fishing.

As he was about to leave the office in which he had been working, a major asked him if he would drop off a set of golf clubs at the officers' club on his way to the barracks. The private said yes, and took the clubs. As he walked into the officers' club with the golf bag, a general casually asked him if he was going to play a little golf.

The private replied, "No, sir, I'm going to do a little fishing."

The private was restricted to the base for the next forty-eight hours.

Camouflage

A sergeant yelled at a soldier, "You're in trouble, mister. You didn't show up for camouflage training."

The soldier replied, "How do you know?"

Citizenship

In the aftermath of World War II, a former German soldier immigrated to Canada and began farming on the Prairies.

About a year later, he wrote home to his brother to say that he had decided to apply for Canadian citizenship.

His bother wrote back, asking, "How could you do such a thing? Why would you want to become a citizen of a country which had twice fought against Germany?"

The man replied, "Are you jealous because we won both wars?"

Tricky Question

If America and Canada got into a war, where would all the draft dodgers go?

Falklands Crisis

This joke made the rounds during the Falklands Crisis in May 1982.

To assist Britain during the crisis, Canada sent three destroyers and two cruisers.

The three destroyers were Pierre Elliott Trudeau, Marc Lalonde, and Jean Marchand.

The two cruisers were Maggie Trudeau and Claude Charron.

Naval Plans

Peter C. Newman tells this story the best. It comes from the column he wrote in the wake of the World Trade Center disaster, "Amen to the Peaceable Kingdom," National Post, September 22, 2001.

With the world drifting toward war, I am haunted by the toast proposed a few years ago by a Canadian naval officer in a ship's wardroom in Halifax.

"We attack at dawn!" he exulted.

"Why dawn?" asked one of his buddies, suspecting that he was being set up as a straight man.

"That way," was the triumphant reply, "if things don't work out, we haven't wasted the whole day."

Air Transat

Muslim terrorists hijacked two U.S. commercial jet aircraft and crashed them into the twin towers of the World Trade Center, 9:15 a.m., September 11, 2001. Within hours the following joke made the rounds. It refers to the fact that a month earlier an airplane operated by the Canadian charter airline Air Transat ran out of fuel in mid-flight (but landed safely).

NEWS ANNOUNCEMENT

It has just been learned that two Air Transat commercial jet aircraft have been hijacked. It is believed that the two planes are headed for Toronto's CN Tower.

Military and aviation authorities maintain that the hijacked planes pose no safety problems. It is expected that they will run out of fuel before they hit their targets.

American War on Terrorism

The Canadians will finally help America with the war on terrorism.

They have pledged two of their biggest battleships, 600 ground troops, and six fighter jets.

After the exchange rate, America ends up with two Mounties, one canoe, and a flying squirrel.

Terrorists

Q. Why are Canadians allergic to terrorists?
A. Our constitution has no stomach for nuts.

Paddy and Saddam

Saddam Hussein was sitting in his office, wondering whom to invade next, when his telephone rang.

"Hello! Mr. Hussein," a heavily accented voice said. "This is Paddy from St. John's, Newfoundland. I am ringing to inform you that we are officially declaring war on you."

"Well, Paddy," Saddam replied, "this is indeed important news. Tell me, how big is your army?"

"At this moment in time," said Paddy, after a moment's calculation, "there is myself, my cousin Sean, my next door neighbour Gerry, and the entire dominoes team from the pub—that makes eight."

Saddam sighed. "I must tell you, Paddy, that I have one million men in my army waiting to move on my command."

"Begorra!" said Paddy. "I'll have to ring you back."

Sure enough, the next day Paddy rang back. "Right, Mr. Hussein, the war is still on. We have managed to acquire some equipment."

"And what equipment would that be, Paddy?" Saddam asked.

"Well, we have two combine harvesters, a bulldozer, and Murphy's tractor from the farm."

Once more, Saddam sighed. "I must tell you, Paddy, that I have 16,000 tanks, 14,000 armoured personnel carriers, and my army has increased to one and a half million since we last spoke."

"Really?" said Paddy. "I'll have to ring you back."

Paddy rang again the next day. "Right, Mr. Hussein, the war is still on. We have managed to get ourselves airborne. We've modified Ted's ultra-light with a couple of rifles in the cockpit, and the bridge team has joined us as well."

Saddam was silent for a minute, then sighed. "I must tell you, Paddy, that I have 10,000 bombers, 20,000 MiG-19 attack planes, my military complex is surrounded by laser-guided surface-to-air missile sites, and since we last spoke, my army has increased to two million men."

"Faith and begorra!" said Paddy. "I'll have to ring you back."

Sure enough, Paddy called again the next day. "Right, Mr. Hussein, I am sorry to tell you that we have had to call off the war."

"I'm sorry to hear that," said Saddam. "Why the sudden change of heart?"

"Well," said Paddy, "we've all had a chat, and there's no way we can feed two million prisoners."

Wall Around Afghanistan

This joke made the rounds in the 1980s without any reference to Osama bin Laden. Following the attack on the World Trade Center, September 11, 2001, it made the rounds again, but this time it featured the name of the Saudi Arabian–born Al-Qaeda terrorist who masterminded the attack.

Three guys, Johnny Canuck, Osama bin Laden, and Uncle Sam are out walking together one day. They come across a lantern and a genie pops out of it.

"I will give each of you one wish; that's three wishes total," says the genie.

Johnny Canuck says, "I am a farmer, my dad was a farmer, and my son will also farm. I want the land to be forever fertile in Canada."

With a blink of the genie's eyes, poof, the land in Canada is forever made fertile for farming.

Osama bin Laden is amazed, so he says, "I want a wall around Afghanistan, so that no infidels, Jews, or Americans can come into our precious state."

Again, with a blink of the genie's eyes, poof, there is a huge wall around Afghanistan.

Uncle Sam, a former civil engineer, asks, "I'm very curious. Please tell me more about this wall."

The genie explains, "Well, it's about 15,000 feet high, 500 feet thick, and completely surrounds the country; nothing can get in or out—virtually impenetrable."

Uncle Sam says, "Fill it with water."

I Am Canadian . . . Forces

This item came as e-mail on February 11, 2002, five months after the World Trade Center disaster. It distinguishes between members of the Canadian Armed Forces and those of the U.S. Army. It was sent to me by Alec Shipman, a firearms specialist, who wrote, "I received this from a friend. This is food for thought!" It is not a humorous item, per se, but it is . . . thoughtful.

I wear combats, not fatigues.

I work for a "lef-tenant," not a "loo-tenant."

I drive an Iltis, not a Jeep or Humvee.

The weapon I carry for my protection is a C-7, not an M-16.

I observe from, or take cover in, a slit trench, not a foxhole.

I don't just speak English or French; I can speak many languages.

Although I am trained to fight wars, I don't cause them.

I try not to take sides, and I believe in treating all humans equally.

I don't just go on patrols, I clear land mines to make regions safe for everyone.

When I am not deployed on a peace mission, I travel all over my country fighting forest fires, battling floods, rescuing lost souls, or repairing damage caused by ice storms.

In my off-duty hours on deployments, I occupy myself by rebuilding schools or playgrounds, and I teach children in war-torn countries about peace and harmony.

I am my country's best ambassador, and I am respected the world over for what I do best.

I carry my country's flag proudly and hold my head high wherever I go.

CF Tribal Wisdom

Alec Shipman also e-mailed me this gem, which he says he received "from an army friend of mine." He added, on February 7, 2002, "It is truly wonderful what our government has done to one of the finest armed forces in the world."

The tribal wisdom of the Dakota Indians, passed on from generation to generation, dictates: "When you discover that you are riding on a dead horse, the best strategy is to dismount."

However, in the modern Canadian Forces, a whole range of much more advanced strategies are often employed:

1. Buy a stronger whip from Bombardier.
2. Change riders.
3. Appoint a committee to study the horse.
4. Arrange to visit other countries to see how other cultures ride dead horses.
5. Lower the standards so dead horses can be included.
6. Reclassify the dead horse as "living impaired."
7. Hire outside contractors to ride the dead horse.
8. Harness several dead horses together to increase speed.
9. Provide additional funding and/or retraining to increase the dead horse's performance.
10. Do a productivity study to see if lighter riders would improve the dead horse's performance.
11. Declare that because the dead horse does not have to be fed, because it is less costly, because it carries lower overhead, it therefore contributes substantially more to the bottom line of the economy than do other horses.
12. Rewrite the expected performance requirements for all horses.
13. Promote the dead horse to general.

Politicians, Politics, and Malarkey

An argument is being waged in this country between two groups of citizens: those who think the country is overgoverned and those who think the country is underregulated. Politicians, elected to represent the desires and aspirations of the majority of Canadians, are caught in the middle—or in the muddle.

It is no wonder that we consider our politicians—municipal, regional, provincial, and federal—to be a bad lot generally. There is a lot of discontent because there is hardly any consensus on municipal, regional, provincial, or federal issues.

Some of our bitterest humour is political in nature, as these jokes, anecdotes, and instances of lore amply show.

Political Mosaic

There is a political saying that goes like this:

In Atlantic Canada, politics is a tradition, in Quebec it's a family affair, in Ontario it's a business, on the Prairies it's a religion, in the North it's survival, and in B.C. it's entertainment.

On the Hustings

A political candidate stood on a platform and announced to the assembled crowd that he was going to fight radicalism, socialism, communism, and anarchism.

One old man snorted and said, "I'll vote for you when you can do something about rheumatism."

Thomas D'Arcy McGee

Thomas D'Arcy McGee was an Irishman with the gift of the gab. He was also one of the Fathers of Confederation. (Perhaps the two go together!)

McGee rose to speak in the House of Commons and to his surprise was heckled. He continued to speak.

That evening, having a drink with his buddy Prime Minister Sir John A. Macdonald, he explained the incident in the House this way:

"You know, Johnnie, they were hissing a Liberal devil who spoke before me. They hissed him down. And would you believe it, Johnnie, when I rose to speak, they started to hiss him all over again!"

Queen Victoria

Sir George Etienne Cartier met Queen Victoria when in London in April 1865 while arranging the passage of the BNA Act, establishing the Dominion of Canada.

The Queen spoke to him (in French, to his surprise and joy) about Montreal's new Victoria Bridge. She asked him, "How many feet is it from shore to shore?"

Cartier delighted her with his reply. He said, "When we Canadians build a bridge and dedicate it to Your Majesty, we measure it not in feet but in miles."

Politician and Statesman

What is the difference between a politician and a statesman?

A politician is a man who has a tongue that has mastered the art of public speaking.

A statesman is a former politician who has mastered the art of holding his tongue that has mastered the art of public speaking.

Parliament

Here is a definition of Parliament:

Parliament is a place where a man gets up to speak, says nothing, and nobody listens. Then everyone disagrees.

Nova Scotia Premier

Q. What would you call the premier of Nova Scotia?

A. The bossa nova.

News Story

A reporter walked into his editor's office and said, "I've got the perfect news story."

"What is it?" asked the editor. "Man bites dog?"

"No, not man bites dog. Bull throws politician."

Inebriate

A farmer in Saskatchewan was reading a newspaper and commented to a friend, "I always thought that M.P. of ours drank too much. Says here in the news he made a speech from the floor of the House."

Rural Riding

A man who was canvassing a rural area, trying to dig up votes for the Progressive Conservative Party, met with stubborn resistance at the door of one farmer.

"I've never voted Tory," said the farmer. "And I never will. My parents were Liberal. My grandparents were Liberal. So I'll always be Liberal."

"Well, that's no way to decide how to vote," said the Conservative supporter. "What if your parents and grandparents had been thieves?"

"In that case," said the farmer, "I guess they'd have been Tories."

Mitch Hepburn

Mitch Hepburn is remembered as the populist premier of Ontario. Running for elective office for the first time in 1926, he travelled from farm to farm across the Elgin West riding, drumming up votes.

In one backyard he came upon a young girl milking a cow. He had started talking to her when the girl's mother stuck her head out of the back door and called out, "Mary, who is that guy you're talking to?"

"He's a politician, Mom!"

"You come into the house right now," commanded the mother. Then she added, "If that guy says he's a politician, you'd better bring the cow with you."

Mitch Hepburn

Mitch Hepburn could convulse an audience in his home township of Yarmouth as he ridiculed the financing policies of CCF leader Edward Jolliffe. They reminded him of a school board deciding to build a new school. First it resolved to build the school; then it resolved to use the materials from the old school; and finally it planned to use the old school while the new one was being built.

Mitch and Ned Sparks

Mitch Hepburn was the Liberal leader and premier of Ontario in the 1930s. He possessed the common touch.

So too did Ned Sparks, the vaudeville performer and silent-film star, who made much of the fact that he was born in St. Thomas, Ont. Sparks was the originator of the deadpan—no matter what happened to him on stage or screen, he never smiled! In fact, it was said that he was insured by Lloyd's of London against ever being caught with a smile on his face by a photographer.

Mitch and Ned had a meeting in the former's office at Queen's Park, here described by a reporter for the St. Thomas *Times-Journal*, December 4, 1934.

"Mr. Sparks' father," the premier said, "had been a staunch St. Thomas Liberal, and the Hollywood star just wanted to see whether the premier had a bust of Sir Wilfrid Laurier in his office."

He saw the bust, the premier observing that Sir Wilfrid had once "patted" Ned on the head.

"He made a dent," added Mr. Sparks.

Arthur Meighen and Mackenzie King

Here is an excerpt from a letter written by retired politician Heath Macquarrie.

"I have a memory of a prime minister who was anything but disingenuous. In the mid-1950s, before I entered the House of Commons, I made several visits to Arthur Meighen to talk with him about Sir Robert Borden.

"It was my custom to write down my recollections as soon as I left his office. (It was not the time nor the man for taped interviews.)

"One of his most brilliant comments was about Mackenzie King's tendency to regard himself as the genius behind Canadian independence. As Meighen saw it, all the real achievements in that field had come during Borden's prime ministership. In fact, all that was left for King to do was 'to burst heroically through open doors.'

"A brilliant put-down but I could not find it anywhere. My friend Roger Graham is long since dead. It's hard to believe that Mr. Meighen coined that put-down during that conversation."

Viscount Bennett

R.B. Bennett had the misfortune to hold the office of prime minister during the worst years of the Great Depression. He was unpopular during the 1930s, and even less popular some years later when, out of office, he pushed for a peerage. In 1941, the British authorities acquiesced and titled him Viscount Bennett of Mickleham and of Calgary and Hopewell.

Charles Ritchie was a consular officer with the Canadian High Commission at the Court of St. James. As he recorded in his diary entry for July of that year: "Bennett's peerage provides me with the headache of writing to him. Lord Stampede of Calgary is the best title suggested."

Leading Mandarin

Jack Pickersgill was one of the wily mandarins of Ottawa.

In his capacity as a member of the public service, he advised prime ministers on policies and procedures. As a member of Parliament, he represented Newfoundland's Bonavista-Twillingate riding.

He was Liberal to the core. In fact, he has been described as the heart, head, and hands of the Liberal Party of Canada.

He had a simple, partisan faith.

He once shared his belief system with some dignitaries who were visiting Parliament Hill.

"The Conservatives are the Party of Opposition," he informed them. "The Liberals are the Party of Government."

Last Living Father of Confederation

J.R. (Joey) Smallwood, a master orator, brought Newfoundland kicking and screaming into Confederation.

He was speaking in an outport community, drawing attention to the benefits of Confederation, when he ran into some organized resistance.

"Go ahead and tell us what's on your mind," a heckler yelled at him. "It won't take very long!"

"I'll do better than that," Smallwood yelled right back. "I'll tell you what's on my mind and what's on your mind as well. It won't take any longer."

Newfoundland Dam

There was a proposal to erect a hydroelectric power dam on the St. Mary's River in the interior of Newfoundland.

To the surprise of Premier Joey Smallwood, the member of his government who represented this region was dead set against the proposal. Joey summoned the recalcitrant member to the Premier's Office and asked him to explain his sudden and unexpected opposition.

"Don't you realize that this dam will bring prosperity to the region, to members of your constituency, and to all Newfoundlanders? It will generate electricity, and we badly need this source of inexpensive power, and it will allow us to harness all the waters of the St. Mary's River and regulate them and make them available for irrigation purposes and that this will increase our overall agricultural production?"

"That's just it, Joey," replied the member. "It's that last part of what you say that bothers me."

"How's that?" Joey asked.

"You see, those engineers, they plan to extract all that energy from the water to generate their hydroelectricity. Then that water will be without energy and it will be just useless, and all our fields will be damaged if that water is used to irrigate the soil!"

Joey Again

A group of students were touring the Confederation Centre of the Arts in Charlottetown, P.E.I. In the art gallery, they were shown Robert Harris's celebrated group portrait called *Fathers of Confederation*.

One student looked closely at the group of distinguished men arranged around a table and asked, "Where's Joey Smallwood?"

The guide answered, "Well, originally, Newfoundland did not want to join Confederation." Then he added, "But to keep Joey happy, the other men let him take the picture."

Parliament Hill

The following quip has been attributed to John Diefenbaker (as well as to many other leading politicians).

"When you arrive on Parliament Hill on your first day, you wonder how you ever got there. After that, you wonder how the other Members got there."

Diefenbaker and Newman

There was no love lost between Prime Minister John G. Diefenbaker and investigative journalist Peter C. Newman, who wrote the definitive book on the Conservative leader, *Renegade in Power*.

A colleague told Diefenbaker, "I don't think that any investigative journalist ever plunged so deeply into the well of information."

"And came up so dry," rejoined Diefenbaker.

John G. Diefenbaker

Prime Minister Diefenbaker was hard of hearing.

At least that is what his aides maintained. His critics said he was hard of listening.

One day he arrived at his office on Parliament Hill wearing a brand-new hearing aid. He exclaimed, "At considerable expense I have acquired the latest-model hearing contraption."

"Marvellous! Does it work well?"

"Half-past three."

Lake Diefenbaker

Diefenbaker was inordinately proud that a lake in Saskatchewan had been named in his honour.

"Two weeks ago, I had a lake named after me," he told the members of the annual convention of the Conservative Party in Toronto in 1967. "They never named one after Sir John A. Macdonald because he wasn't addicted that way."

Dirty Pool

Diefenbaker, shaking hands with a group of Saskatchewan farmers, notices that one of them is wearing a cap with the letters MF.

"What does MF mean?" he asks.

"Why," the farmer replies, "it means 'master farmer.'"

Then he notices another farmer is wearing a cap with the letters AE.

"What does AE mean?" he asks.

"Why," the farmer replies, "it means 'agricultural expert.'"

Then he notices yet another farmer wearing a cap with the letters POOL.

"What does POOL mean?" he asks.

"Well," the farmer replies, "I won't tell you what the P stands for, but the OOL stands for 'on Otto Lang.'"

Dief and Joel

Joel Bonn told me the following story of his second encounter with John G. Diefenbaker. Bonn, one of the country's fastest readers, a one-man literacy campaign, has taught more Canadians to read without moving their lips than any other instructor.

In Ottawa in the early 1960s, I taught John Diefenbaker to speed-read.

I met him again at the Commonwealth Games held in Edmonton in 1978.

"I know you," he said to me. "What do they call you?"

"Bonn, sir."

"Bonn! I remember your last name. It's your first name that escapes me."

Donald Fleming

This bit of wit and wisdom was noted by Peter C. Newman in a review of Fleming's memoirs in The Globe and Mail, *September 14, 1985.*

Donald Fleming was the self-important Minister of Finance in the administration of Lester B. Pearson.

After delivering his first financial report to the House of Commons, December 6, 1957, he added by way of aside: "May I say very humbly that seventeen to eighteen hours work per day and one hundred hours work per week are an insignificant price to pay for the high privilege of serving Canada."

James Sinclair, Liberal Finance critic, whispered in reply: "If conceit is the small man's sword, Don's the best-armed man in Canada."

Prime Minister

Lester B. Pearson is remembered as having been a good prime minister.

One of the reasons for his success was that he surrounded himself with strong and interesting people—called "pearsonalities."

What It Means to Be a Diplomat

The following definition of what it means to be a diplomat has been attributed (on no evidence whatsoever) to the late Lester B. Pearson, the former prime minister and at one time a leading member of what was in the past known as the Department of External Affairs.

"If a diplomat says 'Yes,' he means 'Perhaps'; if he says 'Perhaps,' he means 'No'; and if he says 'No,' it means he's not a diplomat."

Getting It Up

John G. Diefenbaker and Pierre Elliott Trudeau put aside their political differences and met over a drink: water for John G. and wine for Pierre E.

Trudeau said, "Tell me something, Dief. At your age, can you still . . . uh . . . get it up for the ladies?"

Diefenbaker replied, "Most certainly, Pierre. I just pull it out and bang it a couple of times on the foot of the bed and it stiffens right up."

Trudeau thought about this for the rest of the evening. When he went home, Maggie was already asleep in bed. He decided to try Diefenbaker's method. He pulled out his dick and banged it a couple of times on the foot of the bed.

Right away, Maggie sat up and said, "Is that you, Dief?"

Robert Stanfield

Robert Stanfield, a man of principle, was loved in the Maritimes and admired as a kind of Lincolnesque figure throughout the rest of Canada.

He led the Conservative Party but was never elected prime minister of Canada. "He was," Dalton Camp once boasted, "the best prime minister we never had."

When Stanfield agreed to step down as leader of the party, he told the party faithful the following story.

"A poll has been taken of the members of my caucus. The results show that its members are unanimous in the choice of a successor.

"When asked to name the best possible successor, they all answered 'Me.'"

24 Sussex Drive

Private donors covered the cost of the installation of an indoor swimming pool at the prime minister's official residence at 24 Sussex Drive in Ottawa. The prime minister at the time was Pierre Elliott Trudeau.

Opposition members in the House of Commons criticized the expenditure. If it came from the public purse, it was extravagance; if it came from private coffers, it was influence-peddling.

Trudeau would have none of it. He singled out one Opposition member in the House and made an offer: "You may come over at any time to practise your diving in the pool. Come right away, even before the water is in."

Trudeau and Sasha

Pierre Elliott Trudeau and his son Sasha were on a plane flying over Alberta.

"Look, Daddy!" exclaimed the youngster, waving a $1,000 bill, his week's allowance. "If I dropped this $1,000 bill out of the plane, some Albertan would be really happy!"

Trudeau smiled. "If you dropped two $500 bills out of the window, you could make two Albertans happy."

"And if I threw ten $100 bills out of the window, I could make ten Albertans happy!" chortled the youngster.

Just then the plane's intercom system clicked on and the voice of the pilot boomed out, loud and clear: "If you threw your father out the window, you could make all the Albertans happy!"

Trudeau through McLuhan's Eyes

Tom Wolfe Jr., essayist and author, was intrigued with what Marshall McLuhan had to say about Trudeau.

"One time I asked him how it was that Pierre Trudeau managed to stay in power as prime minister through all the twists and turns of Canadian politics. Without even the twitch of a smile, McLuhan responded, 'It's simple. He has a French name, he thinks like an Englishman, and he looks like an Indian. We all feel very guilty about the Indians here in Canada.'"

Trudeau's Cabinet Shuffle

Just prior to the 1979 election, Prime Minister Trudeau shuffled his cabinet. It did him no good, as he lost the election to Joe Clark.

Heath Macquarrie sat on the new Parliament in "the other place." He observed to Clark, "I've attended many funerals but never was at one where a change of pallbearers revived the corpse."

"Clark told me," Macquarrie recalled, "he would use that remark in his campaign."

Trudeau the Good Sport

Trudeau was a sportsman but no sports enthusiast.

Christina McCall-Newman tells of one incident which took place in 1973 that proves the point. It seems Trudeau wanted Senator Keith Davey to act as his campaign organizer.

"Davey was in the Senate lounge watching a Stanley Cup playoff game on television when he was summoned to answer Trudeau's call. After asking him to take on the job, Trudeau said politely that he hoped he wasn't interrupting Davey's dinner. Davey told him he was watching hockey and added that the Buffalo Sabres were winning the game. There was an awkward pause at the other end of the line and then Trudeau said, 'Oh, I see. What inning are they in?'"

Pierre and Mao

Pierre Elliott Trudeau visited the People's Democratic Republic of China.

He was received by Mao Tse-tung, who showed him all the impressive achievements of Communism.

"These achievements are all due to the enthusiasm of the eight hundred million Chinese people for their political system," explained Mao.

"But aren't there also some people who are opposed to your system?"

"Oh, there certainly are some," Mao conceded. "Maybe eight million or so."

"No problem," replied Trudeau. "In Canada, that's about the population of Quebec."

Trudeau on Government

Canada is considered to be a difficult country to govern.

Prime ministers as unalike as Mackenzie King and John Diefenbaker, Lester B. Pearson and Brian Mulroney, John Turner and Jean Chrétien, are all on record as attesting to this fact and as stressing the degree of difficulty of the governance of this land.

Conrad Black recalled a conversation with Pierre Elliott Trudeau. According to Black's account, as noted by the essayist Calvin Trillin in "Paper Baron," *The New Yorker*, December 17, 2001, "Canada was difficult to govern partly because French-speaking Canadians boo the loser and English-speaking Canadians boo the winner."

Trudeau

Q. What is it that God never saw, Pierre Elliott Trudeau seldom saw, but you and I see every day?

A. An equal.

Joe's Cufflinks

Joe Clark is taken by surprise to be presented with a gift-wrapped box by the members of the caucus of the Progressive Conservative Party of Canada.

He opens the box and finds it contains a pair of cufflinks.

He is at a loss for words as he delivers his thank-you speech. "I'll have to have my wrists pierced, I guess," he adds.

Joe and the Students

Joe Clark was visiting an elementary school. In one class, he asked the pupils if anyone could give him an example of a tragedy.

A little boy stood up and said, "If my best friend who lives next door to me was playing in the street and a car came along and ran over him, that would be a tragedy."

"No," said Joe. "That would be an accident."

A little girl stood up and said, "If a school bus was carrying fifty children and it drove off a cliff and everyone died, that would be a tragedy."

"Not really," said Joe. "That is what we would call a great loss."

The pupils were silent, none of them volunteering to answer the question.

"You mean to say," asked Joe, "that no one here can give me an example of a tragedy?"

Finally, a little boy in the back seat stood up and said, "If an airplane carrying Joe Clark and Maureen McTeer exploded in mid-air, that would be a tragedy."

"Wonderful!" Joe beamed. "True! And can you tell me why that would be a tragedy?"

"Well," said the little boy, "it would be a tragedy because it wouldn't be an accident and it certainly wouldn't be a great loss!"

The Clark Family

This classified advertisement appeared not too long ago in a column of the *High River Times*:

"Used gravestone for sale. Ideal gift for a family called Clark."

Joe Clark

Joe Clark, fending off the press, explained, "Not only do I have no plans, I have no plans to have plans."

The Problem with the French

Conservative leader Joe Clark met with his party's economic critic in the House of Commons to discuss the state of the Quebec economy. They agreed it was not performing as well as it should.

"The problem with the French in Quebec," Clark confided, "is their language. They don't have a word for entrepreneur."

Joe Clark and the Russian Ambassador

A long time ago, for a short time indeed, Joe Clark served as prime minister of Canada. He held the highest elected office in the land for approximately nine months, between 1979 and 1980.

It is said that after the defeat of his government, he had a sobering conversation with Alexandre Yakolev, Soviet ambassador to Canada from 1973 to 1983, and close friend and adviser of Mikhail Gorbachov.

Yakolev said, "You know, there is one feature of the Russian political system that you in your country might consider copying."

Clark. "What is that?"

Yakolev: "In my country, when a politician is through, he's finished."

John Crosbie in Heaven

John Crosbie dies and goes to Heaven. St. Peter meets him at the Pearly Gates and takes him on the grand tour.

As Crosbie is walking around, he notices on the wall of one of the heavenly buildings a great many clocks with nameplates fastened above them. He sees nameplates that identify Jean Chrétien's clock, Preston Manning's clock, Lucien Bouchard's clock, and the clocks of many other Canadian politicians. He observes that the hands of the clocks are revolving at different speeds. No two are telling the same time. Some are moving a little faster, others a little slower.

He is curious about the various speeds, so he asks St. Peter what it is all about.

St. Peter tells him that each clock represents a person's life. When someone tells a lie, his clock ticks off a minute of his life.

Crosbie looks around and sees clocks for all the politicians he knows, except for the clock of one politician. So he clears his throat and asks St. Peter a question: "I haven't seen Brian Mulroney's clock. Where is it?"

"Well," says St. Peter. "God Himself keeps Brian Mulroney's clock in His office. He uses it as a fan."

Mulroney's Debt

A father and a son are discussing the address to the nation delivered by Prime Minister Brian Mulroney. The purpose of the address is to draw attention to Canada's mounting debt.

"My son," the father says. "Our country has great faith in your generation. Just look at the size of the national debt we are expecting you to pay."

Mulroney Again

Q. Do Brian and Mila do it with Brian on the top or with Brian on the bottom?

A. He's on the bottom because all he can do is fuck up.

Q. Why did Brian Mulroney cross the road?

A. He didn't. He just said he did.

Mulroney and Bush

Prime Minister Brian Mulroney called George Bush Sr. and he asked him, "Why the hell did you take Dan Quayle as vice-president?"

George says, "He passed the intelligence test."

"What was that test?"

"I asked him, 'If your mother has a baby and it's not your brother and not your sister, who is it?' And Dan answered, 'It's me.' So I hired him."

"Good idea!" says Brian. "I'll try that on my Finance Minister."

So he asks Joe Clark the same question. Joe says, "Well, can I give you an answer in a day or two?"

"No problem."

Joe is completely in the dark, so he asks Jean Charest the same question. Jean answers, "It's me, of course."

Happy now, Joe goes back to Brian and says, "I've got the answer to your question: If my mother has a baby who is neither my brother nor my sister, it's Jean Charest."

Shaking his head Brian says, "You are such a dork! It's Dan Quayle, you idiot!"

Mulroney's Operation

Once out of office, Brian Mulroney had major surgery—a charisma bypass.

Jean Charest

Jean Charest contested the leadership of the Conservative Party but lost to Kim Campbell.

Many observers feel that he emerged the winner, not the loser. He turned out to be a more credible politician than Campbell, who, calling the next general election, lost not only her own seat but all but two of the party's one hundred and sixty-nine seats.

Charest's face was new. He is fluently bilingual. He is a family man. And he is a federalist.

There is only one thing that is against him. Once upon a time he telephoned a judge to put in a good word for a friend who was having legal problems. The judge refused to take the call so no harm was done, except to Charest's career. He was visiting Australia when his indiscretion became public knowledge. He immediately submitted his resignation and it was accepted.

He did it in a unique manner. "I am the first Member of any cabinet to submit his resignation—by fax," he explained.

Funny Thought

Early every morning Brian Mulroney would wake up in the master bedroom that he shared with his wife in the prime minister's official residence at 24 Sussex Drive in Ottawa.

He would turn to Mila and say, "Mila, think of all the wonderful things that I could do for Canada today—if only we did not have our everlasting deficit and debt."

Mulroney Road Sign

Brian Mulroney was the second most despised prime minister in Canadian history. (Pride of first place goes to R.B. Bennett, who had the supreme disadvantage of coming into the highest office during the depths of the Great Depression.) A correspondent drew my attention to the following, which was spotted on a road sign, a professionally produced affair, on a country road near Cole's Island, N.B., in 1990.

If you Drink and Drive,
Run over Mulroney!

Brian and Kim

Political commentators could find no differences between the election platforms of Kim Campbell and of her predecessor, Brian Mulroney.

Jean Chrétien, Liberal leader, in April 1993 quipped, "What is the difference between Brian Mulroney and Kim Campbell? One of them wears a shirt."

Mel Hurtig, leader of the National Party of Canada, expressed it more vividly: "She's Brian Mulroney with lipstick."

Conservative Rout

In the 1993 general election, which saw the victory of Jean Chrétien's Liberals and the downfall of the Conservatives, the only two Tory members to survive were Jean Charest and Elsie Wayne. Even Kim Campbell, the party's leader, was defeated in her own riding.

The next day, suitably subdued, Jean and Elsie sat down to dine in the Parliamentary Dining Room.

The waiter approached them and asked, "Chateaubriand?"

At the end of the meal, he asked, "Will that be one cheque or two?"

Passionate Nationalist

Mel Hurtig, publisher and nationalist, is talking:

"I like to tell the story of the time I spoke to a big convention at the Hotel Vancouver.

"I went to bed just before eleven. Soon after, I was wakened by a knock on my door. I wrapped a towel around my waist and opened the door a crack. There stood a beautiful blond woman, wearing a black mink coat. 'Hello,' I said, wiping the sleep out of my eyes. 'Hello, Mr. Hurtig. I heard your speech tonight and I thought it was marvellous. I'm a very passionate nationalist and I'd really like to meet you.' So, to make a long story short, I sold her a membership in the Committee for an Independent Canada."

Bob Rae

Joe Clark accused Bob Rae of being "a silver-spoon socialist."

After all, argued Clark, the Ontario NDP leader was the son of an Ottawa diplomat, his sister had dated Pierre Trudeau, and Rae himself was a Rhodes scholar who studied at Oxford.

Rae was not amused, and wittily replied, "That's not true. I resent that. My nanny resents that. And my chauffeur resents that."

PC Supporter

A supporter of the Progressive Conservative Party of Canada was canvassing a neighbourhood, trying to see how much support his candidate could expect in the coming election.

He knocked on one door and introduced himself as a representative for the PC's.

"What!" exclaimed the man at the door. "The Tories! Why, I wouldn't vote for one of those crooked, lying bastards if he was the only person running. I've never voted Tory in my life and I never will. Every election, I vote ABC—Anything But Conservative!" Then he slammed the door shut.

The PC canvasser took out his little book, and beside that address he wrote, "Doubtful."

Politician

Reporters were getting annoyed with a politician who wouldn't give them a straight answer on anything.

Finally one of them said, "What's your favourite colour?"

He replied, "Plaid."

Circular Letter

Circular letter noted by John G. Diefenbaker, April 6, 1966. Ross Thatcher served as premier of Saskatchewan from 1964 to 1971. Thatcher, like Hazen Argue, left the CCF party to join the Liberals. Diefenbaker was, of course, a Conservative.

Dear Sir or Madame,

We have the distinguished honour of being members of the committee to raise $50 million to be used for commissioning a statue of Ross Thatcher and placing it in front of the Parliament Buildings.

This committee was in quite a quandary about selecting the proper location for the statue. It was not thought wise to place it beside the statue of the late Arthur Meighen, who never told a lie, or beside the statue of Mackenzie King, who never told the truth, since Ross Thatcher could never tell the difference.

After careful consideration, we decided that it should be placed next to the statue of Christopher Columbus, the greatest Liberal of them all, in that he started out not knowing where he was going, and upon arriving did not know where he was, and upon returning did not know where he had been, and he accomplished all of this on borrowed money.

Five thousand years ago, Moses said to the children of Israel, "Pick up your shovels, mount your asses and camels, and I will lead you to the Promised Land."

Nearly five thousand years later, R.B. Bennett said, "Lay down your shovels, sit on your asses, light up a Camel, because this is the Promised Land."

Now Ross Thatcher is stealing your shovels, kicking your asses, raising the price of your Camels, and taking over the Promised Land.

If you are one of the few citizens who has any money left over after paying taxes, we expect you to send a generous contribution for this worthy cause to:

Leadership Solidification Committee,
c/o Hazen Argue,
Assiniboia,
Sask.

Damn Unions

There is an amusing quip about Mike Harris, the right-wing ideologue who served as the Progressive Conservative premier of Ontario from 1995 to 2001.

The quip, attributed to the lacklustre NDP leader Howard Hampton, was recalled upon news reports that Harris was planning to announce his resignation. It appeared as such in "Mike Harris in Quotes," National Post, October 16, 2001:

Last week Mike Harris was interviewed on the Weather Channel about why weather patterns have been so strange.

Mr. Harris had his own explanation . . . it was all caused by those damn unions.

Mike Harris's Goodbye Letter

I have titled this piece of urban lore "Mike Harris's Goodbye Letter." It was faxed to me on December 6, 2001, by a friend who has sources within the civil service of the Government of Ontario. The draft letter appeared following the announcement by Ontario premier Mike Harris (here called Duffer Harris) that he would not seek another term as premier, as Conservative member of the Provincial Legislature, and as leader of the Conservative Party of Ontario. The draft letter is surprisingly rich in specific details of the premier's personal and public lives, catches the voice of its supposed author, and gives vent to long-simmering resentments felt by members of the civil service and the general public. The Ontario trillium appears at the beginning and the province's tourism slogan at the end. Making allowances for some blurs in the fax, I have reprinted the text as it appeared.

We have obtained a copy of the first unpublished draft of the letter of Ontario premier Duffer Harris, October 16, 2001. We present it in its entirety.

ONTARIO

During my time at Queen's Park, I have travelled back and forth to my riding at least 1,000 times. Half the time I flew and half the time I drove—depending on how eager I was to spend another tension-filled weekend with my wife and kiddies. This year the limo was in the shop.

Flying home to the old ball-and-chain for Thanksgiving this year (don't ask), I saw the world as I had not seen it for several years, mainly because I'd been in T.O. stuffing a certain ex-bingo-caller's gobbler, if you catch my drift. This turned out to be one of the most nerve-wracking experiences of my life—to fly over the miles and miles of autumn colours and, after a couple of complimentary cocktails, imagine an armed Indian hiding behind each and every brightly coloured tree.

Over a few more free Scotches—no water, no ice, for Chrissakes! You don't know where that crud comes from!—I had time to stop and reflect. I realized if I had it all to do differently, I'd make pregnant welfare bums cut them all down—all those useless trees. And I'd make those shiftless teachers spend their summers chopping them up. And I'd make those greedy nurses pile them up until their hands bled. And then I'd, why I'd . . .

As the booze began to take the edges off, I thought about my twenty-plus years at the public trough and my eleven-plus years as leader, and I thought, hey, not bad for a six-toed drifter too boring to teach, too porky to ski, and too much of a hacker to get a job at a mini-putt. But mostly I thought about the past six years as premier and the progress I've made turning Ontario into the Mississippi of the North.

I thought about all of this and the hostile pinko media who've made a such big frigging deal out of each and every little fatality on my watch. Hey, shit happens!

But, hell, it doesn't take a genius to read the writing on the wall—unless it's in Arabic or French or something. So I spoke to our caucus this morning and told them, I'm outta here, although that certainly doesn't mean I'm through sucking on the public teat.

Why, until some other dismally mediocre, middle-aged white guy is sworn into office, I will continue to hang around Queen's Park, taking long lunches and sorting through the inevitable deluge of corporate directorship offers. Time to cash in the chips, suckers. Hey, look at Muldoon when he left office—didn't have a pot to piss in, not one that actually belonged to him anyway—and now look at him.

You know, it is the people of Nipissing who entrusted me to represent them on six consecutive occasions. And to them I say, what the hell were you thinking? Granted, I was the only guy in the riding who owned a suit and wasn't afraid of having their nipples forcibly pierced by crack-addled squeegee kids at the Toronto border.

As premier of Ontario, I have done things I did not dream I would do growing up in Callander and North Bay, Ontario—like grovelling in front of those greedy old quints. Hell, Sharon had to put me on Viagra after that.

Next week, our party will undoubtedly present an even nastier and more brutish vision of humanity at our convention. It's a little something we call Seizing Tomorrow's Gonads, or something like that. Anyway, it's occasions like this that let the grassroots of the party get liquored up, play grab-ass, and think their R.B. Bennett vision of the world actually matters. Hell, that's how we got that Common Sense bullshit rolling.

Anyway, I entered political life to make a differ-ence, to make my little corner of the world a meaner, dumber place. And I'm pretty proud of what I've accomplished on that front.

As a father, I can honestly say that I have given my two sons, Michael and Jeffrey, a better future full of greater opportunities—thanks to my gold-plated pension and upcoming stock options. That's how you get ahead in this world—not through spoon-feeding people.

That's why we restored economic and class advantages in our education system. We alienated our teachers and drove away our health-care workers. We made the halt, the lame, and the maladjusted perform Stupid Welfare Tricks. We sent out big black smoke signals that Ontario is open for business. Remember, more asthma means more cheap jobs. Suck it up, people—get an inhaler and get to work.

I believe government is a blunt instrument to be used to beat up on people. That is not an end in itself, but it sure has been fun.

I want to thank my party. And I want to thank all the interchangeable drones throughout the 905 area code who have supported us. I particularly want to thank all members of my sometimes family and my friends—I'm going to be reminding you who you are— for their unwavering support. The rest of you whiners can kiss my big blue butt.

YOURS TO DISCOVER

Retirement

One Canadian politician left public life the hard way; he didn't write a book.

Styles of Address

A little boy was asked by his teacher how he should address the Pope.

"Your Holiness," the little boy replied.

"And the Queen of England?"

"Your Majesty," the little boy replied.

"Very good! And what about Stockwell Day?"

"Your Funda-mentality," the little boy replied.

Stockwell Buys Stamps

Stockwell Day goes to his local postal outlet to buy stamps to mail his Christmas cards.

He says to the clerk, "May I have fifty Christmas stamps?"

"What denomination?" the clerk asks.

"Oh, my God! It has finally come to this!" exclaims Stockwell. "Give me six Catholics, twelve Protestants, and thirty-two Baptists."

Stockwell Day

Stockwell Day, the first leader of the Canadian Alliance, was not much of a wit. So perhaps he did not originate the following remark.

"A fundamentalist is a man who feels repentance on Sunday for what he did on Saturday and is going to do again on Monday."

Day and Night

The following remark has been attributed to Canadian Alliance leader Stockwell Day. (Decades earlier it was attributed to the Duke of Devonshire.)

"The other night I dreamed that I was addressing the House of Commons. Then I woke up and, by God, I was!"

Invitation Missing

A reception is being held in the Château Frontenac in Quebec City.

Stockwell Day is invited, but he misplaces his invitation. He arrives on time but is stopped by the security personnel at the doorway.

"Who are you?"

"I am Stockwell Day. I'm an invited guest."

"Where is your invitation?"

"I must have misplaced it."

"Sorry, I am not permitted to let anyone in without an invitation."

"But I am Stockwell Day, former leader of the Canadian Alliance."

The security personnel are having none of it. Indeed, since they are newly arrived in Quebec, being French-speaking Haitians, it is doubtful that they have even heard of the Canadian Alliance.

"Your name is not on the list. How do we know who you really are? However, one hour ago we admitted Liona Boyd because she had her guitar with her. Half an hour ago we admitted Dave Broadfoot because he was wearing his Mountie outfit."

"Who are Liona Boyd and Dave Broadfoot and what have they got to do with admitting me?"

"Say no more," the security personnel say. "We have no doubt you are the leader of the Canadian Alliance."

Canadian Alliance

Q. How is the Canadian Alliance like a jigsaw puzzle?

A. Every time it faces a problem, it goes to pieces.

Doris Day

One of the planks in the campaign of the Canadian Alliance in the federal election of 2000 was the promise to hold referenda on all national matters as long as 3 percent (or 350,000) of the voting population signed a petition requesting one.

The crew of Salter Street Productions and *This Hour Has 22 Minutes* devised just such a referendum. It read: "We demand that the Government of Canada force Stockwell Day to change his first name to Doris." To put this into effect, they needed only 350,000 signatures by November 27, 2000.

Instead they got close to one million votes and a lot of publicity. They turned Stockwell into a laughing stock!

Sheila Copps

A lively Liberal member of Parliament and sometime cabinet minister in various Chrétien administrations, Sheila Copps believes in the two-party system: one during the day in the House of Commons, the other during the evening in a bistro in Hull.

Speechifying

A reporter on Parliament Hill approached Art Eggleton, then the Minister of Defence in the Chrétien cabinet, and asked the following question: "Sir, many of your constituents can't understand from the speech you delivered in the House yesterday just where you stand on the purchase of new helicopters for the Armed Forces."

"Good. It took me a long time to write it that way."

In Heaven

Joe Clark, Stockwell Day, and Jean Chrétien are flying from Ottawa to Vancouver when the prime minister's executive jet develops engine trouble and crashes into the Rockies.

The trio find themselves in Heaven standing before the throne of God.

First, God addresses Joe Clark, the leader of the Conservative Party: "Joe, what do you believe in?"

"Well, other things being equal, I believe the Clarity Bill is evil personified. I believe the Liberals are the Devil incarnate. I believe Quebecers have legitimate aspirations that must be met."

God replies, "Fine, fine. I can live with that. Come and sit at my right side."

Then God turns his attention to Stockwell Day, the leader of the Canadian Alliance. "Stock, what do you believe in?"

"I believe in unfettered free enterprise. I believe abortion is the work of the Devil. I believe the earth was created six thousand years ago."

God replied, "Fine, fine. I can live with that. Come and sit at my left side."

Finally God turns his attention to Jean Chrétien, prime minister and leader of the Liberal Party. "Jean, what do you believe in?"

"Uh," replies Chrétien. "I believe . . . I believe . . . you're sitting on my throne."

Who Would Be Saved?

Q. If Jean Chrétien and Paul Martin were on a sinking ship, who would be saved?

A. The country.

Change

Some school children are touring the Houses of Parliament on Parliament Hill.

In the Senate Chamber, they are introduced to an older man, a senator who is approaching the mandatory retirement age of seventy-five years.

"You must have seen a lot of changes over the years," says one of the children.

"I sure have, son," replies the senator, "and I've been against every one of them!"

Two Lions

Two lions escaped from a circus visiting Ottawa. They went their separate ways, but after a week they met in a downtown park.

One lion said, "I'm having a hard time finding food, and people are always trying to catch me."

The other lion said, "I found a great hiding place in the Senate. I eat a senator every day, and nobody even notices anyone missing."

PCs

The Progressive Conservative Party stands for progress, change, and innovation. But not right away.

Jokes about Tories

Q. How many Tories does it take to screw in a light bulb?
A. None. You will live in the dark for the next four years!

Q. Why did the Tory cross the road?
A. Because that's where his BMW was parked.

Q. How does a Tory turn on the light?
A. He opens the fridge door.

Q. What does a Tory woman call a Tory man?
A. Master.

Q. What does a Tory call mass unemployment?
A. Progress.

Q. What does a Tory call pay equity?
A. Sexual harassment.

Q. What is a Tory's idea of a good Canadian magazine?
A. TV *Guide.*

Q. What's the Tory equivalent of Grade 13?
A. Workfare.

Q. How can you tell if a Tory loves you?
A. You're barefoot and pregnant.

Q. What does a Tory call the sound of a hungry child's stomach growling?
A. Purring.

Q. What is a Tory's idea of a good vacation?
A. One that lasts for the rest of your working life.

Q. What do you call a dead Tory?
A. His-Tory.

Prime Ministerial Qualifications

In Canada, everyone may aspire to serve as prime minister as long as he or she is bilingual, a Liberal, a lawyer, and a Quebecer.

Small-l Liberal

A Member of the Canadian House of Commons was in London, England, where he was trying to explain his political preferences to his British colleagues, who were singularly unimpressed.

"I am a member of the Conservative Party of Canada," he explained, "but I am really a small-l liberal."

One of the Britishers, nonplussed, replied, "Small l? At which end?"

Senatorial Styles

Q. What's the difference between senators in the United States and senators in Canada?

A. In the United States, you have to win an election to become a senator. In Canada, you have to lose one.

Prime Ministerial Libraries

Heritage Canada announced on July 1 that it will proceed with plans to establish three prime ministerial libraries.

Each library will function as an archives and research centre devoted to the contribution of a former prime minister of Canada. The libraries are being modelled on the U.S. presidential libraries, which are popular with scholars and students as well as with tourists and members of the general public.

Each prime ministerial library will be dedicated to preserving the papers and personal effects of a former prime minister of Canada. The names and locations of the first three libraries were announced.

The John G. Diefenbaker Library for the Study of Western Canada will be built in Regina, Sask.

The Lester B. Pearson Library for the Study of International Affairs will be located in Ottawa, Ont.

The Joe Clark Library for the Study of Big Little Books and Comic Art will be opened in High River, Alta.

the french fact

15

The jokes and anecdotes in this chapter are told throughout the country and elsewhere in the English-speaking world. I am sure that the majority of them originated in the province of Quebec because informants from that province, particularly from Montreal and the Eastern Townships, passed them on to me.

Invariably jokes here are all about language issues, separatist threats, and the grievances of minorities against majorities, whether English or French.

I have made no attempt to make consistent use of such terms as Canadien, French Canadian, Québécois, and so on. Their usage should be determined by the period of the joke. What I have done is relay them to the reader in the words in which they were told to me.

The Maple Leaf Flag

CANADA		CANADA
CANADA	eb	CANADA
CANADA	q uebe c	CANADA
CANADA	uebe	CANADA
CANADA	q uebe c	CANADA
CANADA	eb	CANADA
CANADA		CANADA

Quebec

Q. How many provinces has Canada if you call Quebec a state?
A. Ten. Calling Quebec a state does not make it a state.

Q. What do Quebecers eat for breakfast?
A. *Huit heures* bix!

Q. What's a *pièce de résistance?*
A. A Quebec virgin.

Jean-Baptiste

This joke requires the reader to recall that Jean-Baptiste was the name of the stock French-Canadian dimwit of the 1920s. As well, it requires the reader to imagine the joke-teller engaging in some indicative action. Here goes . . .

The Canadien woodsman Jean-Baptiste had an argument with his wife and decided he was going to leave her. So he got in his canoe and started to paddle away.

"I 'ave 'ad enough of you, woman. Jean-Baptiste is leaving." (Teller does paddling motions here.)

On shore, his wife cried out, "Jean-Baptiste, you 'ave forget your big axe."

"Keep de axe, woman. Jean-Baptiste is leaving you." (Motions of paddling.)

"Jean-Baptiste, you 'ave forget your gun."

"Keep de gun, woman. Jean-Baptiste is leaving you." (Motions of paddling.)

Then his wife takes off her dress and stands naked on the shore. "Jean-Baptiste, you 'ave forget someting else."

Jean-Baptiste looks around. (Motions of paddling backwards, rapidly.) "One of dese days, I leave dat woman."

Quebec Lumberjack

An Ontario lumber company advertises for a lumberjack.

The next day a skinny little fellow from Chicoutimi shows up at the camp carrying his own axe.

The foreman takes one look at the guy's build and tells him to get lost.

"I'm a strong lumberjack," says the fellow. "Give me a chance to show you what I can do."

"Okay," says the foreman. "See that giant spruce tree over there? Take your axe and cut it down."

The fellow heads for the tree, and within five minutes he's heading back and beckoning to the foreman. "I cut the tree down," he says.

The foreman can't believe what he hears. So he checks for himself. He asks, "Where did you learn to chop down trees like that?"

"In the Sahara Forest," says the puny man.

"You mean the Sahara Desert?" says the foreman.

"Sure, that's what they call it now."

Another Quebec Lumberjack

Young Jules hears that a fortune can be made by working as a lumberjack in northern Quebec. So off he goes. When he arrives at the camp, he asks the foreman for a job.

"Okay, sonny," says the foreman, "but you'll have to pass a test before I hire you. If you can chop down one hundred trees tomorrow, you're hired."

Early the next morning, Jules gets his chainsaw and goes into the woods. He happily saws away the day. But when the trees are counted, he has felled only ninety. "Oh well," says the foreman. "You'll get another chance tomorrow."

The next morning, it is the same story, but this time it was ninety-five trees. "I don't believe this," says the foreman. "A big strong fellow like you should be able to cut down two hundred trees in a day. I believe you can do it, so I'll give you one more chance. I'll join you in the woods and show you a trick or two."

The next morning, young Jules and the foreman go into the woods. On arrival at the previous day's clearing, the foreman puts the chainsaw on the ground and starts the engine.

"For crying out loud!" exclaims young Jules, who has had his back to the foreman all this time. "How can you cut trees with all that racket?"

Two Quebecers

Two Quebecers, Louis and Clarence, lived on opposite sides of the St. Charles River.

It was a good thing the river flowed between them because Louis and Clarence did not like each other at all. Every day they would yell insults across the river at each other. Louis would tell Clarence, "One day, I go over dere and punch your face."

Clarence would reply, "Anytim' you want to try, I be waiting for you."

This went on for years, but neither of them ever crossed the river. Then the government built a bridge across the river.

Louis and Clarence kept up their war of words until one day Louis's wife, growing weary of it, said, "Louis, dere is a bridge now. Why don't you go over dere like you brag, and punch Clarence in de face?"

Louis huffed himself up and said, "I do dat right now!" And off he went. He was back in ten minutes.

"Well," asked his wife. "Did you fix dat Clarence?"

"No, by God," gasped Louis. "I did not know he was so big. Dere is a sign on dat bridge dat say, 'Clarence, 8' 6".'"

Quebec Official

An official in rural Quebec is arrested for accepting a bribe from a contractor.

A friend visits the official in jail and asks, "How are you going to get out of this mess?"

"Easily," replies the official. "I got into trouble for accepting a bribe; I'll get out of it by offering another."

Corruption

A young member of the Union Nationale Party pays a personal visit to the Minister of Public Works at his residence on the Grande-Allée. He is staggered at the wealth and opulence of the establishment.

"How did you manage to acquire so much wealth so quickly?" the young member asked. "I know that you did not inherit money. I also know that the salary of a cabinet minister is not all that high."

"Do you really want to know?"

"Yes, of course. I'm curious."

"Then wait until tomorrow and I will explain fully."

The next day the minister drove the young member a dozen or so kilometres in his Cadillac along the highway. He stopped the car and they both got out. The minister pointed out a spot in the valley along the river. "Do you see that big bridge over there?" he asked.

"Yes."

"Half the cost of the bridge went into my pocket."

The young member said nothing.

Two years later there was an election and the Minister of Public Works lost his seat. The young member, having served his apprenticeship as a backbencher, was appointed the new Minister of Public Works. Two years after that he was visited in his residence by his old friend, the former Minister of Public Works.

"My God," explained the former minister, "you have beaten me all hollow. Such a mansion, with servants, and a Mercedes-Benz! Tell me, how did you manage it?"

"I will tell you tomorrow," said the new minister.

The next day the new minister drove the old minister along the same highway two dozen or so kilometres. He stopped the car at a vantage point that overlooked another valley. He pointed to a spot down the valley and asked, "Do you see the bridge over there?"

"I see no bridge," replied the old minister.

"Quite right," said the new minister. "The entire cost of the bridge went into my pocket."

Salutation

One of the primary concerns of rural constituents in Quebec in the 1920s was the electrification of the villages. Maurice Duplessis, leader of the Union Nationale Party and premier, was not a politician to avoid such an issue while on the campaign trail.

He began some of his campaign speeches with three words of greeting: "Electors, electresses, electricity!"

The Scots Question

The gentleman who represented the association of English-language schools in the province of Quebec requested an interview with Premier Duplessis and received it. At some length he argued the case for increased provincial funding of English-language schooling.

Duplessis was unreceptive to the argument. "I have not increased the allocation for French-language schooling. Why should I increase the funding for English-language schooling?"

The representative continued to argue his case, but Duplessis cut him off. "You English," he said, "you always insist on having more than the other fellow!"

With that the representative, who was a Scot, exploded. "What do you mean, 'You English'? I am not English. I am a Scot, and we Scots were the allies of the English, until the Battle of Culloden, in which we were mercilessly defeated. Indeed, we fought along-side you French against the hated English! For hundreds of years the Scots supported the French against the Sachenachs!"

"You are right," Duplessis said wearily. "I was wrong."

"And besides, we Scots have married you French. Our soldiers married your women, and look at the result—the Yvette McCrimmons, the Marie McCarthys!"

Duplessis suddenly brightened up. "Yes," he said. "It is the best of both worlds. The French are very tight, and the Scots are very hot!"

Maurice Duplessis

Maurice Duplessis was as outspoken as the Leader of the Opposition in Quebec's National Assembly as he was later in his career as the leader of the Union Nationale Party and the premier of Quebec.

While a member of the Opposition, he served on the Public Accounts Committee. He found that its membership was largely drawn from Liberal members of the National Assembly—members of the hated Liberal Party!

During one of its meetings, he declared, "Mr. Chairman, half the people in this room are crooks!"

An uproar resulted and the chairman ordered Duplessis to withdraw the remark.

Duplessis looked incredulous but complied with these words: "All right, half the people in this room are not crooks."

Jean Drapeau

Jean Drapeau, Montreal's long-time mayor and the prime mover of Expo 67, was a tiny man with a towering ego.

He took pride in the description of himself as "Montreal's elected king."

He was never without a grand scheme. He seldom lost an election.

Here is one story that is told about him.

First person: Did you hear about Mayor Drapeau's accident?

Second person: No, what happened?

First person: He was out taking his usual morning walk, when a motorboat crashed into him!

Influence

Mayor Jean Drapeau of Montreal and Paul-Emile Cardinal Léger met at a reception in Montreal in 1967. The cardinal congratulated the mayor on his many successes, including that of Expo 67.

Cardinal Léger: It would not surprise me if you tried to move our next Vatican Council to Montreal.

Mayor Drapeau: That is the last time I shall confide in you.

Vat '69

The diplomat John E. Robbins was appointed Canada's first ambassador to the Vatican in 1969.

He amused audiences by assuring them that the Pope's telephone number in Vatican City was not VAT 69.

Réal Caouette

Before he became Créditiste leader, Réal Caouette had to master the English language. It was hard for him.

He came from the Abitibi region of Quebec, where he heard little English as a child, and as an adult he was quite unsophisticated. Yet he practised speaking English as often as he could. He had a lot of trouble with English idioms.

At his first political reception, he shook the hand of an English-speaker, who said, "How do you do?"

Caouette turned beet red, then ashen white. He thought, "This man wants to know if I am performing sinful acts. He knows that I am from the Abitibi region and that there we avoid using direct terms about such things."

Caouette struggled with his English. "How do I do?" he said. "Well... I don't do... because I'm a bachelor!"

Separatist Tongue Twister

Repeat the following tongue twister briskly:

Can Canada Can Quebec or Can Quebec Can Canada.

FLQ Sympathizers

It is Quebec in the early 1960s.

A couple of FLQ sympathizers are comparing notes on the state of their discontent with the status quo.

"Did you hear our comrades are setting off more bombs in mailboxes in Westmount?"

"It's a terrible way to arrange a revolution!"

"You're right. I agree with you, but it's better than no revolution at all."

The Statue

A man finds an old bronze statue of a rat in an antique store.

The shopkeeper says, "It's $10 for the statue, but $100 for the story that goes with it."

The man skips the story, hands over $10, and starts to walk home with the statue under his arm.

On the way, hundreds of rats start to follow along behind him. The man runs to the nearest bridge and throws the statue in the water. To his amazement all the rats follow the statue and leap off the bridge to their deaths.

When the man returns to the store, the owner says, "You've come back for the story of the statue."

The man says, "No, I was wondering if you might have a bronze statue of a separatist."

Lucien Bouchard

Q. Did you hear the one about Lucien Bouchard and Jean Charest drinking in a bar in Quebec City?

A. Hey, is this some kind of sick joke?

Q. What part will Lucien Bouchard play in the *John Bobbitt Story*?

A. He's the dick that separates.

Leaders and Leaners

Q. Why did the Parti Québécois under Lucien Bouchard lean to the left?

A. Because it had only one leg to stand on.

Q. Why does the Parti Québécois under Bernard Landry lean to the right?

A. Because it is not very bright.

Q. Why does the Bloc Québécois under Gilles Duceppe lean first this way and then that way?

A. Because it stands on an incline leading to a decline.

If Quebec Were to Separate . . .

Quebec premier Lucien Bouchard and former Quebec premier Jacques Parizeau, not the best of friends in the best of circumstances, are discussing the consequences of the separation of Quebec from the rest of Canada. Specifically, Bouchard is concerned with how to define the new status of Quebec once separatism has become a reality.

"I don't know what to do, Jacques," Bouchard admits. "If I call it a kingdom, people will call me a king. If I call it a principality, people will call me a prince. If I call it an empire, people will call me an emperor. If I call it a duchy, people will call me a duchess."

"Well, Lucien," says Parizeau, "I think it would be most appropriate if you called it a country."

Quebec Sports

When Jacques Parizeau retired from public life—in disgrace, some say—he and his wife Lisette took up residence in the south of France.

Once there, he entered into a conversation with a Spanish lady they met who proved to be as opinionated and outspoken as Parizeau. She said, "So you come from Quebec. I understand hockey is the most popular sport in Quebec. In Spain we find it revolting."

"Madame," he said, "I am surprised by what you say. After all, you come from a country where the most popular recreation is bullfighting. Quebecers find that sport revolting. But you expressed a negative opinion about sport in Quebec. You are wrong on two accounts. Hockey is not Quebec's most popular sport—revolting is."

Speedster

A middle-aged Quebecer going through a mid-life crisis rewarded himself by purchasing a brand-new Mercedes convertible SLK.

He admired it and then turned on the engine. He eased it carefully through the dense traffic of downtown Montreal, but once he reached Highway 2, he cut loose. When he hit the Trans-Canada Highway, which would take him to Toronto, he accelerated up to 140 km/h. He particularly enjoyed the smooth ride and the sensation of the wind blowing through what little hair he had left on his head.

"This is great," he thought and floored it. But when he checked his rearview mirror what he saw there was a Sûreté du Québec patrol car catching up to him, blue lights flashing and siren whining.

"I can get away from him with no problem at all," thought the driver, as he continued to floor it, practically flying down the highway, at over 160 km/h.

Then he thought, "What am I doing this for? I'm far too old for this kind of thing." Reluctantly he slowed down and pulled over to the side of the highway and waited for the patrol car to catch up to him.

The police car pulled in behind the Mercedes. The patrolman got out and walked over to the man. "Monsieur," he said looking at his watch. "My shift ends in thirty minutes and today is Friday the 13th. If you can give me a good reason why you were speeding, a reason that I have never heard before, I'll let you go."

The man looked up at the patrolman and said, "Last week my wife ran off with a member of the Sûreté du Québec and I thought you were bringing her back."

The patrolman said, "Have a nice day."

Montreal Phone Book

A man in a Montreal bar was boasting to a friend.

"I have an excellent memory," he said. "I can recite from memory all the names on three pages of the Montreal phone book."

His friend did not believe him and bet him $10 he couldn't do it.

The man took the bet, and then began to recite, "Richard, Richard, Richard, Richard . . ."

Bilingual Restaurant

A diner in a restaurant in Montreal went to the washroom, turned on a tap, and got scalded.

"This is an outrage!" he screamed at the proprietor. "Why aren't your taps marked properly? I turned on the tap marked 'C' thinking it would be cold and I got scalding water!"

The manager was patient. He led the injured diner back to the washroom. "Look," he said, "the tap is marked 'C' correctly. That stands for Chaude, and Chaude means Hot. You should know that if you live in Montreal."

The diner stood abashed for a moment. Then he made a discovery. "But look again," he cried, "the other tap is marked with a 'C' also. What about that?"

"Ah," said the proprietor, "that stands for Cold. This is a bilingual restaurant, my friend."

Barber in Trois-Rivières

Q. Why would a barber in Trois-Rivières rather cut the hair of two francophones than that of one anglophone?

A. He makes twice as much money.

Mount Royal

Pierre Sévigny was a popular raconteur and federal government minister. He had a devilish sense of humour.

He tells the story of the Englishman, visiting Montreal, who climbs to the summit of Mount Royal, and from the lookout point yells, "Hell-ooo!"

He is astonished to hear his echo: "Bon-jooo-uuu-rrr!"

Boy and Girl

A French-Canadian family had to move to Toronto and found itself in a mainly WASP suburb. The six-year-old son quickly made friends with the six-year-old daughter of the family next door.

The two children were playing with the sprinkler in the backyard, and since they were getting their clothes all wet, they decided to take them off and play naked. When the little girl saw that the boy had something she didn't, she said "Wow! I didn't know that French-Canadians were that different!"

French-Canadian Postal Workers

Pierre and Claude, two French-Canadian postal workers, were chatting over lunch.

"How is your wife?" asked Pierre.

"She's in bed with laryngitis," replied Claude.

"*Mon dieu!*" said his friend. "Is that damned Greek around again?"

Visitor

A visitor from Down Under arrived in Quebec, knowing no French.

He quickly came to the conclusion that all he had to say was, "*Moi aussi*" and everyone would know "I'm Australian."

French Immersion

French immersion classes, rare in the 1960s, are commonplace in the 2000s.

"Now, *étudiants*," said the teacher. "In the glorious French language, when we refer to a married woman, she is *madame*. When we refer to an unmarried woman, she is *mademoiselle*."

Having made that point, the teacher turned to one *étudiant* and asked him, "What is the difference between *madame* and *mademoiselle*?"

The *étudiant* replied with a grin, "*Monsieur*."

Sign Laws

Quebec's sign laws were the butt of much black humour in the 1980s and 1990s.

One particularly odious provincial statute required that with outdoor signage, the French language must take preference. Outside an establishment, only French could appear. Inside the establishment, English words could appear, but only if the equivalent French words were larger and bolder than English words. Enforcement was the responsibility of the so-called language police or "tongue-troopers."

A restaurant on St. Catharine Street in Montreal placed this sign in its window: "*Ici, On Parle Toutes les Langues*."

That attracted the attention of a tongue-trooper, who entered the restaurant and sought out the restaurateur.

"Are all your employees multilingual?" he demanded to know.

"Not one of them," replied the manager.

"Well, then, who speaks all these languages?"

"Our customers," the restaurateur sighed.

State of Duplessis

Late one night a member of the National Assembly in Quebec City was walking on the grounds of the legislature. He paused in front of the impressive statue of former Premier Maurice Duplessis, which stands on its plinth to the right of the legislative building.

He heard a slight rumbling. Then to his astonishment, he heard a man's voice. It was the unforgettable voice of Duplessis. The statue of Duplessis was speaking to him.

"You," the statue said, "I want you to tell me why they have me standing so long."

"I . . . I beg your pardon, sir?"

"Why am I standing so long? I am tired of standing. I want to sit down. I want to be seated. I want to sit on a horse, like the heroic personage that I am. It is only appropriate."

"I . . . I do not know what to say, sir."

"Say nothing. Come back right away with a horse, so I may be seated. And be quick about it!"

The member of the National Assembly quickly left and headed for the bunker and to the office of Bernard Landry. He told the Quebec premier what had happened. Landry knew better than to doubt the sanity of a member of the National Assembly. They decided that something had to be done before the story hit the newspapers. Imagine: The ghost of Maurice Duplessis was discontented!

The member and the premier hastened across the grounds and stood in front of the statue wondering what to do. Before they could say anything, or do anything, the statue addressed them in a loud and angry voice: "I am tired of standing. Now I am sick and tired of you. I am furious! I ask for a horse, and you bring me a horse's ass."

Anaesthetic

Quebec premier Bernard Landry consults a physician for a checkup. The physician informs him that he will require a minor surgical procedure.

"Will it be painful?" asks Landry, apprehensively.

"Not really," says the physician. "You will feel nothing. I will administer a local anaesthetic."

"A local anaesthetic!" exclaims Landry. "That's a relief. I was afraid that you would want to administer a national anaesthetic."

Holy Land

Quebec premier Bernard Landry summons the Minister of Culture and Tourism into the Premier's Office and shares with her his latest grand scheme to advance the interests of his favourite province.

"Last night I had a revelation. It dawned on me that Quebec is the Holy Land." He paused for effect. "We are misreading the Bible when we think that the Holy Land is to be found in Palestine."

The minister says nothing.

He continues, "Imagine the tourism potential if we can prove to ourselves and to people around the world that the events in the New Testament took place not in the Middle East at all, but in the State of Quebec!"

The minister says nothing.

"In fact," he continues, "I am certain that Bethlehem is not to be found in present-day Israel at all. It is to be found in present-day Quebec—at Saint-Basil-le-Grand!"

The minister says nothing.

"Therefore, I am charging you with the following responsibility. Check all the historical records for references to the Nativity. Ask the folklore societies for local traditions about the birth of Jesus at Saint-Basil-le-Grand. And I want you back in my office in one week's time to tell me what you have found."

The Minister of Culture says nothing but does as she is told. One week later she returns to the Premier's Office. Bernard Landry inquires, expectantly, "How did you fare?"

"Poorly," she replies. "I checked the historical record but I could not find Three Wise Men. I also asked the population at Saint-Basil-le-Grand for local traditions but no one could remember even one single Virgin."

French-Canadian Woman

Vertical Limits is an action film about mountain climbers. It was directed by Martin Campbell in 2000.

There is an amusing line of dialogue that will appeal to Canadians.

One female character makes an extremely catty remark about another female character who has pronounced mood swings:

"She's French Canadian. When she's Canadian, she's really quite pleasant. But today she's definitely French."

Quebecistan

It seems an important discussion is taking place between two leading *indépendantistes*. Their names are Gilles Duceppe, leader of the Bloc Québécois, and Parti Québécois cabinet minister Joseph Facal. They are discussing how to give greater symbolic weight to their dream of an independent Republic of Quebec.

Duceppe spoke first: "We are prepared to issue Quebec passports, but no country is willing to recognize them. We are ready to print Quebec currency notes, but no banks will accept them as surety. We are all set to design a Quebec flag, but no one will know what it represents. We must devise an emblem for the Republic of Quebec that is immediately acceptable and recognizable."

Facal spoke second: "I have an idea. Every country has its official bird. I think we should have one, too. We need to adopt a bird that everyone in Quebec and around the world will accept and recognize as characteristic of the Republic of Quebec. Have you any suggestions?"

"Yes," Duceppe replied. "What about the ostrich?"

Bi-Bi Jokes

"Bi-Bi" refers to bilingualism and biculturalism and the ever-present realities of the English and French languages and cultures.

It was Pierre Elliott Trudeau's idea to establish a Royal Commission on Bilingualism and Biculturalism. Eminent among the commissioners appointed to tour the country and prepare the report was F.R. Scott, lawyer, professor of constitutional law at McGill, poet, and wit.

Once the commission's report had been tabled, Scott mused publicly that perhaps the most lasting contribution that he might personally make would be to preserve some of the Bi-Bi jokes and anecdotes that the commissioners had heard during the course of deliberations. So he recorded them, "not to produce laughter but to explain Canadians to each other while they are laughing." He went on to say, "My ideal story is one that only a Canadian can really understand."

The commission disbanded decades ago, and the report (for all its sense of urgency, for all its plethora of noble ideas and ideals) has been gathering dust in the National Archives. But the jokes remain with us, caught in amber perhaps, yet reminders, should we need them, of all the language crises and linguistic concerns we have endured over the last four decades.

At the same time, these jokes remain ever ready to delight and instruct us, thanks to F.R. Scott, who in 1982 preserved them for later generations and, indeed, for all time.

Swimming

Two French Canadians were walking along the shore of Lac. St-Jean when they saw a friend struggling in the water, who called out, "Help! Help!"

One said to the other, "It would have been better for him, instead of learning English, if he had learned how to swim."

Bilingualism

It is said that *Time* sent a reporter to the Prairies to find out the grassroots opinions about bilingualism and biculturalism. He arrived in Alberta and, approaching an old farmer, asked him, "My man, what do you think about bilingualism?"

"What do I think about bilingualism?" he replied. "I'll tell you what I think about bilingualism. If the English language was good enough for Jesus Christ, it is good enough for me."

Restaurant

A French Canadian walked into a restaurant leading a large alligator by a rope. He said to the waitress, "Do you serve English Canadians here?"

"Yes," she replied.

"Then serve one to my alligator."

Student

A certain French-Canadian student enrolled in the Law Faculty of McGill in 1937. Coming straight from a classical college, he had never met any Jews before, and sitting next to a fellow student one day, he said, "There are too many Jews in this faculty." The man he spoke to was a Jew.

Later, when he realized what he had done, he explained to his new classmate, "You know, it is only the lower-class French Canadians who hate the Jews. The upper-class hate the English."

Training

There was a training school for life-saving at the Hamilton YMCA. After the course was over, one of the graduates met a friend, who asked, "Now do you know how to save a man from drowning?"

"Yes."

"Could you save a French Canadian, for instance?"

Puzzled, the young man answered, "I don't know. I wasn't trained for that."

Dog

This story is told of two neighbours living in Ottawa, one English-speaking and the other a French-speaking civil servant. The latter had a dog that used to go into his neighbour's garden, rooting in the plants and causing annoyance. The English wife called out angrily to the dog, "Go away, go home!"

The dog did not move. She shouted at it again, still without result, so she telephoned her neighbour and said, "Your dog is in my garden and won't go away when I tell him to."

The French-speaking neighbour replied, "He probably does not understand you. He only understands French."

Quickly came the reply, "Don't you think it's about time he learned to speak English?"

Doctor

Un canadien français était très malade. Il alla consulter son médecin. Le médecin lui dit, "Vous êtes très malade. Il faut vous opérer. Mais je dois vous avertir qu'après l'opération, votre intelligence sera très diminuée. Mais sans l'opération, vous mourrez."

Alors, le pauvre gars répondit, "Je préfère être vivant et stupide qu'intelligent et mort."

Le lendemain de l'opération, le médecin lui rendit visite à l'hôpital et lui demanda: "Comment allez-vous ce matin?"

Le gars répondit, "I feel much better today, t'ank you, Doctor."

Church

An old man and his wife were coming out of a church in Quebec after Mass one Sunday. The following conversation ensued:

Husband: L'étranger à côté de nous ce matin—il priait en anglais.

Wife: Sais pas si ça compte.

Religion

A village in Cape Breton had only one church, which was Catholic. All the inhabitants of the village were Catholic except for a single Protestant. When he died, the priest was uncertain what to do, so he telegraphed to his bishop and asked, "Can I bury a Protestant?"

The answer came back, "Bury all you can."

Clan

There was a great gathering of the MacLean clan in Montreal some years ago. Sir Charles Hector Fitzroy MacLean, "the" MacLean, came all the way from Scotland to attend. During the evening reunion, when all the people called MacLean were celebrating, three girls in kilts entered—MacLeans from the Lower St. Lawrence, who could not speak a word of English.

They came forward and warmly shook Sir Charles's hand, greeting him with the words, "*Monsieur MacLean, nous sommes aussi des MacLeans.*"

He looked at them in embarrassment and said, "I am sorry—I don't speak Gaelic."

Politeness

A French Canadian, with his usual politeness, once said to an English Canadian:

"*Si je n'étais pas français, je voudrais être anglais.*"

To which the English Canadian replied, "*Si je n'étais pas anglais, je voudrais être anglais.*"

Mail

A letter arrived at the post office in St. Andrews, N.B., addressed "Maître de Poste." It was returned to the sender marked, "Not known here."

B.B.

When Brigitte Bardot (B.B.) arrived in New York, she was asked if she could suggest how to improve the relations between the French and the English in Canada.

She replied, coyly, "If I were to go there, it might help, maybe?"

Thus, as George Bain of *The Globe and Mail* commented, "Instead of having two nations warring in the bosom of a single state, we might have two nations warring over the state of a single bosom."

Marriage

A French Canadian in Montreal wrote to his cousin in Manitoba, giving him the family news. One item was, "My sister Marguerite became pregnant by an English major of the Royal Montreal Regiment, but we dissuaded her from marrying him, because we felt we would rather have a bastard in the family than an English major."

Quebec City

One of the old English-speaking residents of Quebec City died and went to Heaven. Very properly, he was greeted at the gate by St. George, who asked him, "Well, my man, what did you do for the British Empire?"

The man answered, "I will tell you what I did. On the first day of the Quebec Winter Carnival, I walked down the Grande-Allée carrying a Union Jack and singing 'God Save the Queen.'"

St. George asked him, "When was that?"

The man looked at his wristwatch and answered, "About five minutes ago."

Bishop

Some time between the two world wars, an Anglican bishop of Quebec met an old English resident, then over eighty years of age.

"I suppose, Mr. Johnson, when you were a young man you didn't see many French Canadians on the Grande-Allée?"

"Good heavens, no," he replied. "We would never have allowed it."

De Gaulle

A French Canadian asked an English Canadian why English Canada was so disturbed when De Gaulle called out, *"Vive le Québec libre!"*

The English Canadian replied, "Well, it's like this. If you are visiting a married couple and call out, *'Vive l'amour,'* it is quite appropriate, but if you call out *'Vive l'amour libre,'* it is not so suitable."

Chief

A priest once approached the chief of an Indian band and asked him whether he might be allowed to enter the reserve to preach Christianity to the Indians.

The chief pondered for a moment, looking directly at the priest, and then said, "There is a white man's village just across the river. Suppose you go and preach there for three years. Then if I notice that the white man steals less, lies less, and cheats the Indians less, I will be glad to have you come as missionary to my reserve."

Au Secours

Two English Canadians were walking along the Gatineau River near Ottawa when they heard a man cry out from the river, *"Au secours!"*

One man said to the other, "What's that?"

The other replied, "He's either a French Canadian or a terrible snob."

F.R. Scott

Once I returned from the United States to Montreal by air and was questioned as usual at Dorval airport by the immigration authorities.

The questions and replies went like this:

"Where do you live?"

"Montreal."

"What is your nationality?"

"Canadian."

Then I added, because it was clear that my questioner was a French Canadian, *"Je suis né dans la Ville de Québec."*

"Alors, vous êtes deux fois canadien."

Penology

A French Canadian, a student of penology, was visiting St. Vincent de Paul Penitentiary. He got into conversation with an inmate, also French Canadian, who was serving a five-year sentence for a series of burglaries committed in Outremont.

The student of penology asked the inmate, "Why did you commit all your burglaries in Outremont? Why didn't you go into Westmount, where you might have had richer houses to rob?"

"Because I don't like the English."

Biculturalism

"Are you in favour of biculturalism?"

"Yes, as long as it is between consenting adults."

L'habitant

L'habitant qui ne s'entendait pas avec son curé alla lui dire, "Monsieur le Curé, j'abandonne la religion catholique et je deviens protestant."

Le Curé répondit, "T'es pas fou, Jos? Tu ne parles même pas l'anglais!"

Swimming Pool

A mother took her six-year-old daughter to the municipal swimming pool.

Playing on the edge of the pool, the girl fell in and was struggling to keep afloat, not knowing how to swim. Seeing the guard watching her calmly and not helping, the mother cried out, "Save her! Save her! Why don't you go to her rescue?"

To which the guard replied, "Sorry, madam, but I don't know how to swim."

"You can't swim!" cried the woman. "Then why are you a guard?"

"Because I am bilingual," he answered.

Anglais

Deux canadiens-français s'embarquaient en train pour Toronto. Ils n'avaient trouvé que des journaux de langue anglais. Ils essayaient de lire en silence, mais après quelques minutes, Joseph demanda, "Pierre, ce mot 'yet,' qu'est-ce que ça veut dire en anglais?"

Pierre: "Yet?" Sais pas. Dans quel contexte?

Joseph: On dit içi "The bullet is in her yet." Quelle partie du corps feminin nomme-t-on-le "yet"?

Pierre: C'est la même chose, je suppose, qu le "now."

Joseph: Son "now"! Qu'est-ce qu c'est que ça?

Pierre: Oh, c'est le même mot qu'on trouve dans la vieille chanson anglais, "I wonder who's kissing her now?"

Polygot

"Qu'est-ce qu'un homme qui parle deux langues?"

"Un bilingue."

"Qu'est-ce qu'un homme qui parle plusieurs langues?"

"Un polyglotte."

"Qu'est-ce qu'un homme qui ne parle qu'une seule langue?"

"C'est un maudi Anglais."

Cat and Mouse

A cat was watching a mouse hole waiting for the mouse. The mouse looked out, saw the cat, and ducked in. So the cat, which was bilingual, barked like a dog. The mouse reasoned that the dog had arrived and that the cat had therefore run away. So it came out of its hole and the cat gobbled it up.

Moral: There are dangers in bilingualism.

F.R. Scott

I was arriving in Montreal on the overnight CNR train from Toronto and the Pullman passengers were standing in the corridor looking out the windows as we passed through the St. Henri district. Two women in front of me were observing the dismal scene.

One said, "Everything in this town is French."

"Yes," replied the other, "even the people."

Ontario

A famous Quebec nationalist once astonished his friends by introducing a private bill in the Quebec legislature to have his name changed from Lavergne to Smith.

His friends said to him, "What on earth has happened? What are you trying to do?"

He replied, "My doctor has just told me that I have an incurable cancer. Now when I die there will be one less Englishman."

Royal Commission

Conversation between a member of the Bilingualism and Biculturalism Commission and a friend at a cocktail party in Calgary:

"Your Royal Commission won't work."

"Why?"

"My son tried to get a job recently and was refused employment because he could not speak French."

"Well, that is exactly what the French Canadians complain about."

"Yes, but my son is English!"

Restaurant

A Montrealer visited Toronto recently and was surprised and delighted to see a restaurant with the title *"Restaurant français."*

He went in, found a bilingual menu, and ordered his meal. When he had finished, he beckoned to the waiter and said to him, *"L'addition, s'il vous plaît."*

The waiter looked at him in astonishment for a moment and then said, "Upstairs, first on the right."

Farmer

A French-Canadian farmer and his young son were sawing a big log with a bucksaw during World War II.

The son asked his father, "Papa, what will happen if the English win this war?"

The farmer thought for a moment and spat over the log. "There will be no change," he said. "I shall be at this end of the saw, and you will be at your end of the saw."

"Papa," asked the son, "what will happen if the Germans win this war?"

Again a pause, and again the farmer spat before he said, "I will be at this end of the saw and there will be an Englishman at your end of the saw."

Echoes

Two English Canadians and a French Canadian were on the Dufferin Terrace in Quebec City talking about their experience with echoes.

One English Canadian said he owned a lake with a hill opposite, and even if you spoke in a quiet voice, the echo came back quite clear and distinct.

The second English Canadian said that he had a lake with several hills around it, and when he called out something, it came back clear and distinct from three different hills at three different times.

Whereupon the French Canadian said he lived in Lévis, and if you stood on the Citadel and cried out, "God save the Queen," before you had even finished, the answer came back firm and clear, *"Mange d'la merde!"*

Trail

When Jean Chrétien was made head of the Department of Indian Affairs and Northern Development, the directors of Banff National Park, which fell under his jurisdiction, realized that they would have to have bilingual signs throughout the park.

They thought it would be nice to make the changes before the minister asked them to. So to a beautiful walk marked "Sightseer's Trail" they added *Sentier des Voyeurs."*

Conference

After a very successful conference of English-Canadian poets at Foster, Que., in 1963, which the Department of Cultural Affairs of the Government of Quebec had financed, there was a meeting to discuss the publication of a volume of proceedings.

A title for the book had to be found. One poet suggested, "Why not call it *The Saxophones among the Anglophones?"*

Foreigners

A French Canadian and his family were in Belgrade one summer.

Their small son, aged six, soon learned to play with some young Yugoslav children his own age, though he could not speak their language.

The father of one of these children asked him in French, "How can you play so well with these foreigners?"

The boy replied, "These are not foreigners, these are Yugoslavs. Foreigners speak English."

Nationality

This story is told of Claire Lalonde, wife of the Hon. Marc Lalonde.

When in England, Mrs. Lalonde was obliged to go to the hospital. When she was checking in at the entrance desk, the following conversation took place:

Head nurse: Nationality?

Mrs. Lalonde: French Canadian.

Head nurse, sharply: Come, come, make up your mind. French or Canadian?

Pessimist, Optimist

A pessimist separatist met an optimist separatist.

The pessimist said, "Do you know, if we separate, we will have to eat crap."

The optimist said, "Well, that's all right, provided there is enough to go around."

Jesus Christ

One day, Jesus Christ decided to visit Quebec City.

As he walked along, he saw a well-dressed man sitting on a park bench, weeping. He said, "My son, what is wrong?"

The man replied, "My wife has left me, my stocks are falling, and my car has been stolen."

Jesus said to him, "My son, go home, and all will be well."

So the man went home, and lo! His wife had returned, the police had brought back his car, and his broker had telephoned to say that the stock market was rising.

Jesus continued his walk through the city and saw a poor man weeping. Jesus asked him, "My son, what is wrong with you?"

The man replied, "My daughter has disappeared, my best friend is near death in the hospital, and I have lost my job."

Jesus said, "My son, go home, and all will be well."

So the man went home, was greeted by his daughter, found a message from the hospital that his friend was recovering, and was shortly telephoned by his employer to ask him to return to work.

Continuing on his way, Jesus found a third man sitting on a curb wringing his hands and weeping copiously. Again Jesus asked, "My son, what is wrong?"

The man replied, "I am a French Canadian."

Jesus sat down and wept.

17
Living in
the Country

Canada is more urbanized than the United States, though that has not always been the case. The vicissitudes of rural life remain deeply embedded in the Canadian psyche. Punkydoodles Corners is an actual place located between Kitchener and Stratford, Ont. Canadians of the past farmed and fished in Birdseye Centre and then Juniper Junction (both creations of cartoonist Jimmy Frise). Ever green in memory is Crocus, Sask., because at heart all farmers were (maybe still are) Jake Trumper (of radio's "Jake and the Kid") or maybe Don Harron's rustic Charlie Farquharson.

The jokes here tell us city dwellers what life in the country is—or was—all about.

Gender Specific

The Canadian government plans to rename a province.
Manitoba is too gender-specific. It will be renamed Personitoba.

Pioneers

A tourist strolling through a rural area sees an old man chopping firewood with an axe.

He goes up to him and says, "You handle that axe pretty well."

The old man says, "Well, I should. My great-grandfather, who was one of the first pioneers in this area, bought this axe, and it's been in the family for over a century."

The tourist says, "Really? It doesn't look that old."

The old man replied, "That's because it's had four new handles and three new heads since great-grandfather had it."

NDP Salmon

A company selling tins of red salmon was in trouble. People were buying twice as many tins of pink salmon as they were tins of red salmon.

The company's owner decided to consult a leading advertising agency. He explained the problem and waited for the advertising specialists to come up with their solution.

He waited a week. They recommended changing the label. The wording on the new label should read: "Authentic Red Salmon—Guaranteed Not to Turn Pink."

Beaver

A beaver was bragging to the other animals that he could cut down any tree in the forest.

"I can honestly say," he boasted, "that I have never been stumped."

Beavers

Q. Why do beavers have webbed feet?
A. To stamp out fires.

Q. Why do bears have flat feet?
A. To stamp out burning beavers.

Beaver in the Bar

The beaver walks into a bar and asks, "Is the bar tender here?"

Rabbit and Beaver

A rabbit and a beaver were staring at the big new hydroelectric dam that now spanned their favourite river.

The rabbit asked the beaver, "Did you build it?"

The beaver replied, "No, I didn't build it. But it's based on an idea of mine."

Sasquatch

Q. How does the sasquatch tell time?
A. With his Swatch.

Elephant at Large

An elephant escapes from a circus in Cape Breton. It makes its way across country and into the yard of a farm, where it begins to help itself to the vegetables in the garden.

In the house the farmer's wife is working in the kitchen. This woman has never seen an elephant in her life—never seen a picture of an elephant, never heard of an elephant, has no idea that elephants exist. She looks out the window and is astonished at what she sees helping itself to the vegetables in the garden.

She shouts to her husband, "George, come quick! There's a monster in the garden... and it's pickin' up the cabbages... with its tail! And if I told ya what he's doin' with 'em, ya wouldn't believe me!"

Old Angus

Old Angus the Cape Bretoner was dying.

He was in his bed in a little room at the top of a steep, twisty stairway. A group of his friends came over to try to cheer him up, and with their jokes and laughter and encouraging words, they soon had him feeling pretty good—thinking that maybe he was going to recover after all.

Then, as they were leaving, one of them banged his head on the low doorway at the top of the stairs and said, "Lord Jesus, but we're gonna have a hell of a time gettin' the coffin down these stairs!"

Small Town

Anonymous small-town saying:

You don't see much, but what you hear makes up for it.

Talking Horse

A man's car broke down while he was driving through Alberta. He was at the side of the highway, with the hood up, looking in to see if he could find the trouble.

A cowboy on a horse came along, and stopped to see what was happening. Suddenly the horse said, "Looks like the carburetor to me."

The man was astounded. "Good heavens!" he said to the cowboy. "Did you hear that?"

"Sure," said the cowboy. "But don't pay him no mind. He don't know nothin' about cars."

The Saskatchewan Cow

The only cow in a small Alberta town stopped giving milk. The townsfolk did some asking around and found that they could buy a cow just across the border in Saskatchewan for $200. They bought the cow from Saskatchewan and it was wonderful. It produced lots of milk all the time, and the people were pleased and very happy.

The townsfolk decided to acquire a bull to mate with the cow to produce more cows like her. They would never have to worry about their milk supply again. They bought the bull and put it in the pasture with their beloved cow.

However, whenever the bull came close to the cow, the cow would move away. No matter what approach the bull tried, the cow would move away from the bull, and he could not succeed in his quest. The people were upset and decided to ask the veterinarian, who was very wise, what to do.

They told the vet what was happening. "Whenever the bull approaches our cow, she moves away. If he approaches from the back, she moves forward. When he approaches her from the front, she backs off. An approach from the side, she walks away to the other side."

The vet thought about this for a minute and asked, "Did you by chance buy this cow in Saskatchewan?"

The townsfolk were dumbfounded, since no one had ever mentioned where they had bought the cow. "You are truly a wise vet," they said. "How did you know we acquired the cow in Saskatchewan?"

The vet replied, with a distant look in his eye, "My wife is from Saskatchewan."

Chess Match

A man walking through a park saw an old-timer sitting at a picnic table, playing chess with a dog. To his astonishment, the dog stretched out a paw and moved his queen.

"That's incredible!" the man cried.

The old man turned around and whispered, "Not really. I've got him beat in two more moves."

Motto of P.E.I.

It seems Prince Edward Island has a new provincial motto.
   It goes like this: *Cogito ergo spud.*
   It translates, "I think, therefore I yam."

P.E.I.

Q. How does a Prince Edward Islander count his wealth?
A. One potato, two potato, three potato, four.

Potatoes

Q. Why was the P.E.I. farmer driving a steamroller across his fields?
A. He thought he could get a better price for his potatoes if they were already mashed.

Harvest

A man asked a P.E.I. farmer how things were going.
   "Just fine," he replied. "First a storm came along and blew down some old dead trees I wanted to clear out. Then lightning struck the pile of fallen wood and burned it away for me."
   "So what are you doing now?"
   "Waiting for an earthquake to bring up the potatoes so I can harvest them."

Ten Percent

A man asked an Island farmer how he could make any money on his potatoes when he always sold them at discount prices to his friends.
   The farmer said, "Well, I sell the spuds to my friends at ten percent off the regular price because they're friends of mine.

Then I take ten percent off the hundredweight, because I'm a friend of theirs."

Potato Farmers

Two P.E.I. farmers were talking.

The one farmer said, "Why did you vote for that candidate in the election?"

The other farmer replied, "Well, he promised to do something that will benefit all of us here on the island."

"What's that?"

"He promised that he's going to stop the importation of French fried potatoes."

Potato Bug

Three P.E.I. potato farmers were complaining about a particularly nasty potato bug.

The first farmer said, "They ate my whole crop in two weeks."

The second farmer said, "That's nothing. They went through my whole crop in two days, then sat in the trees to watch and see if I was going to plant more spuds."

The third farmer said, "You think you've got trouble. They ate up all of my crop in a day, and the next day I saw them at the general store looking at the ledger to see who'd bought seed."

German Tourist

A German tourist visiting Prince Edward Island is having a problem with the German pronunciation of the island's name.

"Excuse me," he says to a local person, "do you pronounce 'Edward' with a 'v' sound or with a 'w' sound?"

"It's Edvard."

"Thank you."

"You're velcome."

Milking the Cows

A city boy asked a farmer how long cows should be milked.
The farmer replied, "The same as short cows."

Exaggerations

A little boy ran into the house yelling, "Ma, I just saw a dog as big as a horse."
His mother said, "Oh, Billy, I've told you fifty million times to stop exaggerating!"

Psychiatrist

"Doctor, my husband thinks he's a horse."
"I think I can help him, but it's going to be costly."
"Money's no problem. He just won the Queen's Plate."

Some Medicine

Two farmers met in town one Saturday.
"I had problems with my prize bull," said one. "He was impotent. The vet gave me some medicine for him, and now he's fine."
"What's the medicine called?" asked the other.
"I don't know. But it tastes like chocolate."

Mail-Order Company

A farmer in Morden, Man., called a mail-order company to ask the price of a box of toilet paper.
The man on the other end of the line said, "You'll find that information on page twenty of our catalogue."
The farmer replied, "Mister, if I had your catalogue, I wouldn't need the toilet paper."

Windy Prairie

A farmer was asked how windy it gets on the Prairies.

He said, "I had a hen that laid the same egg six times."

Animals on the Farm

The animals in Farmer Brown's barn were having a meeting.

The meeting was being chaired by the chicken. "What we need from everyone here is commitment," she announced. "I have commitment. I produce eggs every day. The cow has commitment. She produces milk every day."

The pig grunted and said, "You call that commitment? Try producing ham."

Alberta Branding

A New York family bought a ranch in Alberta, where they made preparations to raise cattle. Friends came from Manhattan to visit and asked them if the ranch had a name.

"Well," said the would-be cattleman, "there are problems.

"I wanted to call it the Bar-J.

"My wife favoured the Suzy-Q.

"Our son liked the Flying-W.

"Our daughter wanted the Lazy-Y.

"So, we're calling it the Bar-J-Suzy-Q-Flying-W-Lazy-Y."

"Wow! That's quite a mouthful! So, where are all your cattle?"

"So far, none of our cattle have survived the branding."

Subscriber

Years ago, the proprietor of *The Star*, the weekly newspaper published in Wainwright, Sask., was really annoyed.

Old Farmer Jones had not paid his subscription for years, and stubbornly refused to do so.

Then one day the editor got a phone call. Relatives phoned to say that old Farmer Jones had just died. He thought to himself, "Well, I guess that means I can finally cancel his subscription."

Herd of Cattle

An agent from the federal Department of Agriculture was inspecting dairy farms in the Codroy Valley on the Prairies.

He walked into the farmer's yard, flashed his identification, and walked toward the cows, despite the farmer's warning to stay behind the fence.

A huge bull charged toward him, and the terrified agent shouted to the farmer, "Call him off!"

"Show him your I.D., b'y!" the farmer yelled. "He don't know who you are!"

Prize Bull

A farmer was using his prize bull to plough a field.

His neighbour saw him and could not believe his eyes. "What the hell are you doing, using that blue-ribbon bull to pull a plough?"

The farmer replied, "I'm just letting him know that life ain't all fun."

Sandstorm

In the summer of 1988 there was a fierce sandstorm in Saskatchewan. A farmer found a hat lying in his field. He picked it up and found beneath it the head of his neighbour, very much alive.

"Wow!" exclaimed the farmer. "I'll get a shovel and dig you out!"

"You better bring a backhoe," was the response. "I'm sitting on a horse!"

Rancher's Legacy

A rancher died, leaving seventeen horses to his three sons.

His will specified: "One-half to the oldest son, one-third to the second son, one-ninth to the youngest."

The cowboy who was the executor of the will had a problem sorting that out. To solve the problem, he added his own horse to the lot, making a total of eighteen horses.

He gave one-half (9) to the eldest son.

He gave one-third (6) to the middle son.

He gave one-ninth (2) to the youngest son.

Adding up 9, 6, and 2, he came to a sum of 17.

So he got on his own horse and rode away happily.

Two Frogs

Two frogs are sitting on a lily pad, when a big swarm of flies comes along. They start shooting out their tongues, gobbling up the insects.

After a while one frog says, "You know, time's fun when you're having flies."

The Talking Horse

A man from Toronto is driving through the Cape Breton countryside. He stops at an intersection, and before he pulls away, he hears someone say, "Hi, how ya doin'?"

He looks around, but all he can see is a horse in a field by the highway. "Yeah," says the horse. "It's me talkin' to ya."

"My God!" the man exclaims. "A talking horse! What are you doing out here?"

"Well, it's a long story," the horse says. "I used to be a great race horse. Even won the Kentucky Derby once. But I got old, and they put me out to pasture, so here I am."

"Who owns you?" the Torontonian asks.

"The Cape Bretoner who lives up in that farmhouse."

"Do you think he'd sell you?"

"Wouldn't hurt to ask. I'd sure like to get out of here."

So the Torontonian goes up to the farmhouse and knocks on the door. The Cape Bretoner answers and says, "What can I do for you, b'y?"

"I was wondering if you'd consider selling that horse you've got down in the field."

"I don't know, buddy. That's a pretty special horse. What'll you give me for it?"

"I'll give you $100, cash."

"Naw. Better make it $150."

So the Torontonian pays the money and goes to get his horse, rejoicing at his luck. A talking horse for only $150!

Meanwhile, the Cape Bretoner goes into the next room where his wife is and says, "I just sold that old horse. Got $150 for it. Boy, I sure put one over on that fella."

"Why do you say that?" his wife asks.

"That lyin' bastard never won the Kentucky Derby."

Lucky Turkey

A man runs a turkey farm. One turkey always seems to avoid being chosen for the dinner plate every year when people come to pick birds for Thanksgiving. It seems that the turkey always has something wrong with it, which causes customers to pass it by.

One year, for example, it has a terrible cough. As soon as it sees a person looking over the turkeys, it starts going, "Carf, carf, carf, carf!" Of course, no one wants to buy a sick bird.

Another year, the turkey has a very pronounced limp. Of course, nobody wants a turkey with only one good drumstick.

This goes on year after year, with the turkey surviving several generations of its fellows. Then, one year, on the eve of Thanksgiving, the farmer sees the turkey walking across the yard, from all appearances in perfect health. He sneaks up behind the turkey and says, "Aha! I caught you!"

The turkey turns around, looks up with a squint, cups a wing to one ear, and says in a cracked voice, "Eh?"

Producing Cow

A farmer's best milk cow had not been producing very well.

One morning the farmer went into the barn and gave her an ultimatum: "What's it going to be—milk or hamburger?"

Farmer's Life

A farmer hit it big on the 6/49 lottery.

A reporter asked him, "What are you going to do, now that you're a millionaire?"

The farmer replied, "I guess I'll just keep on farmin' until the money runs out."

Farmer Jones and Honest Al

Farmer Jones had bought every car he'd ever owned from Al Smith, proprietor of Honest Al's car dealership in town. He'd always felt that Honest Al had stuck it to him on prices, but had done it in such a slick way that it was hard to prove.

One day Honest Al decided that he wanted to invest in cattle, and he went to see his old customer Farmer Jones to buy a starter cow. Farmer Jones helped him select a cow, and then presented him with the following bill of sale to get his own back:

Bill of Sale

Basic cow: $400
Two-tone extra: $90
Extra stomach: $150

Produce storage compartment: $120
Dispensing device (four spigots at $20 each): $80
Genuine cowhide upholstery: $250
Dual horns: $30
Automatic flyswatter: $70

Total: $1,190

Warning to Passengers

Here is the wording that appeared on a sign belonging to the Great Northwest Stage Coach Company, 1880.

Notice / Abstinence from liquor is requested, but if you must drink, share the bottle. Forgo smoking, as smoke and odour are repugnant, especially to ladies. Chewing tobacco is permitted. Gentlemen must refrain from strong language. Don't snore loudly, or friction with fellow travellers may result. Firearms may be kept, but don't fire them for pleasure—the sound frightens the horses. Gents guilty of unchivalrous behaviour toward lady passengers will be put off the stage. It's a long walk back.

A Lesson in Survival Technique

One of the Gallants from North Rustico moved from P.E.I. to Toronto, where he purchased a donkey from an old farmer for $100. The farmer agreed to deliver the animal the next day.

But the following afternoon, the farmer drove up and announced sadly, "I'm sorry, but I have some bad news. The donkey died last night."

"Well, den," said Gallant, "jus' give me my money back. Okay?"

"I can't do that, sir. I went and spent the money."

"Okay, den. Jus' unload dat donkey."

"What are you going to do with him?"

"I'm gon' to raffle him off."

"You can't raffle off a dead donkey, you dumb fisherman."

"Well, dat's where you are wrong. You wait and you learn how smart we are on Ile-du-Prince-Edouard."

A month later, the farmer ran into Gallant and asked, "What happened to the dead donkey?"

"I raffled dat donkey off. I sold five hundred tickets at $2 a piece and made $998."

"Didn't anyone complain?"

"Jus' dat guy who won. So I gave him his $2 back."

Farmer's Field

A man is driving down a country road near London, Ont., when he spots a farmer standing in the middle of a field of wheat. He pulls his car over to the side of the road and notices that the farmer is just standing there, doing nothing, looking at nothing.

The man gets out of his car, walks all the way out to the farmer, and asks him, "Hello, excuse me, but is there something wrong? What are you doing?"

The farmer replies, "I'm trying to win the Nobel Prize."

"How's that?" asks the man, genuinely puzzled.

"Well, I hear they give Nobel Prizes to people who are out standing in their fields."

The Farmer's Sign

Farmer Brown lived on his farm beside a rural road that over the years had turned into a highway. Its traffic increased at an alarming rate. In fact, there was now so much traffic that his chickens were being run over at a rate of from three to six a day.

One day the farmer called the country roads department and said, "You've got to do something about all of these people driving so fast and killing all my chickens."

"What do you want me to do?" asked the manager.

"I don't care. Just do something about those drivers."

So the next day he had the department erect a sign that read: SLOW — SCHOOL CROSSING.

That did not help, so three days later the farmer called the manager and said, "You've got to do something about these drivers. The School Crossing sign seems to make them go faster."

So, again, the manager orders the county roads department to erect a new sign that read: SLOW — CHILDREN AT PLAY.

That did not help either, so three days later the farmer called the manager yet again and complained, "Your signs are doing no good. The traffic is faster than ever. Is it all right for me to put up my own sign?"

The manager told him, "Sure thing. Put up your own sign." The manager was ready to agree to anything, so long as the farmer stopped calling him.

Thereafter the manager got no more calls from Farmer Brown.

Three weeks passed since the farmer's last call. The manager was curious so he decided to call the farmer. "How's the problem with those drivers? Did you put up your sign?"

"Oh, I sure did," the farmer said. "And not one chicken has been killed since then. I've got to go. I'm very busy." He hung up the phone.

The manager thought to himself, "I'd better go to the farmer's house and look at that sign. There might be something there that we, the county roads department, could use to slow down drivers."

So the manager drove out to Farmer Brown's farm and he saw the sign on the highway that the farmer had raised. It was a whole sheet of plywood on which Farmer Brown had painted in large yellow letters the following words: SLOW — NUDIST COLONY.

Cowboy and Horse

A cowboy took his horse to the vet and said, "This horse has no get-up-and-go in him, Doc. You got anything that will give him some energy, make him go a little faster?"

The vet said, "Sure do," and got some white powder from his cabinet and put some in the horse's mouth. The horse neighed and took off like a shot. In a few moments the horse was out of sight.

"Wow!" said the cowboy. "That stuff sure works! You got some for me, Doc?"

"Why for you?" asked the doctor.

"Because now I've got to catch that horse."

The Lawyer and the Farmer

A big-city lawyer went duck hunting in rural Saskatchewan. He shot and dropped a bird, but it fell into a farmer's field on the other side of a fence.

As the lawyer climbed over the fence, an elderly farmer drove up on his tractor and asked him what he was doing. The litigator responded, "I shot a duck and it fell in this field, and now I'm going to retrieve it."

The old farmer replied, "This is my property, and you are not coming over here."

The indignant lawyer said, "I am one of the best trial attorneys in Ontario, and if you don't let me get that duck, I'll sue you and take everything you own."

The old farmer smiled and said, "You may know the law in Ontario, but apparently you don't know how we do things in Saskatchewan. We settle small disagreements like this with the Saskatchewan Three-Kick Rule."

The lawyer asked, "What is the Saskatchewan Three-Kick Rule?"

The farmer replied, "Well, first I kick you three times, and then you kick me three times, and so on back and forth until someone gives up."

The attorney quickly thought about the proposed contest and decided that he could easily take the old farmer, who looked pretty frail. The lawyer agreed to abide by the local custom.

The old farmer slowly climbed down from the tractor and walked up to the city feller. His first kick planted the toe of his heavy workboot into the lawyer's groin and dropped him to his knees. His second kick to the midriff sent the lawyer's last meal gushing from his mouth. The barrister was on all fours when the farmer's third kick to his rear end sent him face first into a fresh cow pie.

The lawyer summoned every bit of his will and managed to get to his feet. Wiping his face with the arm of his silk suit jacket, he said, "Okay, you old coot. Now it's my turn."

The old farmer smiled and said, "Naw, I give up. You can have the duck."

Quickies

Q. Why does Santa have three gardens?
A. So he can hoe, hoe, hoe.

Q. What is Smokey the Bear's motto?
A. "Piss on it!"

Q. What's the difference between mosquitoes and flies?
A. Mosquitoes can fly, but flies can't mosquito.

Q. What do you get if you cross a Canadian with a groundhog?
A. Six more weeks of hockey.

Trees

In the forests of British Columbia, it's sometimes hard to cedar woods for the trees.

A Farmer's Complaints

Here are a farmer's complaints:

"It all started back in '66 when they changed from pounds to dollars—that doubled my overdraft. Then they brought in kilograms instead of pounds—my cows' milk production dropped in half. After that they changed rain to millimetres and we haven't had an inch of rain since. If that wasn't bad enough, they brought in Celsius and we got frost in August. No wonder my wheat won't grow. Then they changed acres to hectares and I ended up with only one-half of the land I had. By this time I'd had enough and decided to sell out. I put the property on the market and then they changed from miles to kilometres. Now I'm too far out of town for anyone to buy this place."

18
Here, there, and everywhere

It is people who make jokes and anecdotes funny, but sometimes the humour is enhanced by the joke's setting—its locale, its physical place in the country, and its psychological place in our minds.

A joke about Rosedale really works when the teller and the listener know that Rosedale is an affluent residential district in Toronto, or that Niagara Falls, for all its natural wonder, happens to be a tourist's bazaar, or that Vancouver seems to be plagued with persistent downpours (according to Torontonians at least). A reference to Moose Jaw or Medicine Hat is certain to attract attention and titters, according to playwright Mavor Moore.

In this chapter you will find wisecracks, wit, humour, jests, quips, and banter about Canadian locales, towns, cities, districts, provinces, regions, and even the country itself.

Playing Cards

A man was hired to work as a communications engineer at the remote post of Alert, N.W.T.

314

The boss handed him an emergency survival kit that consisted of a flare gun, a radio, and a deck of cards.

"I know what the survival kit is for, I know what the radio is for, and I know what the flare gun is for. But what's the deck of cards for?" the man asked.

The boss replied, "If nobody responds to your flare, and if you can't reach anyone on the radio, break out the cards and start playing Solitaire. In no time at all someone will come up behind you and say, 'Put the red nine on the black ten.'"

Driver Identification

How to identify where a driver is from:

One hand on wheel, one hand on horn, driving 20 km/h over the speed limit:
>   Montreal

One hand on wheel, one finger out window, and a Starbucks coffee between their legs, driving 0.2 km/h over the speed limit:
>   Toronto

One hand on wheel, one finger out window, cutting across all lanes of traffic:
>   Ottawa

One hand on wheel, one hand on newspaper, foot solidly on accelerator:
>   Moncton

One hand on wheel, one hand on non-fat, double-decaf cappuccino, cradling cell phone, brick on accelerator, gun on lap:
>   Los Angeles (all right, so Los Angeles isn't in Canada . . . so sue me!)

Both hands on wheel, eyes shut, both feet on brake, quivering in terror:

Saskatoon, but driving in Toronto

Both hands in air, gesturing, both feet on accelerator, head turned to talk to someone in the back seat:

Quebec City

One hand on twelve-ounce, double-shot latte, one knee on wheel, cradling cell phone, foot on brake, mind on radio game, banging head on steering wheel while stuck in traffic:

Vancouver

One hand on wheel, one hand on hunting rifle, alternating between both feet being on the brake and both feet on the accelerator, throwing McDonald's bag out the window:

Calgary

Four-wheel drive pick-up truck, shotgun mounted in rear window, beer cans on the floor, raccoon tails attached to the antenna:

High River

Two hands gripping wheel, blue hair barely visible above windshield, driving 40 km/h on Hwy 401 in the left lane with the left blinker on:

Any place in Ontario

One snowmobile mitt on steering wheel, one snowmobile mitt scraper in hand out front window scraping frost, The Guess Who's "American Woman" playing on an eight-track, hockey equipment smelling up car interior, waiting at lights for snow-removal equipment to finish clearing intersection:

Winnipeg

Texas and Quebec

Tommy Hunter recalls this incident in his memoir, My Story (1985).

The American country singer Tex Ritter agreed to be a guest on Tommy Hunter's popular *Country Holiday* television show. A few minutes before showtime, Tommy talked with Tex, who asked about the political situation in Quebec. This was during the mid-1960s, when the issue of Quebec separatism was beginning to come up in the news. In conversation they agreed to take a pass on the subject.

When the show started, Tommy introduced Tex. Then Tex said, "Thank you, Tommy. And now that I'm here in Canada, I ought to tell you folks that there's been a lot of talk down in the States about Quebec seeking its independence."

"Oh, no," Tommy thought.

"Now, maybe you folks don't know this," Tex continued, "but Texas once sought its independence, too, and now I'm thinking we should seek it once again. Maybe then we could dig a hole in the ground in the middle of Texas, another hole in the middle of Quebec, and run a pipeline between the two, and let Texas and Quebec form a new country."

He paused for a moment. Tommy was worried.

"Now, Texas would probably want top billing, so we could call the new country Tay-Beck; but then, if Quebec insisted it come first, we'd just have to call it Que-Ass!"

The audience burst into uproarious laughter, Tommy too.

Border Signs

When you cross the Canada-U.S. border on your way south, you can see a billboard that says, "Welcome to the United States of America. We have Bob Hope, Johnny Cash, and Stevie Wonder."

On your way back north into Canada, the sign reads, "Welcome to Canada. Here we have no Hope, no Cash, and no Wonder!"

Border Crossing

I first encountered this joke, hoary with age and hoarfrost, in the 1970s, when it was told about a Polish family on the Russian-Polish border.

An elderly woman lived on a small farm in Canada, just yards from the North Dakota border. Her land had been the subject of a minor dispute between the United States and Canada for years.

The widowed woman lived on the farm with her son and three grandchildren. One day, her son came into her room holding a letter. "I just got some news, Mom," he said. "The government has come to an agreement with the people in North Dakota. They've decided that our land is really part of the United States. We have the right to approve or disapprove of the agreement. What do you think?"

"What do I think?" his mother said. "Sign it! Call them right now and tell them we accept! I don't think I can stand another Canadian winter!"

The Consultant

On the Prairies a farmer was leading his sheep in a remote pasture when suddenly a brand-new Jeep Cherokee advanced out of a dust cloud toward him. The driver, a young man clad in a Brioni suit, Gucci shoes, Ray-Ban sunglasses, and an Yves St. Laurent tie, leaned out the window and yelled to the farmer, "If I can tell you exactly how many sheep you have in your flock, will you give me one?"

The farmer glared at the young man and then surveyed his peacefully grazing flock. He calmly answered, "Sure!"

The young man parked the Jeep Cherokee, whipped out a notebook, connected it to a cell phone, surfed to a NASA page on the internet, called up a GPS satellite navigation system, scanned the area, and opened up a database and some sixty Excel spreadsheets filled with complex formulas.

At long last he printed a one-hundred-and-fifty-page report on his high-tech miniature printer, turned round to the farmer, and said, "You have here exactly one thousand, five hundred, and eighty-six sheep!"

The farmer looked surprised. "This is correct," he said. "As agreed, you can take one of the sheep." He watched the young man make his selection and bundle the animal in his Jeep Cherokee.

Then the farmer said, "If I can tell you exactly what your business is, will you give me my sheep back?"

"Okay, why not?" answered the young man.

"You are a consultant," said the farmer.

"This is correct," said the young man. "But how did you guess that?"

"Easy," answered the shepherd. "You turned up here unbidden. Nobody called you. You wanted to be paid to supply the answer to a question that I already knew the answer to. And you don't know anything about my business because you took my sheep dog."

Great City

Toronto mayor Mel Lastman enjoys telling this story about the visit of golfer Lee Trevino to his favourite city in 1999.

It seems Lee takes a seat in a restaurant in downtown Toronto and orders a cigar, coffee, and cake.

He hands the waiter a $10 American bill.

The waiter returns with his change—$11.50 Canadian.

"What a great city!" says Lee.

Disease

Q. What's the latest disease in Toronto's Rosedale?
A. MAIDS. You'll die if you don't get them!

Bible Belt

Canada has its own Bible Belt. It runs through southern Alberta.

An Albertan pensioner was reminiscing to a fellow pensioner about his late wife.

"Yes," he said, "she was a remarkable woman—extremely religious. When she woke up in the morning, she would sing a hymn. Then she would ask me to join her in prayer. Then, over breakfast, she would recite a psalm, and that's how it went all day long—praying, singing, and reciting until she finally climbed into bed, opened her Holy Bible, read some verses, sang a hymn, and said her prayers again. And then, one morning, she was dead."

"What happened?"

"I strangled her."

Greener Pastures

A Ukrainian peasant arrives at the Pearly Gates and is greeted by St. Peter. In the distance he sees what Heaven is like: a luxury hotel with a casino, night club, stretch limousines, a golf course, shapely women who wear bikinis, and so on.

He bows and scrapes before St. Peter and exclaims how he is so happy to be there.

"My good man," says St. Peter. "There has been a terrible mistake. You are not due here for another four years. I am afraid you will have to return to earth. But do not worry. We will send for you at the proper time."

The Ukrainian peasant is sent back. Thereafter, he looks forward to returning to Heaven. So four years later, when he dies, he does so with a smile on his face.

Again he arrives at the Pearly Gates and is greeted by St. Peter. But something is different this time. In the distance he sees what Heaven is now like: old men are working as gardeners, digging ditches, and repairing roads; old women are scrubbing floors, cooking, washing dishes, and doing the laundry.

"This is not the Heaven you showed me four years ago," the peasant protests to St. Peter.

"That is true," replies St. Peter. "The last time you came on a tourist visa. This time you came on an immigrant visa."

Albertan in Heaven

An Albertan dies and goes to Heaven. He is greeted by St. Peter at the Pearly Gates.

"Welcome," says St. Peter. "Where do you come from?"

The man, somewhat bewildered with the rapid transition from earth to Heaven, replies, "Alberta."

"Well," says St. Peter, "in that case, come in. But I warn you, you're not going to be satisfied."

Missing the Ceremony

It was about 8:00 p.m. A group of university students from the United Kingdom was completing the last tour of the Parliament Buildings in Ottawa.

In the Senate Chamber the tour guide pointed out to them the podium behind which British prime minister Winston Churchill had stood when he addressed a joint meeting of the Senate and the House of Commons.

"This is the precise spot," the tour guide said, "that he delivered his famous 'Some chicken, some neck!' address."

"And when was that?" asked one of the students.

The guide replied, "1939."

"Damn it!" replied the student. "We missed the ceremony by about twenty minutes."

Retirement Haven

They say that living in Victoria, B.C., adds ten years to a person's life.

If this is so, those ten extra years can be profitably spent in Toronto or Montreal.

Curious

Q. Where is Sechelt?
A. On the Sey shore.

The Wet Coast

Definition of a Vancouverite:
    A Vancouverite is someone who wakes up in the morning, walks out onto the front steps, peers into the mist, extends his hands, feels the drizzle, and exclaims, "Ah, the rain is beginning to lift."

Like a Desert

Q. In what way is Canada like a desert?
A. Literally. You get the word Sahara, if you substitute *s* for *c*, *h* for *n*, and *r* for *d*.

Tourists Ask the Strangest Questions

Here are some of the questions that tourists asked staff at Banff National Park's information kiosks—according to whoever placed them on the internet, where they appeared November 2001.

1. How do the elk know they're supposed to cross at the Elk Crossing signs?
2. At what elevation does an elk become a moose?
3. *Tourist:* "How do you pronounce 'elk'?" *Park staff:* "Elk." *Tourist:* "Oh."
4. Are the bears with collars tame?
5. Is there anywhere I can see the bears pose?

6. Is it okay to keep an open bag of bacon on the picnic table, or should I store it in my tent?

7. Where can I find Alpine flamingos?

8. I saw an animal on the way to Banff today—could you tell me what it was?

9. Are there birds in Canada?

10. Did I miss the turnoff for Canada?

11. Where does Alberta end and Canada begin?

12. Do you have a map of the State of Jasper?

13. Is this the part of Canada that speaks French, or is that Saskatchewan?

14. If I go to B.C., do I have to go through Ontario?

15. Which is the way to the Columbia Ricefields?

16. How far is Banff from Canada?

17. What's the best way to see Canada in a day?

18. Do they search you at the B.C. border?

19. When we enter B.C., do we have to convert our money to British pounds?

20. Where can I buy a raccoon hat? All Canadians own one, don't they?

21. Are there phones in Banff?

22. So it's eight kilometres away . . . is that in miles?

23. We're on the decibel system you know.

24. Where can I get my husband really, really lost?

25. Is that two kilometres by foot or by car?

26. Don't you Canadians know anything?

27. Where do you put the animals at night?

28. *Tourist:* "How do you get your lakes so blue?" *Park staff:* "We take the water out in the winter and paint the bottom." *Tourist:* "Oh!"

Housing in Canada and Israel

This is a joke book, not a quote book. But I cannot resist the tempta-
tion to include in these pages the following passage from an inspired,
tongue-in-cheek column written by Sam Orbaum and published in the
Jerusalem Post *Magazine. Orbaum's column was titled "I'd Rather*
Live in Israel" and appeared July 13, 2001. It was inspired by the
declaration of the United Nations that as the world's most liveable
country, Canada rates No. 1, whereas Israel rates No. 23. Sam
contends that this declaration is risible, and after all, he should know.
Born and raised in Montreal, he now lives and works in Jerusalem.
Here is what he has to say about housing in the two countries.

Housing is an important aspect of liveability, and here again,
there's no comparison. In Canada, unless you live in an igloo or
at the Salvation Army, you have two or three stories with so
many rooms that a family never sees one another except at
weddings. Like, who needs a living room and a den and an office
and a workroom and a guest room and a spare room, not to
mention a spacious attic and a fully furnished basement, two-car
garage, driveway, front lawn and backyard, and obligatory built-in
skating rink? That's for your basic Canadian three-person family,
and does not include the summer cottage. For a basic, average
Israeli family of six (not including the relatives and neighbours
who come and go), a living room is all we need, and who
doesn't have one?

Heavenly Helper

Here is a story Mel Hurtig told in a speech delivered in Ottawa on
October 19, 1986. It remains a favourite of the nationalist and
publisher.

The story that I've told a few of you that I'll repeat again because
it's so à propos has to do with the mountaineer who always

wanted to climb Mount Robson and he, all of his life, thought that it would be a good idea to try to tackle this gigantic massive peak in the Canadian Rockies on a solo climb. It had never been done before.

So, one day, he set out on an expedition and climbed and climbed and got just below the summit of the mountain, and, as he was almost at the top, he slipped and fell straight down a 10,000-foot precipice. At the last second he reached out and grabbed the only tree that was projecting from the side of the mountain. He hung there and he hung there and he hung there and finally, in desperation, he looked up and he shouted, "Is there anyone up there?"

And a voice came down and said, "Yes, there is."

And he said, "Who is it?"

The voice said, "It's me, God."

He said, "God, would you please, please help me?"

God said, "Don't worry, I will help you."

The man said, "What do you want me to do?"

God said, "Just trust me and let go of the tree."

The man said, "You want me to trust you and let go of the tree?"

God repeated, "Just trust me and let go of the tree."

There was a long silence and finally the climber called out, "Is there anybody else up there?"

The Scotsman and the Fare

A Scotsman was taking the train from Sydney to Halifax. He had with him a huge trunk, which he put on the seat next to him. The conductor came along collecting fares.

The Scot grumbled at the outrageous fares and the amount that he had had to pay for his ticket. The conductor then told him that because his trunk was taking up a seat, he would have to pay an extra fare. The Scot said, "I'm no payin' a fare for a bluidy trunk."

The conductor said he had to. The Scot again refused.

The conductor said, "If you don't pay the extra fare, I'm going to shove that trunk out the window."

The Scot said, "I'm no payin'."

So the conductor grabbed the trunk and shoved it out the window, just as the train was going over a bridge. The trunk bounced off the railing and fell into the river, where it sank.

The Scot said to the conductor, "There! Now ye've done it, laddie. Not only have ye bilked me with your outrageous fares, but ye've gone and drowned my wee boy."

Prince Edward Island

Q. What did the Islander get when he crossed a potato with an onion?

A. He got a potato with watery eyes.

Q. What is the card game that Islanders either love or hate?

A. Bridge.

Q. Who are the biggest celebrities in P.E.I.?

A. Mr. and Mrs. Potatohead.

Saskatchewan

Q. Is it legal for a man in Saskatchewan to marry his widow's sister?

A. No. If he is dead, how could he marry anyway?

Flight from Vancouver

"Did you hear about the man who just flew in from Vancouver?"

"No."

"Boy, were his arms ever tired!"

Yukon

Q. What is the most able part of the country?
A. Yukon. (You can.)

North Pole

Q. Which two letters in the alphabet remind me of the North Pole?
A. I.C. (icy)

Two Drunks

Two drunks broke into a fuel storage room at Toronto airport and stole some gasohol. They took it into an alleyway to drink, then each staggered off to his own flophouse.

In the morning the first drunk woke up because his phone was ringing. It was his buddy. "Hey pal," said his friend on the phone, "you just wake up?"

"Yes."

"Did you fart yet?"

"No."

"Well, don't. Because I did, and I'm calling from Montreal."

Song Lyric

The late American country singer Roger Miller used to say that he could make up a song on the spot about anything anyone suggested to him.

Someone said "Saskatchewan."

Miller took a couple of seconds, and then sang:

Saskatchewan, Saskatchewan,
Show me an itch and I'll scratch you one.

Sign

The following sign appeared at a nudist camp in Ontario:

Nudist Camp
Sorry—Closed for Winter
September–June

Airbase Sign

Sign allegedly seen at the Canadian Forces base, Comox, B.C:
"Absolutely no flying over nudist camp 10 kilometres SSW on a true course of 177 degrees."

Icefields National Park

Driving along the curving highways of Icefields National Park, I marvelled at the scenery. But I also marvelled at the absence of guardrails.

I approached a park warden about this: "The highway is pretty steep and there are lots of bends, curves, and turns. There should be more guardrails."

"Not at all," the warden replied. "Too expensive. Drivers keep knocking them down."

Life in the Barrens

Sam has been in business for twenty-five years and is finally sick of the stress and strain of commercial life.

He quits his job and buys a thousand acres in the Barrens, N.W.T. It is a hundred miles from the nearest community.

He receives mail delivery by air once every two weeks, and grocery supplies are delivered once a month, also by air. Otherwise it's total peace and quiet.

After six months or so of almost complete isolation, someone knocks on his door. Sam opens it. A big, bearded man is standing there.

"Name's Ned . . . your neighbour from a hundred miles away . . . having a party Friday . . . thought you might like to come . . . about five o'clock . . ."

"Great," says Sam. "After six months out here I'm ready to meet some local folks. Thank you."

As Ned is leaving, he stops. "Gotta warn you . . . there's gonna be some drinkin'."

"Not a problem . . . after twenty-five years in the business world, I can drink with the best of 'em."

Again, as he starts to leave, Ned stops. "More 'n likely gonna be some fightin' too."

Sam says, "Well, I get along with most people. I'll be there. Thanks again."

Once again Ned turns from the door. "I've seen some wild sex at these parties, too."

"Now, that's really not a problem," says Sam. "I've been all alone for six months! I'll definitely be there. By the way, what should I bring?"

Ned stops in the door again and says, "Whatever you want, just gonna be the two of us."

Rum-Running Truck Drivers

Two rum-runners, George and Fred from Lawn, Nfld., are smuggling a shipment of rum onto the Mainland.

After carefully mapping out their route, they set out, taking all the backroads through the Maritimes.

Twelve hours later, at 3:00 a.m., on a two-lane road in the middle of nowhere, they pass a sign that reads "Caution—Low Bridge Ahead—Clearance 8'."

The boys from Lawn screech to a stop just before the bridge and get out to assess their situation. Then the driver, George, takes out his flashlight and shines the light on the truck. He reads the notice that says "Height 10'," and asks Fred, "Well, what should we do now?"

Fred replies, "I don't see any cops around, let's go fer it ... !"

Highway Driving

A tractor-trailer is barrelling along the 401 near Oshawa, Ont. The driver sees a sign looming ahead that warns of a low bridge ahead.

He slows down but not quickly enough. There is the awful sound of the scrunch of metal against cement, as the roof of the trailer smashes into the substructure of the bridge. It backs up traffic for miles.

Soon, the Ontario Provincial Police arrive at the scene. An officer gets out of the patrol car and walks over to the driver. He places his hands on his hips and says, sarcastically, "Got stuck, eh?"

The truck driver smiles and says, "No, I was delivering this bridge when I ran out of gas."

Wrong Way on the 401

A man who had recently moved to Ontario was driving along Highway 401 when his car phone rang.

Answering, he heard his wife's voice urgently warning him, "Herman, I just heard on the news that there's a car going the wrong way on the 401. Please be careful!"

"Hell," said Herman. "It's not just one car. It's hundreds of them!"

Holidays

A man decided that for his summer holiday, he was going to pack his wife and the kids into the family van and drive across Canada.

When he got back, a friend asked him how the trip was. He said, "Have you ever been stuck in a van for two weeks with people you thought you loved?"

Camping

A van pulled into a campsite in Algonquin Park.

No sooner had it stopped than the kids piled out and went to work. Two teenagers set up the tent. The twelve-year-old gathered up sticks for the campfire. The seven- and eight-year-olds helped their mother unpack food and set the picnic table.

A man in a neighbouring campsite was watching all this, impressed. He walked over and said to the father, "You sure have a cooperative bunch of kids there."

"It's a system I worked out," said the father. "Nobody is allowed to go to the bathroom until camp is set up."

CN Tower Time

Three guys were at the top of the CN Tower. The tour guide told them that if any one of them could throw his watch over the side and then run down and catch it, he would win $1 million.

The first guy threw his watch over the side. When he reached the bottom of the tower, he found it shattered in a million pieces.

The same thing happened to the second guy and his watch.

The third guy threw his watch over, went home, had a shower and dinner, and then came back and caught his watch.

They all wondered how he had done it.

"I set it two hours fast," he said.

Favourite Railroad

Q. What is a lawyer's favourite railroad?
A. The Soo Line. (Sue, Sault)

Train to Moose Jaw (No. 1)

A man running to catch a departing train yells out to the conductor, "Can I take this train to Moose Jaw?"

The conductor replies, "You can't take this train anywhere— it belongs to the CPR."

Train to Moose Jaw (No. 2)

A man running to catch a departing train yells out to the conductor, "Can I take this train to Moose Jaw?"

The conductor replies, "Why would you want to? It's going there anyway."

Grand Trunk

The president of the Grand Trunk, Georgian Bay, and Lake Erie Railway Company sent a letter to the president of the Canadian Pacific Railway. In the letter he requested a pass that would permit him to ride the full length of the CP line. In exchange, the GT president offered to grant the CP president reciprocal rights, a pass that would permit him to ride the full length of the shortline railroad.

"What good is that?" asked the CP president. "It's not much of an exchange! Our railroad is a hundred times longer than your railroad!"

"Ah," said the GT president, "that may be true. But our railroad's just as wide!"

CPR Theft

In the early twentieth century, there were many coal mines in operation in the Canadian Rockies, including some in what is now Banff National Park. On Saturday nights, many a miner would ride into Banff for a cup of tea or glass of lemonade or, just possibly, something stronger.

Very late one Saturday night, an inebriated miner missed the last train home. He wandered across to the rail yard, found an engine in steam, boarded it, backed it out onto the main line, drove it to his mine, stopped it on a siding, and went to the bunkhouse, where he fell sound asleep.

The next day he was charged with "theft of a locomotive" by the Canadian Pacific Railway. His defence was that he could remember nothing about the so-called theft.

The trial went like this:

Defence counsel: Was the engine on CPR property before my client moved it?

CPR: Yes.

Defence counsel: Was it on CPR tracks when he left it?

CPR: Yes.

Defence counsel: Did it at any time leave CPR tracks?

CPR: No.

Defence counsel: Then where is the theft?

Magistrate: Case dismissed.

Railroad Accident

In a terrible accident at a railroad crossing, a CPR train smashed into a car and pushed it nearly four hundred yards down the track. Though no one was killed, the driver of the car took Canadian Pacific Railway to court.

At the trial, the CPR engineer insisted that he had given the driver ample warning by waving his lantern back and forth for nearly a minute. He even stood and convincingly demonstrated how he had done it. The court believed his story, and the suit was dismissed.

"Congratulations," the lawyer said to the engineer when it was over. "You did superbly under cross-examination."

"Thanks," he said, "but he sure had me worried."

"How's that?" the lawyer asked.

"I was afraid he was going to ask if the damned lantern was lit!"

19

Cities of Renown

In the 1940s there was a chain of gas stations across the country called Cities Service.

Like those gas stations, this chapter performs a service for a few of the biggest cities in the country. Because Canada is so urbanized a country, it is not surprising that much of our humour is local and mainly urban.

"Man may find God in nature," wrote the architect John C. Parkin, "but when they look at cities they are viewing themselves."

Charlotte Whitton

Charlotte Whitton was the first woman to be elected mayor of a Canadian city. The year was 1951 and the city was Ottawa.

She was impish and irrepressible. The story is told of the time she met the Lord Mayor of London. For the occasion both the mayor and the Lord Mayor were suitably attired. Mayor Whitton had a corsage of roses pinned to her evening gown, and the Lord Mayor wore around his shoulders the symbolic Chain of Office.

The Lord Mayor asked, "If I smell your corsage, will you blush?"

The mayor of Ottawa replied, "If I pull your Chain of Office, will you flush?"

Government Man

A man is finding it difficult to think things through, so he makes an appointment with his doctor to see if there is something seriously the matter with his mind.

The doctor examines him and says, "If you will leave your brain with me, I'll go over it carefully. It won't take long. You can call back for it in a few days."

The man agrees, leaves his brain, and goes off.

Time passes and he does not call the doctor. After some weeks, the doctor telephones him: "You know, I have that brain of yours. Aren't you coming for it?"

"Oh that," says the man. "I don't need it now. I've got a job with the government."

Civil Servants

Q. Why do civil servants wear brightly coloured shirts when they're at the cottage?

A. So they can tell when they're on vacation.

American Tourist

Q. How can you tell an American tourist in Montreal?

A. He stands by the Metro sign asking where the subway is.

Flight

A man went to the ticket counter at the airport in Calgary and asked for a ticket to Toronto.

The attendant asked, "So, you want to go to Toronto?"

"No, I have to."

CN Tower

Q. Do people leap off the top of the CN Tower very often?
A. No, just the once.

Texan in Toronto

A Texan was visiting Toronto for the first time. He got a cab at the airport and told the driver to take him on a tour of the city. As they drove past city hall, the Texan said, "What the hell is that?"

"That's our city hall," the taxi driver replied. "We're very proud of it. It took two years to build."

"Hell," the Texan exclaimed. "In Texas, we'd build that in two weeks."

A little later they passed the SkyDome. "What's that?" the Texan asked.

"That's the SkyDome," the driver answered. "It took over a year to build."

The Texan laughed and said, "In Texas, we'd build that in less than a week."

Then the Texan looked up at the CN Tower and said, "What in tarnation is that?"

The driver replied, "I don't know. It wasn't there yesterday."

Torontonians Only

A distinguished couple from New York City was driving down Bay Street in downtown Toronto.

"Oh, look," the wife exclaimed, "they have a Temperance Street in Toronto."

The husband looked at the names on the street signs and responded, "Yes, but you'll notice they keep it at Bay!"

Toronto Transit Commission

Q. What does TTC stand for?

A. "Take the car."

Toronto Subway

Two drunks were riding the Toronto subway system.

As the train pulls into a downtown station, one drunk asks the other, "Is this Wellesley?"

"Naw," says the other drunk. "It's Thursday."

"Thursday?" asks the first drunk.

"Sure am!" says the second drunk. "Let's get off and go for a drink."

Toronto Stammerer

On a Toronto bus a man with a stammer turns to the passenger next to him and asks directions:

"P-p-p-pardon m-m-m-me. C-c-c-could you t-t-t-tell me when we g-g-g-get to B-B-B-Bloor Street?"

The passenger doesn't respond.

The man asks a second time and then a third, his stutter getting worse and worse as the passenger continues to ignore him.

Finally, a woman sitting behind them leans forward and advises the man that they have reached Bloor Street. The man thanks her and gets off.

The woman then leans forward again and says to the silent passenger, "That was very rude of you. Why didn't you answer that poor man?"

"L-l-l-lady, you th-th-th-think I want a p-p-p-punch in the f-f-f-face!"

Things You Hear on the GO Train

A Newfoundlander and a guy from Ontario were talking while taking a run on the GO Train to work.

"You guys down in Newfoundland don't have buildings like this," said the Ontarian, looking toward Bay Street.

"Sure we do, b'y," said the Newfoundlander, "'cept we turns them on their sides and calls them shopping malls."

Toronto Tourism

"Tourism Toronto's New Collection of 'Quirky Questions'" was a *press release issued January 15, 2002.*

Tourism Toronto is the Convention Visitors Association for the City of Toronto. Its call centre handles over 200,000 visitor bookings, requests, and inquiries each year. Most callers are interested in booking their vacations and getting information on Toronto, but there are always a few exceptions.

Tourism Toronto's travel counsellors at the call centre are happy to answer any and all questions, including the "quirky questions" they get from time to time. The following are a few of the funny ones the call centre has collected over the past couple of years:

- Do you have a hotel that rents toboggans?
- Is there a dress code in downtown Toronto? Can you wear shorts?
- I would like to stay at the Bank of Montreal Tower; are you able to help me?
- Is Canada considered part of the United States?
- How do you drive in Toronto?
- Is Cirque du Soleil an astronomer?

- Do you celebrate Christmas the same day as in the United States?
- Does Ontario have a plaid?
- Does the currency rate of exchange fluctuate with the change of seasons?
- How do you spell "CN Tower"?
- My wife and I are going to Hanlan's Point for the nude beach. She wants to keep her bottom on; will we be separated if she does?
- Can I have information on the city of Ontario?
- How many hours does it take to drive out to Vancouver? Three or four?

Snail's Pace

A Japanese tourist flies into Vancouver. He takes a taxi to the centre of town. Along the way he observes that everything in British Columbia seems to move at a much slower pace than it does in Tokyo.

Unable to contain himself, he says to the cabbie, "Your taxis are too slow. Japanese taxis go very fast! Look at your buses. They move at a snail's pace. In Japan, buses run like hell! Look at the speed of your motorcycles. Japanese motorcycles barrel along!"

At the end of the journey, the taxi fare has amounted to $70.

"What!" exclaims the furious Japanese tourist. "Your taxi meter runs too fast."

"Yes, why not?" replies the cabbie. "It's made in Japan, after all!"

Performers on Call

20

The "star system" was introduced into the country in 1962 when the federal government, much to the dismay of commercial broadcasters, imposed its Canadian content regulations. Up until that time, cultural organizations—including Canadian Broadcasting Corporation, National Film Board, National Ballet, Canadian Opera Company, National Theatre Company, Canada Council, and some book publishers—had to contend with the fact that the media (and to some degree the public) knew little and cared even less about the talent and indeed the genius of the performers and creators who lived and worked among us. The result has been brand-name recognition across the country for leading creative and performing artists.

Let me offer you the first names of one dozen performing and creative artists and you may supply their last names: Alice, Anne, Atom, Bryan, Céline, David, Glenn, Leonard, Margaret, Michael, Michel, Randy. (That you are able to supply their last names is a result of the effectiveness of the star system and the Canadian content regulations, despite the stiff opposition of private broadcasters at the time and even today.)

The jokes and anecdotes in this chapter are about these creators. They assume that you are familiar with them and their work.

Canadian Content Television

From the internet, October 2002

The Government of Canada is always going on about Canadian content in broadcasting and telecasting. However, we all want to watch American shows.

There is a solution. Put Canadian content into the titles of the programs, leaving the American shows alone, and allow the public to watch them and enjoy them with a clear and patriotic conscience.

Change:

* *Magnum P.I.* to *Magnum P.E.I.*
* *Buffy the Vampire Slayer* to *Buffy St. Marie Vampire Slayer*
* *My Favorite Martian* to *My Favourite Monctonian*
* *Star Trek Voyager* to *Star Trek Voyageur*
* *Deep Space Nine* to *Deep Space Nanaimo*
* *Little House on the Prairie* to *Little House on Portage La Prairie and Main*
* *Rat Patrol* to *Muskrat Patrol*
* *This Old House* to *This Old Igloo*
* *L.A. Law* to *L.A. Law* (with L.A. standing for Lake Athabaska)
* *South Park* to *North Park* (the creators are Canadian, y' know)
* *All the President's Men* to *All the Prime Minister's Men*
* *Cops* to *Mounties*

How Canadian Can You Get?

Radio and television personality Bernie Braden got his start on stage and radio in his native city of Vancouver. He moved to Toronto, where he became a mainstay of CBC Radio, and then to England, where he found fame and fortune as a talk show host, specializing in what he called "chatire."

The English press, unsure what to make of him, kept referring to Bernie Braden as "the Canadian Stephen Leacock."

Who's Who

Ernest (Ernie) Bushnell, the pioneer broadcast executive, was well known and well respected by people in radio and television.

There is a story about how he was introduced to a prairie audience in the 1950s. The chairman of the meeting was suitably impressed with Bushnell's qualifications . . . almost too suitably impressed.

He said, "The best way I can give you an idea of how important Mr. Ernest Bushnell is, is to say his Who's Who is eight inches long!"

Actor's Pun

The distinguished Broadway actor Hume Cronyn was born of "old stock" in London, Ont.

To Londoners that is nothing to be "Cronin" about. Instead they want to know for "Hume" the bell tolls.

Betty Oliphant

Q. What is the one thing that Betty Oliphant and Bobby Orr can never do?
A. Wear monogrammed clothes.

Lorne Greene

Lorne Greene discovered how profitable it was to be a rancher late in life when he was cast as Papa Cartwright in the long-running television series *Bonanza*.

They said of him he was the only rancher with spurs on his slippers.

Mr. Fix-It

Peter Whittall was a regular on CBC Radio's Farm Broadcast. Between 1952 and 1964 he was known as "Mr. Fix-It," the original handyman on radio and then TV. Jack Brickenden recalls this anecdote about his years as a young reporter in Winnipeg in the 1930s in Signing On: The Birth of Radio in Canada *(1982) by Bill McNeil and Morris Wolfe.*

One day he took his wife, who was about to give birth, to hospital and then continued to the CBC to do his broadcast. When he was on the air someone passed him a note saying the baby was born; it was a small girl, weighing only five pounds. Pete read the note on the air and ended with the comment, "I hardly got my seed back," which is a farm expression for a poor crop. It almost cost him his job.

Young Reporter?

A young man leaves his hometown of Sydney, N.S., and heads for Toronto.

Looking for work, he walks into the Toronto Star building. At the time, it was still located on King Street. He asks to see the managing editor, as he has decided he would like to write for Canada's largest newspaper.

The managing editor invites him into his office and asks him, "What experience do you have?"

The young man replies, "I have no particular interests and I have no genuine talents, but I enjoy belittling the artistic endeavours of others."

"Fabulous!" retorts the managing editor. "We just happen to have an opening for a theatre critic."

Newspaper Critic

In his day, Nathan Cohen was the country's leading drama critic. He reviewed all the plays staged by local and travelling companies in his controversial *Toronto Star* column. He also attended musical concerts, though he seldom reviewed these.

He attended a concert by violinist Yehudi Menuhin at Massey Hall. Upon leaving, he was assailed by a local violinist, an impassioned member of the audience.

"Wasn't that a wonderful concert!" the local violinist exclaimed. "Wasn't that superb playing! Wasn't that a great occasion!"

Cohen looked irritated. "Yes," he replied in a measured fashion, "but only if you can stand perfection."

Acting

There is a simple difference between an optimist and a pessimist.

Ask them to name a great Canadian actor.

The optimist says, "Christopher Plummer."

The pessimist says, "William Shatner."

Odd Information Department

Elvis Presley's favourite singer was Anne Murray.

Famous American

Al Waxman, the veteran radio, television, and stage performer, became famous when he created the character of the curmudgeonly merchant Larry King for CBC-TV's *King of Kensington*. A statue was raised in his memory in the adjacent park.

Between 1975 and 1980, one hundred and eleven episodes of the popular television series were shot on location in Toronto's Kensington Market, which is located not all that far from Al's birthplace.

The television series made him instantly recognizable, a true Canadian personality.

He was on location in Kensington Market one day when a shopper recognized him. Approaching him, she identified herself as a Canadian and a fan of the show.

She added, "I hope you enjoy your visit to Canada."

Movie

The Far Shore was the title of the Canadian feature film based on the romantic life of the painter Tom Thomson.

It was said that the film was so poor that patrons had to sit through it four times to get their money's worth.

An Actor in Heaven

A Canadian actor dies and appears before St. Peter, who tells him that he will have to labour for the souls of others for fifteen billion years in purgatory or go straight to Hell for eternity. The actor asks if he can see Heaven and Hell before he makes his decision.

Down they go into Hell. It turns out to be a steamy, dungeon-like kitchen in which actors toil away, shouting food orders, while cooks swear at them and threaten them with kitchen knives and a hulking maître d' tells them to "Hurry! hurry! hurry!"

"No," screams the actor, "that's what my life was like on earth! Show me Heaven!"

Up they fly to Heaven. It turns out to be a steamy, dungeon-like kitchen in which actors toil away, shouting food orders, while cooks swear at them and threaten them with kitchen knives and a hulking maître d' tells them to "Hurry! hurry! hurry!"

"No," screams the actor. "This is the same as Hell. I had enough of that on earth!"

"Oh, no! It is not the same," St. Peter replies. "These actors have agents."

Stratford Festival

The editor of *Frank* magazine dispatched its leading gossip columnist to Stratford to "do a piece" on the actors at the festival. This meant to write about their love lives.

"Give me some background," the gossip columnist said, during the course of an interview with one of the festival's leading romantic actors. "Do you subscribe to the theory, held by some Shakespeare scholars, that Hamlet had a sexual relationship with Ophelia?"

"I have no idea what the Bard had in mind," the actor replied with a leer, "but I usually do."

Stratford Again

In the early days, when the Stratford Festival was still known as the Stratford Shakespearean Festival, there was a dearth of trained actors. The festival's first director, Tyrone Guthrie, and some of its leading actors interviewed everyone who applied for a part.

One applicant was an old man with a thick German accent. He informed Guthrie and the actors, "I vant to be an hectah. I vant to play Hemlet."

"You want to be an actor?" Guthrie boomed. "I am afraid not. Perhaps I could arrange a minor part as an extra. Maybe you could carry a spear."

"No," the old man insisted. "I vant to try for de part of Hemlet."

"Oh, all right," Guthrie agreed. "Go ahead, do 'Hemlet.'"

Guthrie and the actors leaned back in their seats as the old man stepped on to the stage. Then, in a deep voice, speaking English in dulcet tones, as if he were "to the manor born," he began his recitation of Hamlet's famous soliloquy:

To be, or not to be, that is the question,
Whether 'tis nobler . . .

Guthrie and the leading actors looked on in astonishment. They maintained total silence as the old man held them spellbound.

When he recited the last lines of the soliloquy, Guthrie exclaimed, "That's fantastic!"

"No," the old man replied in his thick accent, "dat's ecting!"

The Ungilded Lillie

She was called "the funniest woman in the world." Noël Coward, friend and collaborator, regarded her as "the greatest comedian in the world."

Beatrice Lillie referred to herself as "the ungilded lily." It was a pun on her name—and perhaps also on her modest birth in Toronto.

She attended Gladstone Avenue School, along with the young Gladys Smith, later Mary Pickford, when the principal of the school was Alexander Muir, the composer of "The Maple Leaf Forever." While still a youngster, she sang and danced with her sister and mother on the city's stages.

She crossed the Atlantic (with her mother) and made her London debut in variety in 1914, and then recrossed the

Atlantic and made her Broadway debut in burlesque in 1924. Thereafter she was, as they say, the "toast" of two continents, and she saw her name on marquees of the West End and Broadway for close to half a century.

When she married England's Sir Robert Peel in 1920, she became Lady Peel. Socialites said she would now be "a Lady in her own wrong." Kenneth Tynan suggested that this was placing a halo on the head of a hurricane.

P.L. Travers said, "You are Mary Poppins." Noël Coward created the part for her of the mad spiritualist Madame Arcati in *Blithe Spirit*. Patrick Dennis modelled the lead in *Auntie Mame* on Bea.

Robert Benchley once quipped, "If we never had Beatrice Lillie, we might better never have been born."

Beatrice Lillie titled her memoirs *Every Other Inch a Lady* (1972). On the last page of that amusing book, she recalls an incident that involved her dog, a Pekinese.

"My first London Peke, Ming-Ki Poo, once was with me in a taxi on our way to the Savoy when I sensed that something was happening on one of my gloves and saw a little trickle on the leather seat. The driver must have seen what had happened, too. Looking back as the doorman helped me out at the revolving doors of the hotel, he jumped out of the cab.

"'Now, then. What do you mean by letting your dog mess in my taxi?' he demanded.

"I turned to him, every inch a lady and at least six feet tall. I pressed a handsome tip into his grimy hand. 'I did it,' I said, and swept into the lobby."

Lillie felt quite at sea on the luxury ocean liners that ploughed the Atlantic between the two world wars.

Departing London aboard the *Queen Mary*, she looked around and quipped, "When does this place get to New York?"

Timothy Findley was a young, aspiring actor learning the trade in London in the 1950s. He recalls in his memoirs how one day he entered a lift at Fortnum & Mason's. On the next floor a strikingly tall woman wearing an extravagant dress and dark sunglasses entered and ignored him.

It took a moment for Findley to recognize Beatrice Lillie. He stared at her in wonderment and was opening his mouth to address her when she raised her glasses, stared at him for a second, and said, "No, thank you." Then she lowered her glasses and ignored him until he stepped off the lift.

Findley could think of nothing to say!

CBC Announcing School

Instructor: I understand you went to a special school for help in curing your stuttering. How did it go?

Trainee: Peter Piper picked a peck of pickled peppers!

Instructor: That's excellent!

Trainee: S-s-sure. B-b-but it's r-r-really d-d-difficult t-t-to w-w-work into a c-c-conversation.

Wayne and Shuster

Nobody in comedy is likely to break or even match the record for longevity and popularity established by the comedy team of Wayne and Shuster.

Johnny Wayne (the short one) and Frank Shuster (the tall one) had a remarkable career that extended from 1941 to 1989. They created their own material and performed highly inventive skits on CBC Radio and then CBC-TV. They were a great hit with Ed Sullivan, who invited them to perform on his Sunday-night television show more often than any other single performer—on close to 60 occasions. (Sullivan called them his "Canuck egghead comics.")

Back at the CBC, they had their own office in one of the corporation's Yonge Street locations. Two doors, each with its own number, led into their single office.

One door said: "1224 – Wayne & Shuster."

The other door said: "1226 – Shuster & Wayne."

Amusing Pun

Johnny Wayne and Frank Shuster were known to work and rework the scripts of their radio or television skits until their humour was finely honed. Witness "The Siege of Troy," one of their most memorable TV skits.

No sooner have the Trojans wheeled the wooden horse into the Trojan camp than a voice is heard asking the following question:

"Is there a doctor in the horse?"

Comics on Humour

Frank Shuster, the tall half of the comedy team of Wayne and Shuster, was interviewed by journalist Ed Gould. During the course of the interview, Shuster revealed the secret of their success. It had to do with their nationality and the subject of their comedy:

"The basis of our humour is Canadian. We find that the thing that unites Canadians everywhere is that they all detest Toronto!"

Sir Ernest MacMillan

Sir Ernest MacMillan was the renowned organist, composer, and conductor of the Toronto Symphony Orchestra and the Mendelssohn Choir. But he was not always recognized on the streets of Toronto.

One day he was stopped by a young man, a tourist, who asked him, "How do I get to Massey Hall?"

Sir Ernest replied, "Practise, my boy, practise."

Maestro MacMillan

Sir Ernest MacMillan was the most widely respected musician in the country. For many decades he was the conductor of the Toronto Symphony Orchestra.

Once, when one of the musicians complained that one of the scores was too difficult to play because part of the orchestra was to play in 4/4 time and the other in 6/4 time, he soothed them by saying, "Well, those playing in 4/4 watch my right hand, and those in 6/4 watch my left."

Glenn Gould

Glenn Gould was Canada's most celebrated eccentric. His eccentricities were recognized—and appreciated—throughout the world of music.

Before he played Brahms's Piano Concerto in D Minor with the New York Philharmonic Orchestra, the conductor, Leonard Bernstein, made a general announcement: "This is the Glenn Gould Brahms Concerto."

The reason for the warning became apparent. In the words of pianist and wit Oscar Levant in *The Unimportance of Being Oscar* (1968): "Gould gave a very languid interpretation to this pretentious work . . . his rendition established a world's record. It lasted fifteen minutes longer than any previous playing.

"Afterward Irving Kolodin, the music editor of the *Saturday Review*, asked Gould why he had done it that way. He replied: 'I felt very baroque.'"

Musical Prodigy

Glenn Gould was a musical prodigy.

He once told an interviewer, "I was always precocious and prolific.

"At three I composed a minuet.

"At four I wrote a symphony.

"And at five I finished a complete opera.

"And at five-thirty, as usual, I went into the kitchen and drank a cup of tea."

Glenn Again

Gould was no fan of the music of Wolfgang Amadeus Mozart. It irritated Gould that Mozart had died at such a young age. (He was only thirty-five years old at the time of his death. Gould himself would die in his fifty-first year.)

It was with some viciousness, according to teacher and accompanist William Aide, that Gould exclaimed as follows:

"It's not that Mozart died too soon; he died too late."

Gould Yet Again

Early in his musical career, when he still toured and performed as a concert pianist, Glenn Gould was taken to one side by fellow pianist Artur Rubinstein.

Rubinstein offered the young pianist this piece of advice: "When you travel, you must always stay at *grande de luxe* hotels. That is the only way to make travelling bearable."

"Hotels?" Gould replied. "I'm a motel man myself."

Gould No More

Someone once recommended that the following couplet, with its delightful pun, serve as the epitaph for Glenn Gould. (It refers to the pianist's habit of humming while playing and recording.)

How strangely silent now this peaceful Glenn,
Only a distant mumble now and then.

Modern Music

Perhaps it was Anna Russell, the musical comedienne and long-time Ontario resident, who first memorably quipped, "Opera isn't always as bad as it sounds."

Dire Straits

The rock group Dire Straits was in Toronto to make a video. The musicians went to the Metro Zoo and told the official that they needed some animals for their video. They wanted the zoo to let them use some rabbits and chimpanzees.

"How much will it cost?" the lead singer asked.

The official said, "It is such an honour to be able to help out a great rock band, there will be no charge at all."

"Great," said the lead singer. "Bunnies for nothin' and the chimps are free."

Mamas and Papas

John Densmore of the Mamas and the Papas rock group told the following story while being interviewed on CBC Radio's *Morningside*.

He and the other members of the group were at a house party in London. The Beatles had been invited, and they were expected to make an appearance. Though Densmore was a pop star himself, he was excited at the prospect of meeting the Fab Four.

Then John Lennon arrived, and the Papa went up to him. Almost simultaneously, the two of them said, "Aren't you—?"

Then Lennon added, "Yes, I suppose we are."

Shania Twain

Shania Twain throws a party for six hundred of her loyal fans. It is held in the largest auditorium in Timmins, Ont.

It is a great success. At the height of the festivities, Neil Young, flying in from Los Angeles on his private jet, enters the crowded auditorium. Shania is so excited she yells out, "Neil!"

All six hundred of her devoted fans kneel down.

Paul McCartney

In Paul McCartney's movie *Give My Regards to Broadstreet*, there is a scene in which Paul's band is going to practise in what appears to be a cold, dank warehouse.

Ringo Starr quips, "Can we get some heat in here? Or are we practising to be Canadians?"

THE WRITTEN WORD

21

Authors and writers are so articulate that it is only right to grant them a chapter all to themselves. They deserve it.

Whereas authors produce books, those I refer to as "writers" adapt words for use in other media; they work as publicists, journalists, columnists, correspondents, editors, critics, commentators, and so on. Our scribes, to a considerable degree, invented and, from time to time, revive or at least revivify the national spirit of Canada.

The jokes and anecdotes here range from the fine arts to unrefined news reports from the popular press.

Mr. Massey and Mr. Harris

Here's an amusing anecdote about diplomat Vincent Massey, artist Lawren Harris, bureaucrat Brooke Claxton, and the naming of the Massey Commission. I have it courtesy the late Louis Applebaum, "The Mermaid Inn," The Globe and Mail, November 20, 1982.

There's a story about Vincent Massey and his arts commission that should be recorded for posterity. I heard it from Guy Sylvestre, our

355

esteemed national librarian in Ottawa, who assures me that it can be verified by Jack Pickersgill, a former Liberal cabinet minister.

The story goes back to the mid-1950s, when Dr. Sylvestre was secretary to Louis St. Laurent. Vincent Massey had returned to Canada about a year earlier after a period of distinguished service as British High Commissioner.

The idea of a commission to study the arts and sciences had been percolating its way through the government while Mr. Massey waited in his Port Hope, Ont., home for a call to further service in Ottawa. After considering other possible appointees, the government eventually arranged a marriage between Mr. Massey's interests and its own with the decision to create the Commission on National Development in the Arts, Letters and Sciences, with Mr. Massey as chairman.

A list of possible commissioners to join Mr. Massey was then drawn up for consideration by Brooke Claxton, a former chairman of the Canada Council. From the beginning, artist Lawren Harris figured high on the list.

A member of the Group of Seven, Harris had achieved great prominence; he was an ardent and effective spokesperson for the arts and was a former chairman of the Canadian Arts Council (now the Canadian Conference of the Arts), which had pressed energetically for the idea of just such a government initiative. Harris was considered a natural for the assignment and his nomination seemed assured.

When Mr. Claxton saw the short list of nominees, he immediately struck Harris from the list. In response to the outcry from his colleagues, Mr. Claxton said: "This is impossible. Can you imagine having an arts inquiry that everyone is sure to call the Massey-Harris Commission?"

Given that both Vincent Massey and Lawren Harris were descendants of the two families that in the early 1890s had merged their large farm-implement companies, Mr. Claxton could be excused for worrying about waggish comments prompted by the juxtaposition of these two prominent Canadian names.

Arts Report

Appointed to chair the Federal Cultural Policy Review Committee were Montreal publisher Jacques Hébert and Toronto arts administrator Louis Applebaum.

The committee's report was expected to assist the government in its dealings with Canadian cultural expression and the Americanization of the entertainment media.

Even before it was released in 1982, it was dubbed (after the names of the commissioners) the "Applebert" Report. But upon its release, it was judged to be a disaster, so the press redubbed it the "H-baum" Report.

Mazo de la Roche

Ron Hambleton, biographer of Mazo de la Roche, tells this story about the author of the Jalna novels, her cousin and companion Caroline Clement, and man-of-letters Kildare Dobbs.

During the 1950s Mazo sent a short story to *Tamarack* (a Toronto literary quarterly) through one of its editors, Kildare Dobbs, who was then also an editor for her Canadian publishers. Dobbs thought the story embarrassing, for it dealt with a topic of which Mazo was ignorant: in terms both sinister and suggestive, she described a convict coming out of prison after twenty years and his reunion with his daughter.

At the editorial meeting Dobbs was asked to return it, which he did, saying that the editors did not like it much. He then received this reply: "I'm not surprised that you didn't like the story. Caroline didn't like it, and I didn't like it very much myself, but as I've never liked any of the stories in *Tamarack*, I thought it might do very well."

Dobbs considered the matter closed, but some weeks later Mazo's son Ren revealed that she had been surprised that Dobbs had not responded. She wondered, "Hasn't Mr. Dobbs a sense of humour?" She might have said, rather, a sense of irony, which in ordinary conversation she herself used skilfully as part of her armour against the bewildering world in which she earned her living.

Yeats and Leacock

W.B. Yeats agreed to meet some Canadian writers in his room at the Ritz-Carlton Hotel in Montreal during his visit to the city in 1932. The poet R.G. Everson agreed to handle the introductions.

When Stephen Leacock arrived, Everson introduced Leacock to Yeats by saying, "Dr. Leacock, professor of economics."

Leacock, wanting to establish his credentials as a published author, said quickly, "I write too."

"A pity," Yeats replied. "So few read."

Stephen Leacock

For many years Stephen Leacock was renowned and respected as a professor of economics who taught at McGill University. It was only in the latter half of his life that he gained fame as a humorist and public speaker.

Shortly after he earned his doctorate in political economy from the University of Chicago, he signed his name with pride on the register of the vessel that was taking him to Europe: "Dr. Stephen Leacock."

During the voyage, a steward rapped on the door of his cabin and asked him, "Are you Dr. Leacock?"

The humorist allowed that he was, and the steward asked him if he would be willing to examine the stewardess's leg.

"Realizing my obligations," Leacock recalled in one of his essays, "I was off like a shot. But no luck! Another fellow got there ahead of me. He was a doctor of divinity."

Earle Birney

Earle Birney, the poet and sometime professor of English at the University of British Columbia, is the author of the narrative poem "David," about an incident that occurs while David and the narrator are climbing a mountain.

Birney maintains that two colleagues told him they overheard the following conversation between two freshmen during fall registration in the 1950s.

"I'm really gonna be sunk in English. You know whose section they put me in?"

"No. Whose?"

"Birney's."

"Who's he?"

"The guy that wrote 'David.'"

"David, who's he?"

"Yuh dope. It's a poem, you had it in Grade 10. He's the son of a bitch who pushed his best friend off a cliff."

"Jeez, you better git a transfer."

The Dog at the Movies

An usher in a movie theatre saw a man and a dog sitting together, watching the film. The dog seemed to be totally wrapped up in the story.

"That's amazing," said the usher. "To see a dog so interested in a movie."

"I'm surprised, too," said the man. "He didn't like the book at all."

Farley Mowat

Farley Mowat, author and adventurer, has travelled through the world writing about its remote locations and their inhabitants. At parties he is inclined to talk at length about his treks through wilderness areas and describe in detail the places he has been, the people he has met, and the things he has done.

At one point he told a group of people at a gathering, "I stood on the rim of the volcano and stared down into its flaming mouth. It was like looking into the very bowels of Hell!"

One young listener raised an eyebrow and said, "My, but you have been everywhere!"

Bard of the Yukon

Q. What is the only way to get a message through to the author of the ballad "The Shooting of Dan McGrew"?
A. Wire service.

John Kenneth Galbraith

John Kenneth Galbraith, the celebrated Ontario-born economist and author, was interviewed on the eve of his ninety-fourth birthday. The interviewer was William Keegan, and he wrote his impressions of the man in the article "Man for All Markets," Guardian Weekly, October 10, 2002. He quoted some of Galbraith's salty observations.

- He referred to his celebrated book *The Affluent Society*, currently out of print: "Things are bad enough so that I haven't noticed any great revival of interest in that book. Perhaps I should have a new edition with a new title. It could be *The Depressed Economy*, and it would face the fact that only a reduced colony of booklovers could afford to buy it."

- He would peruse bookshops to see how his titles were doing. He noticed that one title was never on sale in the old La Guardia Airport in New York. "One night the woman in charge asked me what I was looking for. I was a little ashamed, but came out with the title, *The Great Crash*. She never hesitated: 'That certainly is not a book you could sell at an airport.'"

- *"The Great Crash* has been in print since the mid-1950s, and it still outsells all of my other books. It has a wonderful, built-in salesmanship: Any time anyone complains as to what he or she is suffering in the stock market, there is someone who always says, 'If you think that is bad, why don't you read Galbraith on 1929?'"

- He was appointed American ambassador to India by U.S. president John F. Kennedy: "First he would call me up to ask what to do. Then to tell me what he was doing. Then he would not call me at all."

Editor

A Toronto magazine editor received a story with a letter that said, "If you can't use my story, return it immediately, as I have other irons in the fire."

He sent it back with a note that said, "Remove irons from fire. Put in story."

Star Acquisition

I have this story from David MacDonald, chronicler of the history of the Toronto Star.

In a news release dated October 15, 1975, the publisher of the *Toronto Star* announced that it had acquired Harlequin Enterprises Ltd. The newspaper paid $30 million for the paperback publishing company.

Reporter and correspondent Gerald Utting was not amused. On reading the news release, he wrote the following mock bulletin and posted it on the bulletin board in the *Star's* newsroom:

"The world's largest purveyor of romantic fiction has just been acquired by the world's largest purveyor of romantic fiction."

Heavenly Reward

A writer dies and wakes up to find himself standing in front of the Pearly Gates listening to St. Peter.

"Welcome to Heaven!" says St. Peter. "We have read all your books here and we believe that you are a good writer as well as a good man. So I am happy to inform you that you will be admitted to Heaven, should you choose to reside here for the rest of eternity."

"Where else could I reside?" asks the writer cautiously.

"Why, you could choose to spend the rest of eternity in the Other Place—Hell."

"It's unlikely that I would choose to do that. So show me around Heaven, please."

"Easily done," says St. Peter. So saying, he swings open the Pearly Gates and ushers the writer into Heaven. The Elysian Fields extend before them. In the distance St. Peter points out a resort community.

"Over there is our writers' colony," says St. Peter. "We call it Indigo Place. Let's take a look around."

They are soon there and the writer looks around with incredulity. Here are hundreds of happy-looking writers with pens and pencils and pads of papers, computers and printers, even photocopiers, each with his or her own suite of rooms with a patio that looks out over the heavenly fields.

"I would like to reside here for the rest of eternity," says the writer.

"Not so fast," replies St. Peter. "Before you make up your mind, you have to see what Hell has to offer."

The writer looks dubious but in a flash he is teleported to the Gates of Hell. Standing before the gates is Satan himself, with a sardonic grin on his face.

"Welcome to Hell," gloats Satan, waving his trident. "Before you say anything at all, let me assure you that St. Peter has informed me that you are a writer, and a good one, as well as a good man, and that you are here only to look around. After that you will have to make up your mind where you want to reside for the rest of eternity."

With that, Satan leads the somewhat reluctant writer through the Gates of Hell. To the writer's surprise, the scene that greets his eyes is the same scene he saw in Heaven. Elysian-like fields extend before them, and in the distance he sees a resort community.

"Over there is our writers' colony," says Satan. "We call it Indigo Place, as they do in Heaven. Let us take a look around."

They are soon there and the writer looks on with incredulity. Here are hundreds of happy-looking writers with pens and pencils and pads of papers, computers and printers, even photo-copiers, each with his or her own suite of rooms with a patio that looks out over the heavenly fields.

The writer exclaims, "It looks ideal, but there doesn't seem to be any difference between what a writer can expect in Heaven and what a writer can expect in Hell."

Satan smirks and waves his trident. With that, the writer is teleported back to the Pearly Gates.

"Well, now," says St. Peter. "You have seen what Heaven has to offer. You have seen what Hell has to offer. Where do you wish to reside for the rest of eternity?"

The writer shakes his head. "I can see no difference between eternal life in Heaven and infernal life in Hell. I could live in equal comfort in Indigo Place in Heaven or in Indigo Place in Hell. I did not spot a single difference between them. Is there a difference?"

"Why, yes, there is," replies St. Peter.

"What is that?"

"In Hell," replies St. Peter, "the writers think they are going to be published."

Michael Wardell and the *Daily Gleaner*

I am grateful to retired journalist and writer George Hancocks for telling me this story about his experience as a Canadian Press wire-service operator in 1956. It sheds light on the interests of Brigadier Michael Wardell, confidant of Lord Beaverbrook and autocratic publisher of the Fredericton Daily Gleaner.

My first job on leaving university was as a wire editor for the Canadian Press in Toronto. I was what they called the east TTS operator (short for teletype-setter). It was my job to edit down the thousands of words from the CP log so they would fit into short sections of a daily newspaper with the (CP) byline on them.

On taking over the east TTS job, one of the dailies I fed was the *Fredericton Daily Gleaner*, Brig. Wardell's paper.

The time was 1956. I was a rookie news reporter and editor. Suddenly, everything stopped in the newsroom, then bells began ringing like mad. That was my first experience with the "bells"— news that brings newsrooms to a halt and instantly turns the Fourth Estate in the direction of the Events at Hand. This particular event was the joint British and French invasion of Suez in Egypt.

In a flash I stopped my wire transmissions to the Maritime dailies and sent this bulletin: "Flash. Combined British and French forces invade Suez." I was sure in my belief that this was stop-press news, and that every Maritime paper would want to carry it.

I had not reckoned with the *Fredericton Daily Gleaner*. My standing instructions for the paper was that no matter what happened, I was to continue the daily "run" of stock quotations from the Toronto stock market. On my own initiative I interrupted the run and sent this message to the *Gleaner*:

"Combined British and French forces have invaded Suez. Major international war in the offing. Developments coming rapidly. Do you want me to continue the stock run?"

After a few moments, I received the following message: "Continue stock run. Wardell."

Celebrity

A movie star visiting Toronto suddenly took ill and had to be hospitalized. She did not want any details appearing in the newspapers, so she told her security people to keep reporters away from her. The papers, of course, got wind of it, and decided they'd try to get by the security.

The editor of the *Toronto Star* had one of his reporters dress up as a nurse and go to the hospital to get the story. She was back in the office an hour later. "That was fast," said the editor. "Did you get the story?"

"No," she replied. "I was sent home by the doctor from *The Globe and Mail.*"

Funniest Line?

Peter C. Newman has written many books on contemporary politics and business leaders, as well as innumerable columns of opinion for newspapers and magazines. During the course of an exchange of e-mails, I asked him if he had a funniest line. On November 13, 2002, he replied in the affirmative and offered one of his bons mots:

"I've always thought that my funniest line came from a piece I did after visiting Hollywood, where I wandered around Malibu, the film colony's seaside adult playpen. 'What makes Malibu unique,' I reported at the time, 'is that it has no blacks and no brunettes.'"

Message or Massage?

Communications theorist Marshall McLuhan is identified globally with his famous formulation, "The medium is the message." But then he went on to say, "The medium is the massage."

About the origin of that variation, I have the following story from Mark Federman, chief strategist, McLuhan Management Studies, McLuhan Program in Culture and Technology at the University of

Toronto. It concerns both Marshall and his son, Eric. Mark gave it to me following an appearance at the ideaCity conference in Toronto, June 21, 2002. I am grateful to him for sharing it with me and with my readers.

The story for public consumption with regard to "The Medium is the Massage" always has to do with "a medium working us over," as Marshall was wont to say. Everyone took it for one of the bad puns for which Marshall was infamous. But just recently, indeed it was within the last two months, Eric McLuhan told me what he claimed to be the real story behind it.

We were in Corinne McLuhan's home in Wychwood Park at the time, in the doorway that leads from the kitchen to the hall on the main floor, when Eric asked, "Do you want to know how that title really came about?" Then Eric related this story.

They were in New York at the time, and Marshall had been expecting the proofs of what was going to be the (interim) follow-on to *Understanding Media*, called *The Medium is the Message*, to arrive from the publisher. According to Eric, Marshall was becoming a little perturbed that his famous paradox was becoming—or perhaps more correctly, had become—a cliché.

The package came, and when Marshall unwrapped it and looked at the cover proof, he burst out laughing. The typesetter had mistakenly substituted an "a" for an "e" in "message," giving him the probe and a whole new twist to the aphorism.

He apparently said, "This is wonderful! A medium works us over like a good masseuse. This is perfect!"

So McLuhan adopted the remark "The medium is the massage."

He also punned, on yet another occasion, "The medium is the mess-age." I often wonder about the story of that variant.

McLuhan's Celebrated Quip

Mention the name Marshall McLuhan and what comes to mind is his celebrated aphorism "The medium is the message."

But remember that McLuhan was a Canadian, Edmonton-born to boot. What he meant to say was "The median is the message."

The Bicycle Built for Two

Marshall McLuhan was so remarkable a man that his thinking impressed even the youngster who delivered the daily newspaper to the McLuhan household. The following true story was told to me by that former newspaper delivery boy, now a respected journalist in Toronto.

Marshall and his wife, Corinne, raised their one son and four daughters in Wychwood Park, a lovely residential area of Toronto. For their amusement the family owned a tandem bicycle—a bicycle built for two. To be neighbourly, they made it available for the use of youngsters in the area.

McLuhan laid down one regulation: "I will loan it to any three youngsters who ask me if they can borrow it."

"Why three youngsters?" asked the paperboy. "Only two youngsters can ride it at any one time."

"That's right," McLuhan replied, "but I want them to learn how democracy works."

McLuhanism

Q. What do you call McLuhan's book on Euripides?
A. *The Medea is the Message.*

Telegram

In the days before e-mail, facsimile, and low long-distance telephone rates, messages to distant cities were sent by telegram.

Marshall McLuhan decided to send a telegram to a friend who had a dog. He went to the telegraph office and filled out the form. The message read: "Woof. Woof. Woof. Woof. Woof. Woof. Woof. Woof. Woof."

The telegraph clerk took the form, examined it, shook his head, and said, "May I make a suggestion? There are only nine words in your message. The charge is based on ten words. You could send another 'Woof' for the same price."

McLuhan replied, "That would make no sense at all."

McLuhan Bested

Characteristic of the anecdotes that are told about the late Marshall McLuhan, founder of the Centre for Culture and Technology at the University of Toronto, is that he says the most outrageous things, that he makes the most insightful points, and that he does so in the most preposterous ways imaginable. Here is one anecdote (a true one, as it happens) in which he does not have the last word.

C.C. (Kelly) Gotlieb, computer scientist and founder of the university's computer science department, admired McLuhan but felt that the so-called guru of the electronic age knew nothing at all about science and hardly anything at all about computer technology, which in the 1960s was a much discussed subject. Kelly briefly headed the Centre for Culture and Technology.

Kelly surprised McLuhan by asking him, "Do you know what GIGO means?"

"Certainly," McLuhan replied. "It's a computer term and it means Garbage In, Garbage Out."

"No," replied Gotlieb, "it means, Garbage In, Gospel Out."

For once, McLuhan was wordless.

Bear

Marian Engel created a sensation when she published a short novel about a woman who falls in love with . . . and into the arms of . . . a bear. It was titled, appropriately, *Bear*.

Local wits thought it was misnamed. Don Harron quipped that it could be retitled *On Top of Old Smoky* or *A Grizzly Piece*.

Joey Slinger thought it should be called *Gently Ben*.

Engel's novel is something of a folktale, written with deftness and drama. The experience of reading it is not, in the least, unbearable.

Gaffes

Thomas H. Raddall complained about the ignorance and heedlessness shown by copywriters employed by publishers. He wrote in *In My Time: A Memoir* (1976):

"Doubleday's blurb on the jacket of *The Governor's Lady* declared that I lived in Halifax, that one of my books was entitled *Nova Scotia, Warden of the North*, and that Nova Scotia was an island. I got hilarious letters."

For the record, Raddall lived in Liverpool, not Halifax; his book *Warden of the North* was a study of Halifax, not Nova Scotia; and Nova Scotia is part of the mainland, not an island like Prince Edward Island or Newfoundland.

First Child

When Margaret Atwood gave birth to a daughter in 1976, she received many notes of congratulations. As well, she received bouquets of flowers from her publishers in New York City and Toronto.

The former sent her a bouquet with the message: "Babies are Better."

The latter sent a bouquet with a message that read: "Best Wishes for a Speedy Recovery." (The Toronto publisher maintains it was all a mistake.)

Group of Seven (or Eleven!)

If you count them, you will find that the Group of Seven consists of eleven painters, not seven. As someone observed, they were great at drawing but poor at counting.

The funniest tribute to the group is the following routine of Don Harron's. He was performing as Charlie Farquharson, the hayseed from Owen Sound, on a radio commercial for the Art Gallery of Ontario in 1974:

"I'd like to get down and look at them pictures of barns and outbuildings done by them fellas that used to paint by numbers—what they call yer grope of seven. Tom Thomson, Jack Jackson, John Johnson, and Jim Jimson. Now that'd be the kinda culture I could take."

Film Censorship

Film censorship is practised by all the provinces. Over the last century, Ontario's censor board has gone from being iron-handed to being broad-minded.

Mary Brown, Ontario's chief movie and video censor in the 1980s, was one of the restrictive ones. She was often ridiculed in print, but never so well as in the following couplet:

She scissorses all explicit sex,
North of knees and south of neck.

Poetry Reading

The Ottawa poet Duncan Campbell Scott liked to tell the story of how Mackenzie King, after inviting him to read his poetry at a literary evening at Kingsmere, first hushed the company to listen as his little dog Pat beat out a series of horrible discords on the piano, and then turned brightly to the elderly poet, saying, "Now, Scott, it's your turn."

Scott told the story to the portrait photographer Yousuf Karsh, who recalled it for Sandra Gwyn, who recorded it in her book *The Private Capital: Ambition and Love in the Age of Macdonald and Laurier* (1984).

The Corporation

In broadcasting circles a reference to The Corporation is a reference to the Canadian Broadcasting Corporation, the largest public broadcasting service in the world.

Radio likes to regard itself as "the senior service."

Radio broadcasters dismiss television as "radio with pictures."

Radio producers say that television is a "medium" because so little of it is rare or well done.

Radio writers maintain that CBC Television is having a beneficial educational effect. It is driving people to read books.

CBC Radio may be bad but it is bad in a unique way. As one commentator said (adapting a witticism identified with Canadian-born English TV critic Milton Shulman), "It is the least-worst radio in the country."

Little Things

Little things make one's day, the day being Wednesday, March 14, 2001.

Walking past Frontier College on Jackes Avenue just off Yonge Street in Toronto, I decided to investigate the rumour that there was a new condominium complex located behind the college that includes designs or decorations associated with the great innovative American architect Frank Lloyd Wright.

I knew that Wright has some Canadian connections, but I also knew that these were pretty minimal.

I did not have far to go. Outside the building on a tiny island of grass I saw three columns of decorated concrete. They were standing erect, like bulrushes, only larger. Each column is in effect the elongated form of a woman with a rectangular head topped with a triangle.

Each figure looked totally heartless. Together the figures looked merciless, like furies. The figures and their decorations all bore the hallmarks of Wright. They are too uncompromising in conception and completion to be the work of a student of Wright's design.

I entered the condominium's foyer and spoke briefly with the concierge, who had eyed me suspiciously until I identified myself as a passerby and inquired about the statues out front.

"Who designed them?" I asked innocently, waving my arm in their general direction. They were visible through the front windows of the foyer.

"Those statues?" he replied.

"Yes."

"They are the work of a famous artist."

"Yes. Who is he?"

"His name is Andrew Lloyd Wright," the concierge assured me, proudly. "He did them for a Chicago exposition many years ago."

I thanked him and then walked out of the condominium to admire them again. These columnar women with the fierce eyes! All the while I was disentangling the names of Andrew Lloyd Webber (composer of the musical *Evita* and others) and Frank Lloyd Wright (Prairie School architect).

Somewhere in this semantic muddle there might be found lurking the names of Sam Loyd, the puzzle king, and the silent movie comedian Frank Lloyd (or is it Harold Lloyd)?

Literary Fame

The solemn dramas and laboured poems of Charles Heavysege (1816–1876) of Montreal were so highly praised during their creator's lifetime that the public could be forgiven for concluding that Heavysege was a literary heavyweight. The only question to ask was this one: Was he one of the greatest writers of all time, or only the greatest of his time?

The question was answered by a dissenting literary critic, who proclaimed, "He is a writer whose books will be read long after Shakespeare, Wordsworth, and Longfellow are forgotten. But not before."

Time and Dalton Camp

Dalton Camp, advertising executive, Conservative thinker, and newspaper columnist, tells of the conversation he had with an unnamed correspondent for Time *magazine in his autobiography* Gentlemen, Players and Politicians *(1970). It took place when he was a young man considering employment with the news magazine.*

Over a highball he looks at me and says, "How do you think you would like it, working for *Time?*"

I tell him I think I might like it a lot. "How do you like it?" I ask.

"Oh, I like it."

"What's it like?" I ask him.

"Well," he says, thoughtfully, "it's like working in the world's finest whorehouse."

CBC Script

At a party a CBC Radio producer encounters the freelance writer whom he commissioned to produce the script for a mystery series.

Producer: So how are you getting on with the script of the mystery drama that you're writing for my series?

Writer: Well, I've been through three drafts over the last three months and it's still not quite right.

Producer: I guess it's a case of all work and no play!

Titles Canadian and American

Literary agent Beverley Slopen likes to recount the following incident that amusingly highlights the different approaches taken by Canadian and American publishers to book titles and promotion, even for the same book. In passing, she mentions one of her clients, Morley Torgov, ready wit and prize-winning novelist.

I was selling U.S. rights to Judylaine Fine's book *Your Guide to Coping with Back Pain.* That was the title the Canadian publisher McClelland & Stewart used.

We had at least two offers in the U.S., but one American publisher (the one we went with) said they wanted to change the title to *Conquering Back Pain.*

I happened to be speaking to Morley just after I received the call from the U.S. editor. I said, "See, that's the difference between Canadians and Americans: Canadians cope, Americans conquer."

Morley said, "Sure. If Julius Caesar had been a Canadian, he would have said, 'I came, I saw, I coped.' If Oliver Goldsmith had been a Canadian, his play would be titled *She Stoops to Cope.*"

National Literary Expression

Four literary scholars are conversing over drinks after a day at an international meeting. As the drinks begin to take effect, the British expert begins bragging.

"Britain produced the finest form of national literary expression in the sonnet," he says. "It's fourteen lines of perfect romantic expression."

The Irish scholar retorts, "Ireland produced a far more effective and efficient literary form in the limerick. In just five lines,
we can express a variety of thoughts, many of them making fun
of you English."

The Japanese savant calmly says, "In Japan we have perfected
literary expression in the haiku. We express the most profound
concepts in just three lines and seventeen syllables."

The Canadian jumps up and says, "Well, we can beat that.
We've perfected communication with a one-unit literary form,
and we've covered our entire country with it. It's the printing on
the bilingual milk carton."

Nobel Who?

The novelist Robertson Davies used to tell of the response at a
reception in British Columbia when the news came that Lester
B. Pearson, later to be prime minister of Canada, had been
awarded the Nobel Peace Prize.

"Well!" someone said. "Who does he think he is!"

Northrop Frye

Northrop Frye died in 1991, but the man's contribution to literary and social criticism is immense, and his influence is certain
to be valued and re-valued throughout the twenty-first century.

He served in turn as professor, president, and chancellor of
Victoria College, University of Toronto. Generations of his
students are known variously as "Fryedolators," "Fryegians," and
"Small Fryes." They speak of attending "Frye High."

They add, "'Frye' is a four-letter word, not to be spoken lightly!"

According to Peter Yan, a former student and fan, Frye is a
critic for all seasons. He explains:

"The renowned semiologist Roland Barthes is really deep
down a French Frye, as his mythology is what Frye calls an
applied mythology or ideology.

"Deconstruction is Frye's theory in reverse, as Frye shows unity among differences in literature, while deconstructivists show difference among unity.

"Frye is a post-structuralist, reversing the hierarchy of literature over criticism, as Frye inadvertently made literary criticism and literary critics as celebrated as literature and literary writers.

"Frye is the ultimate 'both-and' post-modernist, as his work fuses both the sacred and the secular, mythos and logos, art and social science, literary theory and imaginative vision . . .

"Frye's writing is the operating system adaptable to any platform, the ultimate shareware, the great code which builds upon old programs and allows you to write new ones."

As Yan notes, visitors to Victoria College often pause when climbing the steps to read the inscription above the entranceway: "The Truth Shall Make You Free."

Frye's students have interpreted this to read: "The Truth Shall Make You Frye."

Mordecai Richler and the CJC

The speaker is Mordecai Richler, a native of Montreal, who was being interviewed in Jerusalem by Sam Orbaum, also a native of Montreal but a resident of Jerusalem, in "Make 'em Mad, Mordecai Richler!" Jerusalem Post Magazine, November 6, 1992.

I was enormously helpful to the Canadian Jewish Congress (CJC) about twenty-five years ago.

I received a letter from them, and it said on the letterhead, "Cable Address JEWCON."

So I phoned them and said, "Listen, if I put this on an envelope, you guys are going to attack me as a self-hating Jew. How can you have a cable address like JEWCON?"

Anyway, they changed it.

Irving Layton vs. Patrick White

Patrick White, the Australian novelist, hosted Irving Layton and his Australian-born wife, Aviva, at a dinner party at his home in late February 1974. A year earlier White had been awarded the Nobel Prize for Literature.

After the meal, the Canadian poet usurped the Australian novelist's favourite chair and announced in a loud, clear voice that he thought he would read a superb poem which he had just written. There was a short but palpable silence, Aviva recalled, then White was heard to say, "My dear fellow, whatever for?"

There was another silence, during which Layton considered his response, which came in a still-louder voice: "Now that I come to think of it, I think I'll read two poems."

Then White, in an even more refined way, said: "You do that, dear chap, and I'll read my whole friggin' novel."

Another silence ensued while Layton considered his reply, which was: "That ought to be a fair exchange, Patrick, as two of my poems just about equal one of your novels."

Free Verse

The poet Milton Acorn lived precariously from hand to mouth, supporting himself as best he could on his disability pension augmented by the slim earnings of his poetry.

His medical history was checkered, for he had been disabled during the war. Feeling sick, he made his way to the veterans' wing of Sunnybrook Hospital in Toronto.

The attending physician says, "I'm afraid to inform you that you have only three months to live."

"On what?" asks Acorn.

Fan Letter

James Houston is the artist and arts administrator who spent a dozen years in the eastern Arctic, where he was responsible for launching the

Inuit art movement—all those wonderful sculptures and prints. His life has been one of adventure and achievement, and among his many accomplishments is the authorship of books set in the Arctic, notably the children's book Tikta'liktak *and the novel* White Dawn. *In* Zigzag: A Life on the Move *(1998), the second installment of his memoirs, Houston tells an amusing story about one young reader's enthusiastic reaction to the book* Tikta'liktak.

I still receive hundreds of letters from school children who have read my books . . . There is one favourite letter from Calgary, which I often quote.

Dear Mr. Houston:

I have read your book *Tikta'liktak*. It is the best book I have ever read. It is the only book I have ever read.

Love, Wendy

Barbara Amiel

Friends say that Barbara Amiel, columnist and wife of wealthy capitalist and newspaper publisher Conrad Black, makes no attempt to hide her acquisitive habits.

"It's unfortunately true," she said, "that I tend to spend oodles of money. But that's my own extravagance!"

Talks and Autographs

Richard Bachmann, proprietor of the Different Drummer Bookstore in Burlington, Ont., has for decades sponsored a series of literary talks and readings. At each of the Tuesday morning series held at the LaSalle Park Pavilion, three authors read from their books, discuss their work, and then autograph copies of their books. The series is fully subscribed. There are more than two hundred listeners. The audience is largely made up of women "of a certain age," who certainly know how to concentrate, show their appreciation, and purchase books.

I was invited to address this group, along with fellow authors Richard Wright and Joan Bodger, on November 13, 2001. During his general introduction to the series, Richard pointed out that Vancouver writer and broadcaster Bill Richardson would be appearing soon in the Tuesday morning series.

To the amusement of members of the audience, he went on to say, "Bill Richardson will autograph his books. I understand he may even sign other people's books, if you ask him."

Write the Author

High school teachers frequently encourage their students to address letters to Canadian authors of their choice.

Milton Acorn cherished one letter that he received from a high school student. It read: "I have chosen you as my favourite author. Please write to me immediately and tell me why."

Canadian Book Club

There's a new Canadian Book Club.

You send it your credit card details and for $100 a year it leaves you alone for 365 days.

The Poet and the Felon

The poet Susan Musgrave and her husband, former felon Stephen Reid, are walking along Davie Street in Vancouver when they stop to look in a jeweller's window. Susan says, "I'd love those ruby earrings."

So Stephen takes a brick out of his pocket, smashes the

window, grabs the earrings, and gives them to his wife.

A little farther down the street, they stop to look in another jeweller's window. "Oh, look at that lovely diamond ring!" she says. "I'd just love it."

So Stephen takes another brick from his pocket, smashes a hole in the window, grabs the ring, and hands it to his wife.

A few minutes later they find themselves outside yet another jeweller's window. She says, "I'd really love to have that pearl necklace."

And Stephen says, "That's enough. You must think I'm made of bricks!"

Vanity

George Bowering is a fine poet and a man with a fine sense of the worth of his work. Fittingly, in November 2002, he was proclaimed Parliament's first Poet Laureate.

The story is told that at the press conference in Ottawa to announce the appointment, he fielded reporters' questions. Then he said, "That's enough talk about me and my appointment. Let's talk about what you think of my poems."

Admirably Awful Writing

The Bulwer-Lytton Award is presented each year to the writers of passages of prose that are judged to be truly awful. The award has been made for a dozen or more years by a group of American academics, and it was named after Sir Edward Bulwer-Lytton, the nineteenth-century English author of *The Last Days of Pompeii*, *Zanoni*, and other once-read novels. Today Sir Edward is principally remembered for the opening sentence of his novel *Paul Clifford* (1830). It begins with these seven unforgettable words: "It was a dark and stormy night . . ."

Praise for recognizing that there should be all-time awards to Canadians for their "admirably awful writing," whether in the form of prose or verse, or a blend of the two, should be accorded Herb Wyile, a member of the Department of English at the University of Alberta. He made the proposal to the 300-odd subscribers to the internet's CanLit listserv group on October 21, 1999. The compiler of the present book rose to the occasion and implemented the proposal.

It is my feeling that such awards should be made, from time to time, as passages of "admirably awful writing" (not just prose but also poetry and verse) flow from the pens and personal computers of the authors of Canada, past and present.

Here are some specimens of prose and poetry that deserve to be cherished for the simple reason that they are so bad that they are good! Long may they bring tears to the eyes . . . and laughter to the lips!

1.

Lady Louisa's bosom heaved with various emotions.

> This description comes from the pages of the historical novel *St. Ursula's Convent; or, The Nun of Canada, Containing Scenes from Real Life*, published in two volumes in Kingston, U.C., in 1824. It was written by Julia Catherine Hart at the age of sixteen. Today it is cherished as the first work of fiction to be written and published in Canada.

2.

The vampire of despair had banqueted on their hearts. Their vitality had been sucked, as it were, by its cold and bloodless lips; and little more than the withered rind, that had contained the seeds of so many affections, had been left.

> This is Major John Richardson's description of the state of mind and grief of Madeline and Clara after being taken captive during the attack on Michilimackinac in the novel *Wacousta; or, The Prophecy—A Tale of the Canadas*, published in three volumes in London, U.C., in 1832.

3.

Another gallant deed achieved
Was up at Contrecoeur:
Expecting heads to have been cleaved
Was nothing to allure.

> This stanza of doggerel comes from the verse "Achievements of a Volunteer Corps" in M. Ethelind Sawtell's generous collection of 269 verses written in the same vein titled *The Mourner's Tribute, or, Effusions of Melancholy Hours* (1840).

4.

All hail Our Great Queen in Her Regalia,
One foot in Canada, the other in Australia.

> This deathless couplet may well have been composed in the 1880s by the poetmaster James Gay, who styled himself "Master of All Poets of the Royal City of Guelph, Ontario," as noted by John Robert Colombo and Philip Singer in *Master of All Poets: The Life and Works of James Gay* (1996).

5.

Little Vancouver was born in the west,
The healthiest baby on Canada's breast.
Motherly Canada nursed the wee youth,
And brought it a railroad to cut its first tooth.
And soon it grew out of its swaddling bands,
To slip from the lap and the old nurse's hands.

> These couplets from the verse "Little Vancouver" were composed by E. Pauline Johnson around 1894 and were recalled by Charlotte Gray in *Flint & Feather: The Life and Times of E. Pauline Johnson, Tekahionwake* (2002). She calls them "possibly the worst piece of poetry that Pauline ever wrote."

6.

Nine hundred and seventy-five lines into *Towards the Last Spike*—with hundreds more to go—Pratt's railway builders confront another mountain range:

> This was a range
> That looked like some strange dread outside a door
> Which gave its name but would not show its features,
> Leaving them to the mind to guess at.
>
> But the mind does guess:
>
> This
> Meant tunnels—would there be no end to boring?

"Awfully, admirable, ambiguous, I've always thought"—Mark Baker of the CanLit listserv group noted, explaining that the 1952 epic of railway building written by narrative poet E.J. Pratt is not without its longueurs!

7.

> And 'neath the shelter of these ancient groves,
> The Cariboo with fearless footstep roves,
> Or the gay Moose in jocund gambol springs,
> Cropping the foliage Nature round him flings.

These lines are reprinted from Joseph Howe's long poem "Acadia," which appears in his posthumous collection *Poems and Essays* (1874), with an introduction by M.G. Parks in a 1973 edition.

8.

Only make me over, April,
When the sap begins to stir!
Make me man or make me woman,
Make me oaf or ape or human,
Cup of flower or cone of fir;
Make me anything but neuter
When the sap begins to stir!

This stanza of unintentionally bad verse comes from the poem "Spring Song," *Songs from Vagabondia* (1894), composed by the troubadour Bliss Carman and included in *The Selected Poems of Bliss Carman* (1954) edited by Lorne Pierce.

9.

Take it from me
Thalassa
My eyes
Thalassa O Thalassa
My hands
Water
Wash
Ash

O Thalassa!

Lines from Henry Beissel's poem "Configurations of Sea and Sand," which may be found in his collection *The Salt I Taste* (c. 1975).

10.

I saw the marvelous sun
rise out of the boundless sea

mere words could not discover
its sheer sublimity

> Undying lines from the poem "Celestial Events" included in the
> collection *The Rage of Space* (1992), written by translator and
> sometime poet Philip Stratford.

11.

This does not mean we must bow down before the godlike
figure of carbon, or, in studying the diamond, extend to it some
crucial rite of true affiliation due a distant, albeit mineral,
cousin, though we may, at times, wish to engage . . .

> This is a passage from "The Technology of Alchemy" (a sequence
> of *poèmes* and *pensées*) written by Kim Maltman and published in
> *Technologies/Installations* (1990).

12.

Peggy, Michael, Gwendolyn and David,
only one of them dead
so far,
my generation—we could
throw in Leonard Cohen
and maybe George Bowering.

> Puerile thoughts from the poem "Literary History" in *Ghost Safari*
> (1991), composed by Tom Marshall.

13.

Standing on tiptoe ever since my youth . . .

> This howler is the opening line of the poem "Standing on
> Tiptoe," composed by George Frederick Cameron and included
> in his collection *Lyrics on Freedom, Love and Death* (1887). About
> this line, poet and reviewer Fraser Sutherland opined: "It might

be better put, 'O my aching instep.' Contemporary wrong-footedness should not go ignored."

14.

Our lives so far
sweet-and-sour chicken balls

> Evocation of forty years of married life and, presumably, love, from the poem "Sweet-and-Sour Chicken Balls," included by Raymond Souster in his collection *The Eyes of Love* (1987).

15.

The bum isn't an anus.
The moon isn't green cheese.

> Lines said to find their source and origin in the poem "The Anus," included by innovative sound-poet bp Nichol in his *Selected Organs: Parts of an Autobiography* (n.d.).

16.

Thank you for hanging both parents on the wall.

> Line from the poem "Thank You," included by Gregory M. Cook in his book *My Diary of Earth* (1987).

17.

Beautiful Losers, by Leonard Cohen. A pretentiously poetic extravaganza of perversion, Canadian-style, wrapped around a rambling psychological non-story that in turns titillates, disgusts and bores. McClelland & Stewart, $6.50.

> Brief notice by an anonymous hack of Leonard Cohen's novel *Beautiful Losers* (1966) in *Maclean's*, June 4, 1966.

18.

Alexander Knox spent his childhood in Northern Canada where his father was a Presbyterian Minister in the small lumbering town of Pembroke, Ontario; during this time he got to know some of the Eskimo inhabitants and the Arctic landscape.

> Blurb (that telescopes geography and demography) on the back cover of the Pan Books reprint of actor and author Alexander Knox's novel *Night of the White Bear* (1975).

19.

Christopher Plummer stars in this Canadian murder tale with overtones of Devil worship and drugs. The Quebec actors are splendid and Karen Black has attractive breasts.

> Capsule review of the fine Quebec-made feature film *The Pyx* (1973), said to have appeared in the *Ottawa Journal* in 1974.

20.

You Are Happy is a collection of very modern poetry. This is not a value judgment but a description.

> Opening sentence of a review written by John W. Chalmers and published in *The Canadian Author and Bookman*, spring 1975, of Margaret Atwood's book of poems *You Are Happy* (1974).

21.

In Canadian culture, a liberated woman who wants a new life goes to the north and makes it with a bear. There must be a lesson in that somewhere, but I don't think it's good news for Canadian men.

> A passing reference to Marian Engel's novel *Bear* (1976) made by Martin Knelman in *Weekend Magazine*, June 19, 1976.

22.

"Courses in Canadiana"/No. 150. *Creative Canada*. This unique program is a series of 10 lectures exploring Canadian arts and culture. Topics include painting, sculpturing, native crafts, furniture, architecture and themes in Canadian literature. Babysitting is available. Co-sponsored with "Live and Learn" committee.

Copy from a bulletin about public courses issued by the North York (Ont.) Public Library, December 1976.

In passing, allow the present compiler to extend special thanks to Mark Baker, George Bowering, Gerald Lynch, Fraser Sutherland, and Herb Wyile.

Sex and Other
Vital Matters

The labels "Mature Subject Matter" and "Reader Discretion Is Advised" apply here. There are some X-rated jokes in this chapter.

Readers who are uncomfortable with material of this nature will be happier reading Chapter 8, "Love and Marriage," which go together like "a horse and carriage." The jokes in this chapter simply go together.

Top Ten Canadian Euphemisms for Sex

I received this item via e-mail on September 10, 2002. It purports to be from David Letterman's CBS-TV late-night talk show.

10. Playing Mountie.

9. Fur trapping.

8. Making Peg whinny.

7. Entering Parliament.

6. Pulling the goalie.

5. Doin' it, eh?

4. Putting the "man" in Manitoba.

3. High sticking.

2. Stuffing a beaver—the beaver is our national animal.

1. Oh, oh, oh Canada.

Come From

A little boy asked his parents, "Where did I come from?"

The parents had been expecting the day when they'd have to answer that question, and they were ready for it.

They took the boy into the living room, got out some books with pictures, and began to carefully explain sex, the sperm and the egg, conception, birth, and so on.

When they were finished, they asked, "Does that answer your question?"

"Not really," he replied. "The little girl who just moved in across the street told me she's from Winnipeg, and I just want to know where *I'm* from."

Facts of Rural Life

John Kenneth Galbraith, the economist, wrote in his memoir, The Scotch *(1964), that this incident occurred to him when he was a youngster in Elgin County, Ont. The story is hallowed by or hoary with age.*

A farmer's son and his girlfriend are walking through the fields when they see a bull mounting a cow.

The young man nudges the girl and says, "You know, I'd kind of like to do that."

The girl smiles and says, "Go right ahead. It's your cow."

Hen House

One hen complains to another, "That rooster is always after me for sex."

"Well, it's your own fault," says the other. "You keep egging him on."

Proposition

A young man is trying to get his girlfriend into bed.

"No, Harry," she says, "I can't."

"But why not?"

"Because if I do, I'll hate myself in the morning."

"So, couldn't you sleep until noon?"

Calgary Restaurant

A cowboy from the Alberta foothills went into Calgary to sell a herd of cattle, and since he was in the big city for the first time and had a load of money, he decided to eat in a fancy restaurant. He was shown to a table right next to one occupied by a wealthy, prim, proper, snobbish young lady.

When the waiter came to take the woman's order, she said, "I'll have the virgin chicken breast. Make sure it's virgin. Choose it yourself. You can dress the plate in fresh spring onions. I'll have a cup of coffee, rather mild, not too sweet; stir it with a silver spoon. And (sniff) could you please open a window. I smell horse. I do believe there is a . . . cowboy . . . in here."

The cowboy overheard this and of course was a little annoyed. So when the waiter took his order, he said, "I'll have a big, fat duck, and make sure it ain't a virgin. See to it personally if you have to. You can dress the plate in horse turds. I'll have a mug of booze stronger than Alberta mule piddle. And open up that door, will ya? It smells like a bordello in here. If the madam ain't in here, she sure as hell is nearby."

Kilts Away

A Scotsman newly arrived in Canada insisted on wearing his kilt.

A woman went up to him and asked, "Is it true that you men don't wear anything under your kilts?"

The Scot said, "Why don't you reach your hand under, and find out for yourself?"

She reached her hand under the kilt, then immediately pulled it back and said, "Oh, that's gruesome!'

The Scotsman said, "If you reach your hand under again, you'll find it's grew some more."

Billy and Joey

Two little boys, Billy and Joey, are sitting on the curb across the street from a Winnipeg brothel.

They watch men go up onto the porch, ring the bell, hand a woman some money, go inside, and then come out about an hour later with big smiles on their faces.

"I wonder what they sell in there," Billy wonders.

"It must be something pretty good," says Joey. "Those men all look so happy when they come out."

"Let's put our money together and see if we have enough for one of us to go over there," says Billy.

They pool their money and find they have only $2. "Gee," says Joey, "those men were paying with $20 bills. I don't think we have enough."

"Well," says Billy, "maybe we can just ask for $2 worth."

So they toss a coin, and Billy wins. He heads across the road with his $2 and rings the doorbell. The madam answers the door and looks down at the little boy. "What d' you want, kid?" she asks.

"I want $2 worth of what you sell here."

"Oh, you do, do you?" says the madam. "Well, first of all, you're going to have to pull your pants down for me."

Billy thinks this is a bit odd, but he does it. As soon as his pants are down, the madam sits down on a chair, hauls Billy across her lap, and gives him half a dozen hard whacks on his bare bottom.

"Dirty little boy!" she says. "Two dollars worth of what I sell, eh? Well, here's your $2 worth!"

When she finishes spanking him, she tells him to pull up his pants and be on his way. Tearfully, Billy runs back over to Joey.

"Boy, I'm glad we only had $2," he wails. "I wouldn't want twenty bucks worth of that!"

Peanuts

A man went to the Metro Zoo and was looking in the monkey exhibit. There were no monkeys to be seen. He asked an attendant where the monkeys were.

"Oh, they're all inside their monkey house, sir. You see, this is the time of day that they do their mating."

"Well, I'd like to see them," the man said. "Would they come out for a bag of peanuts?"

The attendant replied, "Would you?"

McGill Biology Class

Prudery was the order of the day at McGill University in Montreal in the 1920s.

A biology professor asked a female student, "What part of the human anatomy, under the right circumstances, can expand to ten times its normal size?"

The young woman was shocked. "How dare you ask me such a question!" she exclaimed. "You dirty old man! I'll inform my father. He'll see to it you never teach in this university again."

The professor quietly put the same question to another female student. That student answered, "The pupil of the human eye, under the right conditions of darkness and light, can expand to ten times its normal size."

"That is correct," the professor said. Then he turned to the first student. "As for you: First, you didn't do your homework. Second, you have a dirty mind. Third, you are in for a major disappointment on your wedding night."

Nothing Like It

A Saskatchewan farm boy with a company of Canadian soldiers in France in World War II got a weekend pass.

He didn't have much money, so the other guys in his outfit pooled their funds so that he could have a big night in Paris, on the condition that he tell them all the details when he got back to camp.

In Paris, he went to the classiest brothel in the liberated city. He told the other guys later, "I never seen nothing like it in Saskatchewan.

"There were silk drapes hanging everywhere, and everything smelled of sweet perfume. They gave me wine that was like nothing I ever had in Saskatchewan.

"They sat me down on velvet cushions, and there was soft, beautiful music playing. I never heard nothing like it in Saskatchewan.

"Then down the stairs came the most gorgeous woman I have ever seen. She had long black hair, deep brown eyes, ruby red lips, soft white skin, and a body like a movie star. I never seen anyone like her in Saskatchewan.

"She took me up to a bedroom that was more beautiful than any room I ever saw in Saskatchewan.

"She kissed me with those warm, moist lips, unbuttoned my shirt with those delicate little hands . . ."

The other guys were almost going crazy now. "What next, what next?" they gasped.

"Well, after that, it was pretty much the same as in Saskatchewan."

Wedding

An old man and an old woman got married. On their wedding night they got into bed and went right to sleep.

In the morning, as they were having their tea, the old man shamefacedly said, "I'm sorry, but I couldn't consummate our marriage last night."

The old woman looked puzzled for a moment, then said, "Oh, that!"

Birth-control Methods

A nurse was conducting a survey on birth-control methods in Vanier, a residential neighbourhood in Ottawa. Some people said they used condoms, others the pill, and so on.

At one house, a very big woman answered the door. When the nurse told her the subject of the survey, the woman said, "Well, my husband and I use the bucket-and-saucer method."

The nurse admitted that she had never heard of that one, so she asked the woman if she could describe it.

"Certainly," she said. "You see, my husband and I like to do it standing up. As you can see, I am quite big, but my husband is very short. He stands on a bucket so he can reach. I keep a close watch on him, and when his eyes get as big as saucers, I kick the bucket out from under him."

Sex Lies

An elderly couple are in a doctor's office in Toronto.

The old man says to the doctor, "Doc, we're having a sexual problem. We thought that if we could do it here in your office, you could check us out."

The doctor tells them to go ahead, so they take off their clothes, get on the couch, and do it. The doctor watches them, and then tells them that he can't see any problem. He says they seem to be functioning quite well for people their age. They thank him and leave.

A week later they're back in his office with the same complaint. Once again, the doctor watches them have inter-course, and again he tells them they're fine.

A week later they're back again. This time the doctor says, "Now look, I've watched you have sex twice, and you seem fine to me. Just what is this sexual problem you say you have?"

The old man says, "Well, we're not married. We're having an affair. We can't go to my house, because my wife is there. We can't go to her house, because her husband is there. A motel costs seventy bucks. A hotel costs a hundred bucks. Your office is fifty bucks, and OHIP pays it."

Double Entendre

Did you hear about the Canadian who went off in the woods with two yanks?

Cheating on One's Wife

Three married guys die and meet St. Peter at the Pearly Gates.

St. Peter asks the first guy, "Did you ever cheat on your wife?"

The guy answers truthfully, "Every chance I got."

Peter points to two doors, telling the guy to enter door number two.

He then turns to the second guy, asking him, "Did you ever cheat on your wife?"

"A couple of times," the guy mutters.

He is directed to take door number two.

St. Peter asks the third guy, a Newfie, "Did you ever cheat on your wife?"

The Newfie thinks for a couple of seconds and says, "Well, once. You see, I was in this saloon in Texas, and I noticed they only had one cowgirl working there to take care of all the guys. I asked the bartender how come, and he said, 'Well, she's all we need. That filly can suck a baseball bat through a garden hose.' So that's when I cheated on my wife."

St. Peter then told the Newfie to enter door number one.

The Newfie asks, "What's the deal? You sent the others to door number two!"

St. Peter says, "Yes, and they are both going to Hell. But you and I are going to Texas!"

Female Company

A Frenchman, an American, and a Newfie were wandering through the European countryside trying to get back to their army squadrons. It had been a long and lonely war, and they were in desperate need of some female company.

By and by they stopped to rest near a small farm. Noticing a sheep grazing peacefully at pasture, the Frenchman said, "*Mon Dieu*, I wish very much that that sheep was Brigitte Bardot."

The American then said, "Hell, I wish it was Marilyn Monroe."

The Newfie matter-of-factly offered, "I wish it was dark!"

Newlyweds

A young couple had just got married and were in the honeymoon suite on their wedding night.

As they were undressing for bed, the husband, who thought himself a macho kind of guy, tossed his pants to his bride and said, "Here, put these on."

She put on his pants but the waist was twice the size of her body. She said, "I can't wear these pants."

The husband replied, "That's right, and never forget it. I'm the one who wears the pants in this family."

With that his wife flips off her panties and tosses them to him and says, "Here, try to get into these."

He tried to pull them on but couldn't quite make it to his kneecaps. He said, "Hell, I can't get into your panties."

She looked at him and said, "That's right, and if you keep that attitude you're never going to!"

Punch Lines to Filthy Jokes

10. And that's why salmon swim upstream!

9. Why do you think it's called "The Big O"?

8. It's the mouth of the mighty St. Lawrence.

7. Now that's a beaver pelt!

6. That's right—the world's tallest free-standing structure.

5. They call them the Edmonton Oilers.

4. Just south of Regina.

3. Hurry! Hurry hard!

2. I get a double-double every morning!

1. Like a moose, baby.

Disco Dancing

A young Maritimer was in Toronto for the weekend and decided to visit a popular disco.

While standing at the bar, listening to the music and watching the people dancing, he turned to the bartender and said, "You know, my Ma invented disco dancing."

The bartender looked sceptical. The young man from out east continued, "She sure did. She took me aside when I was just a lad and said, 'Now boy, look at your feet. Dis' goes here . . . dis' goes there . . .'"

Condominium

A young man from St. John's returns to the small apartment he shares with his wife and excitedly tells her that he has just bought a condominium.

"Oh darling, that's wonderful!" replies his young wife. "Now I can throw away my diagram!"

The Canadian in the Brothel

Bob, a middle-aged Canadian tourist on his first time in Lincoln, Nebr., locates the red light district and enters a large brothel. The madam asks him to be seated and sends over a young lady to entertain the client. They sit and talk, frolic a little, giggle a bit, drink a bit, and she sits on his lap. He whispers in her ear and she gasps and runs away.

Seeing this, the madam sends over a more experienced lady to entertain the gentleman. They sit and talk, frolic a little, giggle a bit, drink a bit, and she sits on his lap. He whispers in her ear and she screams, "No!" and walks quickly away.

The madam is surprised that this ordinary-looking man has asked for something so outrageous that her two girls will have nothing to do with it.

She decides that only her most experienced lady, Lola, will do. Lola looks a bit tired, but she has never said no and it doesn't seem likely that anything would surprise her. So the madam sends her over to Bob. They sit and talk, frolic a little, giggle a bit, drink a bit, and she sits on his lap. He whispers in her ear and she screams, "No way, buddy!," smacks him as hard as she can, then runs away.

The madam is by now absolutely intrigued, having seen nothing like this in all her years of operating a brothel. She hasn't done the bedroom work herself for a long time, but she did it for many years before she got into management. She's sure she has said yes at one time or another to everything a man could possibly ask for.

The challenge is irresistible.

She just has to find out what this man has wanted that has made her girls so angry. And she sees a chance she can't pass up to show off to her employees how good she was at what they do.

So she goes over to Bob and says that she's the best in the house and she is available. They sit and talk, frolic a little, giggle a bit, drink a bit, and she sits on his lap. And Bob leans forward and whispers in her ear . . .

"Can I pay in Canadian dollars?"

Husband and Wife

A husband and wife were having dinner at a fine restaurant when an absolutely stunning young woman comes over to their table, give the husband a big, open-mouthed kiss, then says she'll see him later and walks away.

The wife glares at her husband and says, "Who the hell was that?"

"Oh," replies the husband, "she's my mistress."

"Well, that's the last straw," says the wife. "I've had enough, I want a divorce!"

"I can understand that," replies her husband, "but remember, if we get a divorce, it will mean no more shopping trips to Montreal, no more chalet in Whistler, no more summers in Tuscany, no more Infiniti or Lexus in the garage, and no membership in the Vancouver Yacht Club. But the decision is yours."

Just then, a mutual friend enters the restaurant with a gorgeous woman on his arm.

"Who's that woman with Jim?" asks the wife.

"That's his mistress," says her husband.

"Ours is prettier," she replies.

Chinese Wedding Night

A Chinese couple marry. He's older and experienced. She's young and virginal.

On the wedding night she cowers naked under the bedsheets as her husband undresses. He climbs in next to her and tries to be reassuring. "My darling, I know this is your first time and you are frightened. I promise you I will give you whatever you want. I will do anything you want. What do you want?"

"I want sixty-nine," she replies.

He looks at her, puzzled, and says, "You want beef with broccoli?"

Memorial Research

A young student, studying Folklore at Memorial University in St. John's, is assigned to research a human-interest story about happiness and sadness.

Being from an outport community, he returns to an outport to conduct his research. He heads for the oldest fisherman in the community, introduces himself, and proceeds to explain to the old codger why he is there.

The young man asks, "Has anything ever happened around here that made you very happy?"

The fisherman thinks for a minute and says, "Well, one time one of my neighbour's sheep got lost. We formed a posse and found it. We all screwed it and took it back home."

"I can't print that!" the young man exclaims. "Can you think of anything else that happened that made you or a lot of other people happy?"

After another minute, the farmer says, "Well, one time my neighbour's daughter, a good-looking girl, got lost. We formed a big posse that time and found her. After we all screwed her, we took her back home."

Again, the young man says, "I can't print that either. Has anything ever happened around here that made you sad?"

The old farmer drops his head as if he were ashamed, and after a few seconds looks up timidly at the young man and says, "I got lost once."

The Hereafter

There was a young woman sitting on a bench sunning herself when an old man came over to sit down.

He moved over to her side and said, "Do you believe in the hereafter?"

She said, "Yes."

He said, "Then you know what I'm here after."

Saying the Vows

After being married for forty-five years, Aggie says to George, "George, I'm worried the spark is gone out of our marriage. Why don't we repeat our vows?"

"Yes, m' darlin'," says George. "And where do you expect to honeymoon, Viagra Falls?"

Vaseline

A market researcher knocked on the door of a house. A young woman with three small children running around her answered. He asked her if she minded replying to his questions, and she agreed to.

He asked her if she knew his company, Cheeseborough-Ponds.

When she said no, he mentioned that among its many products was Vaseline. She admitted she knew of that product.

When asked if she used it, the answer was yes.

Asked how she used it, she said, "To assist sexual intercourse."

The interviewer was amazed. He said, "I always ask that question because everyone uses our product and they always say they use it for the child's bicycle chain or the gate hinge; but I know that most use it for sexual intercourse. Since you've been so frank, could you tell me exactly how you use it?"

"Yes, we put it on the doorknob to keep the kids out."

The Airport Ride

George and Aggie were in Boston for the first time to visit their son and his family.

Outside the airport terminal they hail a taxi. As they head for the city, the driver, making small talk, asks them where they are from.

Aggie asks George, "What'd he say, George? I can't hear him!"

The old skipper leans over and yells in her ear, "He asked where we're from."

Then the old skipper says to the driver, "We're from Stephenville."

"Oh," says the driver. "I was stationed there when I was in the air force."

Again Aggie pipes up, "What's the fella saying now, George? What'd he say?"

"He says he's been there."

"I see," says Aggie.

They drive along in silence for a while. Then the driver says, "You know, I went with a girl when I was there, and she was the meanest, most disagreeable hag I ever hooked up with."

"What's he saying now, George. I can't hear him."

The old skipper yells back, "He thinks he knows ya."

Enlargement

Once there was a girl who wanted larger breasts.

So she went to see Dr. Smith, her general practitioner.

Dr. Smith told her to, as an exercise, rub her breasts and repeat the following words: "Scoobie, doobie, loobie; I want bigger boobies."

One day she was running late and decided to do her exercises on the bus, when a guy came up to her and asked, "Are you a patient of Dr. Smith's?"

"Yes," she replied. "How did you know?"

He replied, "Hickery, dickery, doc!"

Wayson Choy

Here is an incident about growing up in British Columbia. It comes from Wayson Choy's *Paper Shadows: A Chinatown Childhood* (1999).

Two friends, Blackie and Alfie, watched as two dogs copulated. Alfie explained the procedure—how the *pee-nis* went into the *regina*. The author adds, "For years, I wondered about the geography of Saskatchewan."

Three Guys

There were three guys, an American, a Canadian, and a Mexican.

They had been travelling for days and were very, very hungry. They came across a farm devoted to mixed fruits and vegetables. While they were eating, the farmer came out and caught them.

The farmer said, "Since I'm in a good mood today, I won't kill you—if you stuff one hundred pieces of your favourite fruit up your ass without laughing."

The American was up first. He chose cherries as his favourite fruit. He got up to seventy-eight and then burst out laughing. So the farmer shot him with a shotgun.

The Canadian was next and chose grapes. He got up to ninety-two but then started laughing. So the farmer killed him too.

When the Canadian and the American arrived in Heaven, an angel asked them why they had laughed. They both replied, "We saw the Mexican had chosen watermelons."

23

Weather in the Course of Human Events

No collection of jokes would be complete without a chapter devoted to the extremes of our weather. The subject and this chapter includes climate, of course, and this affects all of us; indeed, to a greater or a lesser degree, SAD (seasonal affective disorder) is a sad fact of life for many of us.

Our weather conditions are extremely diverse. Not only does Canada have "more weather" than any other country except for Russia, but our weather is extremely variable and changeable.

In the early days of national television, the weather forecaster, or weatherman, was a meteorologist rather than an actor or presenter. The first weatherman (not to be confused with the U.S. vigilante group called the Weathermen) was Percy Saltzman, and he instantly emerged as our infant television industry's first and foremost celebrity.

Here are some jokes and lore about our weather conditions. The chapter begins, appropriately enough, with a ditty associated with Mr. Saltzman, who would conclude his "weather-side chats" with an act of showmanship: tossing a piece of chalk into the air and catching it again.

TV Weatherman

Percy Saltzman, CBC-TV's first weatherman and, some say, Canadian television's first celebrity, was hauled into court for driving too fast.

The judge said, "Today I'll just charge you $50. But if you do this again, you're going to jail."

The man said, "Oh, I get it. 'Fine today, cooler tomorrow.'"

New Rhyme

This is a traditional verse associated with Percy Saltzman, CBC-TV's first weather forecaster.

Whether it's cold,
Or whether it's hot,
We'll have weather
Whether we like it or not.

Curse

A Canadian curse:
May you have a bad back, a big shovel, and wet snow.

Autumn

Autumn is the season when the leaves turn yellow and the teachers aren't too confident either.

Fogo's Weather

A Toronto man visiting Fogo Island, Nfld., complained about the weather.

"Rain and fog, rain and fog," he said to a local man. "Don't you ever have summer here?"

"Sure," the Newfoundlander replied. "Last year it was on a Tuesday."

St. John's Weather

Visitors complain that St. John's gets too much fog, but it was foggy only twice last week; once for four days, and once for just three.

Old Rhyme

The weather may be dry, or the weather may be hot,
But there's never any failure of the dandelion crop!

Imbibing

The melancholy days have come,
    The saddest of the year;
It's a little too warm for whiskey,
    And a little too cold for beer.

Ditty, *Calgary Eye Opener,* June 17, 1916

Weather Report

It's been observed (by actor Robert Morley and meteorologist Dave Phillips, among others) that we are obsessed not only with weather but also with weather reports.

Actor Robert Morley, visiting Toronto in 1972, observed: "Canadians love to sit in the dark trembling with fear at weather forecasts."

Dave Phillips, Dominion climatologist, noted: "If we could predict the weather perfectly, it would take all the fun out of being Canadian."

The most charming weather report of all time has to be the one delivered by the CBC Radio announcer on the Prairies in the 1940s: "There will be a heavy snowfall, followed by little boys on sleighs."

The wittiest weather report by a non-weather forecaster may well be the one delivered by Don Harron in the guise of his Ontario farmer Charlie Farquharson. It comes from his book *Charlie Farquharson's K-O-R-N Filled Allymanack* (1976). The mock weather report goes like this:

> Normal temperatures will prevail. Coastal oceanic areas will be damp tending to wet. Air masses will move from west to east, bringing storms over the Rockies and drying out over the deserts, tapering off to bring eventual relief. The north will get a touch of cooler weather. Seasonal conditions will exist in the south, with not much change in variants. Fog will be patchy, tending to rain in spots, and in northern regions, the winter version of rain, snow or sleet, will make an appearance. Each Canadian is guaranteed a snow job.

Northern Proverb

In the Arctic, winter lasts twelve months. The rest of the year it's summer.

Seasons

Weather has long been a topic of conversation among Canadians.

It's often said that there are six seasons in Canada—summer, fall, winter, winter, winter, and spring.

Perhaps more to the point is the division of the year into five seasons—spring, summer, autumn, fall, and winter.

Unbearable

A baby polar bear asks his mother, "Am I a polar bear?"

She says, "Of course, you are."

"Are you a polar bear?"

"Yes, certainly."

"Dad, are you a polar bear?"

"Yes, for heaven's sake!"

"Is grandma a polar bear?"

"Yes, yes!"

"Is grandpa a polar bear?"

"Yes, yes, yes!"

"How about great-grandma and great-grandpa?"

"Will you stop! Yes, of course they're polar bears! Why are you asking?"

"Because I'm freezing!"

Weather

A farmer returns from a visit to the capital of Newfoundland.

A friend asks him, "How was the weather in St. John's."

"Dunno. So foggy I couldn't tell."

Snowman

Q. What do you get if you cross a snowman with a vampire?

A. Frostbite.

Snowed In

George and Aggie were sitting down to their usual cup of morning coffee, listening to the weather report on the radio:

"There will be three to five inches of snow today and a snow emergency has been declared. You must park your cars on the odd-numbered side of the streets."

George got up from the table and replies, "Jeez, okay."

Two days later, again they both are sitting down with their cups of morning coffee and heard the weather forecast:

"There will be two to four inches of snow today and a snow emergency has been declared. You must park your cars on the even-numbered side of the streets."

George got up from the table and replies, "Jeez, okay."

Three days later, again they both are sitting down with their cups of coffee and heard the weather forecast:

"There will be six to eight inches of snow today and a snow emergency has been declared. You must park your cars on the—" and then the power went out, so George didn't get the rest of the instructions.

He says to Aggie, "Jeez, what am I going to do now, Aggie?"

Aggie replies, "Aw, George, just leave the car in the garage."

Cold Fronts

Americans are getting annoyed about all those cold fronts moving down from Canada.

They want to know if they can weatherstrip the border.

Snowbirds

Snowbirds are Canadians of retirement age who spend the winter in the southern U.S. sun.

French Canadians escape the Quebec winter by living in condos and motels in the vicinity of Hollywood, Florida.

One French Canadian was so homesick living all winter long in Hollywood that he went to Costco, where he bought a cheap television set. He plugged it in but never bothered to connect the antenna.

He wanted to see some snow.

British Columbia Sect

There is a religious sect in the interior of British Columbia. Members of this group are sun worshippers.

They pray to the sun. Everyone else in that province prays *for* the sun.

Feminism

A Canadian woman burns her bra only if she's out of wood.

Winter Shoes

A Canadian woman doesn't worry if her shoes fit her feet as long as they fit in the plastic bag she carries them around in between October and April.

Snow Shovel

A Canadian considers it one of the great thrills of life when snow doesn't stick to his shovel.

Snow

Q. Why do Canadians like snow?
A. It fills the potholes.

Perfect Weather

"The weather here in Vancouver is perfect," a Vancouverite was telling a friend visiting from Winnipeg. "Last month the sun came down in torrents for three weeks."

Vancouver Weather

It never rains in Vancouver.

Scott McIntyre, a publisher who loves British Columbia and lives in its largest city, assures everyone that this is so. It never rains.

"I suppose you are going to tell me the sun shines 365 days of the year," I said, in disbelief.

"Yes, in B.C., the sun shines 365 days a year," he said. "And I might add that that's a conservative estimate."

The Newcomer

A newcomer arrives in Victoria, B.C. It's a rainy day.

She gets up the next day and it's still raining.

It continues to rain the day after that, and the day after that.

She goes out to lunch and sees a young kid. In despair, she asks him, "Hey, kid, does it ever stop raining around here?"

The kid replies, "How should I know? I'm only six."

Victorian Conditions

Q. What did the Victoria native say to the Pillsbury Doughboy?
A. Nice tan.

Q. What does daylight saving time mean in Victoria?
A. An extra hour of rain.

Q. What do you call blue skies over Victoria?
A. A thirty-second time-out.

Q. What do you call two straight days of rain in Victoria?
A. An average weekend.

Q. How do they wash the streets in Victoria?
A. Huh? You're not from Victoria, are you?

Rainstorm

Meteorologists were predicting a gargantuan rainstorm that would inundate the Pacific Northwest coast and create flood-like conditions.

The archbishop of Vancouver Island appeared on cable television's *100 Huntley Street* and declared, "This is your punishment from God. Prepare to meet your Maker."

The prime minister appeared on CBC-TV's *The National* news program and announced, "Our scientists have done all they can. The end is near."

Finally, the *Victoria Evening News* published its daily weather report, which read: "Today's five-day forecast . . . same as usual."

Vacuum Cleaners

In Dawson City, Y.T., even the vacuum cleaners have snow tires.

Judgment Day

A curious fellow died one day and found himself waiting in the long line of judgment before the Pearly Gates.

As he stood there, he noticed that some souls were allowed to march right through the Pearly Gates into Heaven. Other souls, less lucky, were led over to Satan, who flung them into the burning pit. But every so often, instead of hurling a poor soul into the fire, Satan would toss the soul off to one side onto a small pile of souls.

After watching Satan do this several times, the fellow's curiosity got the better of him. So he strolled over to the Evil One and asked a question. "Excuse me, Mr. Satan," he said. "I'm waiting in line for judgment, but I couldn't help but wonder. Why are you tossing those people aside instead of flinging them into the fires of Hell with the others?"

"Ah, those . . ." Satan said, with a groan. "They're all from Victoria. They're too damn wet to burn."

The Chief and the Weatherman

It was a rainy autumn and the people on a remote northern reservation in Saskatchewan approached their newly elected chief to ask him whether the coming winter was going to be cold or mild.

But he was one of the newly elected chiefs, and not one of the old hereditary chiefs, so he knew next to nothing about the traditional ways. As a modern man, nature's secrets were a mystery to him. Whenever he cast his eyes to the sky, he saw no telltale signs of the weather to come.

Nevertheless, to be on the safe side, he told his people, "The coming winter is going to be a cold one. We should collect wood to keep our fires burning through the months of ice and snow."

He thought for several days about the advice he had given his people. Being a prudent man as well as a modern man, he went to the telephone booth when no one was looking and phoned the weather service. He reached the weatherman at Environment Canada. "Is the coming winter going to be cold?" the chief asked him.

"It looks like this winter is going to be quite cold," the weatherman replied.

So the chief went back to his people and said, "The coming winter is going to be even colder than expected. We had better collect even more firewood in order to be prepared for the frigid weather."

One week later he phoned the weather service for the second time. He asked the weatherman, "What are your predictions now? Is it still going to be a very cold winter?"

"Yes," the weatherman replied. "It's going to be a very cold winter."

So the chief went back to his people and said, "Collect every scrap of wood you can find. Stockpile it against the cold of winter."

One week later, the chief phoned the weather service for the third time. "Are you absolutely sure that the coming winter is going to be extremely cold?"

"Absolutely," the weatherman replied. "It looks like it's going to be the coldest winter on record."

"How can you be so sure?" the chief asked.

The weatherman replied, "The Indians are collecting firewood like crazy!"

Work, Work, Work!

The title of this chapter is taken from that once-popular Canadian hymn which begins, ponderously, "Work, work, work! for the night is coming."

Whether the approach of night is imminent or not, work seems to be man's lot (and woman's lot, too) in this world. It is the human lot to labour, to work, to build, to create, to provide, and to realize one's potential.

So here you'll find jokes that tell about hard and heavy labour, about building or growing a business, about ethical trade and professional practices, and about rules and regulations that hobble ingenuity and effort.

I am not sure that work in Canada differs from work in other parts of the Western world, but if it does, these jokes are part and parcel of those labour pains.

Important Notice

Mail Fraud Warning

Warning! Please read immediately! This is Serious!

If you receive in the mail an envelope with the return address "Revenue Canada," DO NOT OPEN IT!

This group operates a scam around this time every year. Their letter claims that you owe them money, which they will take and use to pay for what is described as the operation of essential functions of the Canadian government.

This is untrue! The money that this organization collects is used to fund various inefficient and pointless social engineering projects.

This organization has ties to another shady outfit called the Canada Pension Plan, which claims to take money from your regular paycheques and save it for your retirement. In truth, the CPP uses the money to pay for the same misguided make-work projects that Revenue Canada helps mastermind.

These scam artists have bilked honest, hard-working Canadians out of billions of dollars. Don't be among them!

In a Bar

There are three Canadians in a bar—a man from British Columbia, a man from Ontario, and a Newfie.

They are sitting at the bar drinking, when the man from B.C. looks around and sees seated nearby a middle-aged man who looks exactly the way you would expect Jesus to look: sensitive, holy, with a halo. The man from B.C. waves his hand at Jesus, and Jesus nods back.

Excitedly, the man from B.C. turns to his drinking buddies and says, "That's Jesus over there. I'm going to buy him a drink!"

The drinking buddies look at Jesus and then discuss the matter. They summon the bartender over and ask him to deliver three drinks to Jesus. He does so.

Jesus accepts the drinks with surprise and makes short work of them. Then he stands up and approaches the three men. He places his hand on the back of the man from B.C. and says, "Thank you, my son."

Just then, the man from B.C. stands up straight and exclaims, "My back . . . it's better! You've healed my back. I've been having back problems for years, but now it feels great. Thank you, Jesus!"

Jesus then touches the elbow of the man from Ontario. The Ontarian can hardly believe it: "I've had arthritis in this elbow for years. The doctors said they couldn't do anything for me. Now I have no pain at all. Thank you, Jesus!"

Jesus finally approaches the Newfie and extends his hand. The Newfie backs away, yelling, "Don't touch me! Don't touch me! I'm on workers' compensation!"

Graduate

He has a B.A., an M.B.A., and a Ph.D. The only thing he doesn't have is a J.O.B.

Lachlan Currie

Lachlan Currie, a well-respected, Canadian-born and trained economist, has acted as a financial adviser to the governments of a number of Latin American countries. It is said he had a special influence on the economic policies of the Republic of Colombia.

The story is told that on one of the Caribbean islands, he tried to introduce one of its able-bodied inhabitants to some twentieth-century notions of efficiency and good management.

On the first day there, he met a man sitting on the porch of his shack in the middle of the day with a bottle of beer in his hand. He explained to the loafer that life would be so much better if he got himself a regular job.

"Why?"

"Because then you could make some money."

"Why do I need to make money?"

"Because when you've made enough, you can retire and you won't have to work any more."

"But I don't work now!"

Tickle Me Elmo

A Newfie got a job at a toy factory and was put on the assembly line making Tickle Me Elmo dolls. After a while, there was a major hold-up in the line at the Newfie's workstation.

The foreman went over to see what the problem was. The Newfie had a stack of little bags and a container full of marbles. He would put two marbles in a little bag and then stitch it between Elmo's legs.

He explained to the foreman, "I was told to give each doll two test-tickles."

Butcher's Lesson

A butcher is training an apprentice clerk.

He begins, "When a customer asks the price of two pork chops, say, 'Five dollars.'"

He continues, "If the customer doesn't wince, immediately add on 'and ninety-five cents.'"

He concludes, "If the customer still doesn't wince, say 'each.'"

Insect Spray

A woman went into a Canadian Tire store and picked a can of insect spray off the shelf.

She took it to the counter and asked, "Is this good for spiders?"
"No, ma'am," said the clerk. "It kills them."

Dock Worker

A Cape Bretoner was at a dock in Newfoundland, looking for work on a boat. One of the fishing captains finally hired him on.

The first mate went to the captain and said, "Why did you hire that Cape Bretoner? You know they can't be trusted."

The captain said, "Oh, he looks honest enough to me. I'm sure he'll be okay. Just keep him busy."

The mate gave the Cape Bretoner a mop and told him to swab the deck. He also resolved to keep a close eye on him.

Suddenly, a huge wave hit the boat and washed the Cape Bretoner away. The mate saw it happen and ran to the captain.

"Skipper!" he cried. "That Cape Bretoner you hired! He just took off with the mop!"

Captain Sam's Secret

Captain Sam was the saltiest old skipper in the Canadian Navy. During World War II he commanded a destroyer, escorting convoys across the Atlantic and duelling it out with German U-boats. He was fearless, undaunted by high seas or ocean gales.

After the war he went into the Coast Guard. He led expeditions into the Arctic, rescued more vessels than any other captain, and was the terror of smugglers of every description. The sailors under him loved him for his courage, his seamanship, and his willingness to teach others.

One thing perplexed them. In his cabin, Captain Sam kept a safe. From time to time he would open it, take out a piece of paper, look at it, then lock it up again. He would never reveal what was on the piece of paper. Some said it was a secret code from naval headquarters. Others thought it might be a picture of a long-lost love. It remained a mystery for years.

Then one day age caught up with Sam. He had a mild heart attack while on the bridge of his vessel and had to be airlifted to a hospital. His first mate was obliged to go through his cabin to gather his personal effects. The mate unlocked the safe and took out the piece of paper which had been a puzzle for so long.

On it was written, in Captain Sam's hand, "Starboard is right, port is left."

Insurance Pitch

An insurance salesman was trying to sell a life insurance policy.

"I don't want to pressure you," he said to his potential client. "You sleep on it, and we'll talk about it again tomorrow, if you wake up."

Threatening Letters

A man went into a police station and said, "I've been getting threatening letters and phone calls. Isn't there a law against that?"

"Yes," said the officer at the desk. "There certainly is. Do you know where these letters and phone calls are coming from?"

"The electric company, the gas company, the cable company . . ."

Tricky Questions

In court a lawyer was giving a witness a hard time, telling him that he must answer questions with a simple "yes" or "no."

The witness complained that some questions could not be answered with just a simple "yes" or "no."

The lawyer smirked, "Can you give me an example?"

Right away the witness said, "Sure. Are you still drinking a lot?"

Inheritance

A lawyer asked a colleague who was looking rather glum what the problem was.

"Well," the man said, "a few years ago I had my mother committed to a mental hospital. Last week she died and left me an estate of over a million dollars. Now I have to prove that she was of sound mind."

Parking Space

A salesman in Toronto was having a terrible time finding a parking space. Finally, he parked in a "No Parking" spot and left a note on the windshield that said, "I've circled this block twenty times and couldn't find a spot to park. I have a meeting to attend, and if I'm late, I'll lose my job. Forgive us our trespasses."

When he came back there was a ticket on the windshield with a note that said, "I've circled this block for twenty years. If I don't give you a ticket, I'll lose my job. Lead us not into temptation."

Carpentry

A father was doing some carpentry work in his workshop.

His little boy looked at some boards and said, "Why do some of the boards have holes in them?"

His father replied, "Those are knotholes."

The little boy asked, "Well, if they're not holes, what are they?"

Minimum Wage

People started saying that a certain farmer was underpaying his labour. An official came to check.

"How many people do you employ?" the official inquired.

"Two men," said the farmer.

"I understand that you are paying them below the minimum wage."

"Is that so!" snorted the farmer. He called out to his men. "Now," he said, "tell this fellow what your wages are."

"Five hundred dollars a week," each of them answered.

"Well, that's all right," the official said. He turned to the farmer, "Are you sure you don't employ anyone else?"

"Only the half-wit," the farmer said. "He gets his board and a little cash each week for his tobacco."

"That's disgraceful!" the official said. "Let me talk to him."

"Talk to him?" the farmer said. "You're talking to him now."

Blackboard

The preacher came along and wrote on the blackboard: "I pray for all."

The lawyer came along and wrote under that: "I plead for all."

The doctor came along and wrote: "I prescribe for all."

The Canadian citizen coming by read these carefully and thought for a while before writing: "I pay for all."

Apprentice Smith

A young man in a frontier town was apprenticed to a blacksmith.

The smith decided to start by teaching him to make horse-shoes. He said, "I'm going to get the horseshoe from the fire and put it on the anvil. When I nod my head, you hit it with the hammer."

The blacksmith was out cold for two hours.

Workers' Compensation

"When will your father's leg be well so he can come to work?"

"Not for a long time, I think."

"Why?"

"Because compensation's set in."

Passing a Test

An Ontarian is the foreman at a lumber camp when a French Canadian approaches him, looking for a job. The foreman doesn't want to hire him but is afraid of being accused of bigotry, so he devises a test that he is sure the Quebecer will fail.

He gives him a piece of paper and a pencil and says, "Without using numbers, illustrate 'nine'."

The French Canadian draws three trees.

The foreman asks him how that can be nine.

The French Canadian says, "Tree, tree, and tree; dat make nine."

The foreman says, "Okay, now for part two. Without using numbers, show me ninety-nine."

The Quebecer smudges the pictures and says, "Dere you go. Dirty tree, and dirty tree, and dirty tree. Dat's ninety-nine."

Now the foreman is getting worried, because it looks like he might have to hire the man. So he says, "Last test. Without using numbers, show me one hundred."

The French Canadian draws a little blob at the bottom of each tree.

The foreman says, "You're crazy! How can this represent one hundred?"

The French Canadian replies, "Well, you look around here, and you see how de dog crap at de bottom of each tree? Well, dirty tree and a turd, and dirty tree and a turd, and dirty tree and a turd make one hundred. When do I start?"

What Do You Call?

Q. What do you call a country that lacks a modern telecommunications system?

A. Technologically backward.

Q. What do you call a country that lacks a fully integrated
banking system?
A. Economically underdeveloped.

Q. What do you call a country that lacks a well-connected
public transportation system?
A. Canada.

Oil Patch Millionaire

Allan Anderson, the broadcaster who compiled a series of
books of oral history, tells the story of Smith, a Westerner who
moved East.

Because of the Eastern feeling that everybody is a millionaire
out West, when he was introduced to a very conservative group
of businessmen who were members of the Rotary Club at their
meeting in London, Ont., he felt compelled to set the record
straight.

The head of the Rotary Club said, "I want to introduce you to
my friend who is a new resident of this district. He's from
Saskatchewan, and he just made a million in uranium."

So the newcomer, Smith, stood up and said, "I want to set the
score straight before I say anything else.

"First of all, I'm not from Saskatchewan. I'm from Alberta.

"Second, it wasn't uranium. It was oil.

"Third, it wasn't a million. It was only half a million.

"And, fourth, I didn't make it. I lost it."

New Automobile

The Chrysler Corporation has announced that it is adding a new
car to its production line.

It will be named to honour former U.S. president Bill Clinton.
The Dodge Draft will begin production in Canada this year.

Bank of Canada

David Dodge may be a brilliant economist but his speaking skills leave a lot to be desired. As the Governor of the Bank of Canada he is expected to address the general public as well as members of the financial community. Not only is the sound of his voice grating but he lacks a sense of idiom.

Once, a subordinate stood at the door of his office. Dodge saw him and said, "Why are you outstanding! Please income!"

Auto Workers

Q. How do you get 500 G.M. workers into a Buick?
A. Send in Buzz Hargrove and the rest will follow.

Statue of St. Anthony

An unemployed Italian worker walks into St. Anthony's Church, approaches the big statue of St. Anthony, and says, "St. Anthony, today I've gotta find a job. I ask you to help me, okay? Thank you, St. Anthony."

He leaves the church and goes out searching for a job, but he doesn't find one.

The next day he's back in the church, talking to the statue. "St. Anthony, yesterday I ask you to help me find a job, and you didn't. Now, today, you gonna help me, okay? Thank you, St. Anthony."

He leaves the church and goes out searching, but he doesn't find a job.

This goes on for several days, with the man becoming more and more discouraged, and angrier and angrier.

Finally, he goes into the church and says, "St. Anthony, I give you one last chance. Today, if you don't help me find a job, I come back and I smash you to bits."

He leaves the church without another word.

Two of the priests overhear the threat, and decide they'd better get their beautiful statue out of there. They have it moved to a safe location in the basement, and put a much smaller statue in its place.

Much later, when the Italian enters the church, very angry and armed with a sledgehammer, he says, "St. Anthony, I ... hey, kid! Where's your papa?"

Shoe Store

A man with a speech impediment gets a job in a shoe store.

He goes to take care of his first customer, a young woman wearing a short skirt. He picks up the foot-measuring device and speaks to her. She slaps his face and walks out.

The boss hurries over and asks what happened.

"I don't know," says the bewildered clerk. "All I thaid wasth pleasth thit down and I'll look up your thize."

Assistant Pharmacist

A pharmacist running a drugstore in Cape Breton hires a young woman to help out with the shop. One day he has to go out for a while, and he leaves her to look after the place. When he comes back a couple of hours later, he asks if there had been any customers.

"Yes," she says. "One man came in who was coughing right bad, so I give him a big dose of laxative."

"Laxative!" cried the pharmacist. "That won't stop a cough!"

"Oh yes it will," said the woman. "Look at him out there holding on to that lamp post for dear life. He's afraid to cough!"

Stock Market Rule

One of the gurus of Bay Street was Andrew Sarlos, who made fortunes and lost fortunes investing through the Toronto Stock Exchange.

Peter C. Newman tells an amusing story of a conversation he had with Sarlos. Here is the essence of it from his monthly column in *Maclean's*, August 12, 2002.

Newman drew Sarlos out by saying, "Investing in the market is a gamble as crazy as throwing your money away at a casino."

"That is not true," Sarlos replied. "Casinos have rules." After a pause, Sarlos added, "One stock market rule that must be obeyed is that when a taxi driver tells you what shares to buy, you stop the cab, give the guy twenty bucks, run back to your office, and sell everything."

Newfie Census Taker

Census taker: When's your birthday?
Newfie: 24th of December.
Census taker: What year?
Newfie: Every year!

Census Taker in Cape Breton

A census taker was knocking on doors in a community in Cape Breton.

At one door he knocked on, a little old man answered and said, "What do you want, b'y?"

The man said, "Well, I'm the census taker."

"What the Jesus does that mean?"

"Well, the government sends me out to find out how many people there are in the country."

"Well, buddy, it's no use you comin' around here to ask me, because I don't know."

Census Taker in Manitoba

The census taker visits a farm in Manitoba during the Great Depression and stops to talk with an older farmer, who agrees to answer his questions.

"The Census Bureau of the federal government has asked me to ask you for the answers to these questions. Are you the head of the house?"

"I guess you could call me that."

"How many people are presently living and working on your farm?"

"There are eight people living on this farm."

"Who are they and what work do they do?"

The farmer thinks for a moment and then begins to speak. The census taker writes down everything he says.

"Well, Number One is my wife. She does most of the housework.

"Number Two is my wife's mother. My mother-in-law's pretty old, but she does the housework that my wife doesn't do.

"Number Three is my wife's father. My father-in-law's pretty old, too, so all he can do is occasionally mind the children.

"There are three of those children, all pretty useless around the place. But they're Numbers Four, Five, and Six, I guess.

"Then there's the hired man. He's Number Seven, but he's hopeless because he drinks too much. And when he drinks, he disappears for days on end.

"Then there's the old gaffer, Number Eight."

"The old gaffer? Who's he and what does he do?"

"That's me. What do I do? I do the work."

Cunard Steamship Company Limited

An executive for the Cunard Steamship Company Limited is sent from London, England, to run the office in St. John's, Nfld. Being a high-society, Oxford-educated Brit, he is rather contemptuous of the local people.

One Sunday he decides to take his Rolls-Royce out for a drive around the countryside. He soon gets lost. He pulls into a gas station.

"I say," he says to the man who comes out to serve him, "how do I get back to St. John's?"

The Newfoundlander, however, is really taken with the man's expensive car.

"Say, buddy! That's some nice car you got there, eh?"

"Yes, yes it is. Much nicer than anything you've ever seen before, I dare say. Now would you stop drooling over it and tell me how I can get to St. John's?"

"B'y, a car like this must cost a lot of money!"

"Well, of course it costs a lot of money. It's a Rolls-Royce. Now, how do I get to St. John's?"

"Guess a fella would have to have himself a real good job to be able to drive a grand car like this?"

"You don't pay for a car like this punching a clock from nine to five—or pumping gas. Now would you *please* tell me how I get to St. John's?"

"So, what do you *do*, buddy, to be able to afford a car like this?"

"If you really must know, I work for Cunard!"

"Well, buddy, I works forkin' 'ard too, but I still can't afford a car like this."

Every Day Will Be Labour Day

An accountant with the Canada Customs and Revenue Agency, during an otherwise idle afternoon, calculated that every day is Labour Day. Here are his calculations.

Every regular year has 365 days.

If you sleep eight hours a day, it equals 122 days. This leaves 243 days.

If you rest eight hours a day, it equals another 122 days. This leaves 121 days.

There are 52 Sundays, leaving 69 days.

If you have a half-day off on Saturday, this equals 26 days, and it leaves 43 days.

If you have one and a half hours for lunch every workday, this equals 28 days, leaving 15 days.

Two weeks' vacation equals 14 days.

This leaves only 1 day.

And on Labour Day nobody works.

Louis Laberge

The state funeral held for Louis Laberge in Quebec on July 24, 2002, brought to mind an incident in his public life that helps to explain why he had earned his reputation for being such a fiery, defiant, and outspoken leader of the Quebec Federation of Labour.

The incident took place in Montreal in the early 1970s. Laberge took his seat on a panel to discuss the plight of the Quebec worker within the Canadian Confederation. It was to be a live telecast so the camera operators were busy checking the camera angles and the sound technicians were taking the voice levels of the participants.

The participants identified themselves. They did so in their normal voices, except for Laberge, who dropped his voice to a whisper when he said, "I am Louis Laberge," as if he were having trouble speaking the words. The sound technician asked him to repeat his name to check the level and then increased the volume of his microphone.

Once the proceedings were under way, each participant identified himself. When it was Laberge's turn, he began yelling into the microphone, "I'M LOUIS LABERGE AND I REPRESENT THE DOWN-TRODDEN WORKERS OF QUEBEC WHO ARE BEING VICTIMIZED BY THE GOVERNMENT IN OTTAWA!" The sound technicians scrambled to reduce the volume of his microphone.

That is one of the many reasons why he was seen (and heard) to be such a forceful personality.

Union Matters

Two Toronto union leaders were discussing whether or not they should go to that evening's union meeting.

One of them didn't much feel like it, but the other guy said, "We have a duty to go. It's up to us to get the message across to those fat cats in management that the little guy is important; that the rank and file who work for them have a right to a fair piece of the pie."

The other guy said, "Yeah, I guess you're right. But we'll have to go in your Mercedes. My Jag is in the shop."

Post Office

People complain about the service of Canada Post, but I know of a letter that went from Vancouver to Halifax in one day.

Okay, so it was supposed to go to Victoria.

Postage Costs

If the world is getting smaller, why does postage keep going up?

Top Ten Reasons

Or Why the Canadian Union of Postal Workers
Is Being Legislated Back to Work

I picked up this item on the internet in May 2002 but it clearly refers to events in the news at least two years earlier.

10. Vancouver RCMP in urgent need of five thousand gallons of pepper spray delayed in transit by strike.

9. Preston Manning thinks "back to work" is really "back to slavery."

8. Conspiracy on the part of *X-Files* TV producers, who are running out of things for Scully and Mulder to investigate.

7. Parti Québécois votes *oui* to everything.

6. Hockey fans think if strike ends soon, they can send Mark Messier to Japan Olympics via inexpensive parcel post.

5. Georges Clermont, considering retiring from his $380,000-annual-income job as Canada Post president, wants to make sure he gets his pension cheques promptly.

4. Conservative Party still blames postie union for loss of several hundred seats during previous two elections.

3. Sheila Copps terrified she won't get the latest Victoria's Secret catalogue in time for Christmas shopping.

2. Bill Gates told Jean Chrétien, "Don't negotiate; everyone who counts has e-mail."

1. Roch Carrier still sore about that darn sweater.

Three Men

Three middle-aged Canadians died at the same time and were greeted at the Pearly Gates by St. Peter.

"How much did you earn last year?" St. Peter asked the first man.

The man replied, "A little over $500,000."

"Go and stand over there with the surgeons and the lawyers," St. Peter said.

He then asked the second man, "And how much did you earn last year?"

"About $200,000," he replied.

He was promptly told to stand with the engineers and the accountants.

St. Peter then turned to the third man. "How much did you earn last year?" he asked.

"About $6,000," admitted the man.

St. Peter stopped in his tracks, looked at the man keenly, and said, "And would I have seen you in anything?"

Gold Prospector

A gold prospector trips and falls down a neglected mine shaft at Williams Creek in Cariboo country, B.C., and wakes up dead.

Dusting himself off, he looks up to see the Pearly Gates and St. Peter guarding the entranceway to Heaven.

He heads for the gates, but St. Peter bars his way. "Sorry, nothing personal, but there's absolutely no room in Heaven for another gold prospector. We work on a quota system, and we've filled our quota."

The prospector is momentarily nonplussed. Then an idea occurs to him. He stands up straight, puts his hands to his mouth, and yells as loudly as he can: "Gold Discovered in Hell!"

Thereupon hundreds of prospectors rush through the gates and head in the direction of Hell.

"Very ingenious," says St. Peter admiringly. "You may now enter."

"No thanks," says the prospector, already heading in the opposite direction.

"Where are you going?" asks St. Peter.

"Down there. After all, there might be some truth to the rumour."

Colonial Paints

Oil paints were a valuable commodity in the days of the British Empire. Paint companies in the Old Country made a fortune manufacturing and shipping cans of paint to merchants in the far reaches of the Empire, including to purchasers in St. John's and Halifax.

One company sent a clipper full of red paint across the Atlantic. During a terrible storm, it had the bad luck to collide with another clipper full of blue paint. The result of this disaster was that both crews were marooned.

Wheelbarrow Smarts

The strong young man at the construction site was bragging that he could outdo anyone in a feat of strength. He made a special case of making fun of one of the older workmen. After several minutes of this, the older worker had had enough.

"Why don't you put your money where your mouth is?" he said. "I will bet a week's wages that I can haul something in a wheelbarrow over to that outbuilding that you won't be able to wheel back."

"You're on, old man," the braggart replied. "Let's see what you got."

The old man reached out and grabbed the wheelbarrow by the handles. Then, nodding to the young man, he said with a smile, "All right. Get in."

Worst Business

A salesman went into a men's clothing store in a small town. He asked the manager how business was.

"Business was real bad on Wednesday," the manager said. "I sold only one suit. Thursday was even worse. I didn't sell a single thing. But Friday was the worst of all."

"How could that be possible," the salesman asked, "if you didn't sell anything on Thursday?"

The manager replied, "The man who bought the suit on Wednesday brought it back."

Pilot

These two East Coasters came to Toronto looking for work. Finding nothing in the papers, they went to an employment agency.

The first one went in and asked for a job as a woodcutter. The agency person said, "This is Toronto. There are no woodcutting jobs here. All those jobs are up north."

So the guy left the agency and told his buddy that there were no jobs for him. His buddy went in anyway and came back out in five minutes with a job. He told his friend about his job.

A little annoyed, the first guy went back into the office and said, "You don't have a job for me as a woodcutter, but my friend gets a job."

The clerk replies, "Yes, your friend said he was a pilot."

The guy said, "Yeah, sure. If I don't cut the wood, how can he pile it?"

Today's Stock Market Results

I am indebted to writer and speaker Eric McLuhan for this amusing piece of lore, which he sent to me by e-mail on August 7, 2002. It seems to say something about the cycles of the stock market.

Helium was up, feathers were down.
Paper was stationery.
Fluorescent tubing was dimmed in light trading.
Knives were up sharply.
Cows steered into a bull market.
Pencils lost a few points.
Hiking equipment was trailing.
Elevators rose, while escalators continued their slow decline.
Weights were up in heavy trading.
Light switches were off.
Mining equipment hit rock bottom.
Diapers remain unchanged.
Shipping lines stayed at an even keel.
The market for raisins dried up.
Caterpillar stock inched up a bit.
Sun peaked at midday.
Balloon prices were inflated.
And Scott Tissue touched a new bottom.

New Element Discovered

Ottawa's National Research Council (NRC) recently announced the discovery of the heaviest chemical element yet known to science. The new element has been tentatively named Governmentium.

Governmentium has 1 neutron, 12 assistant neutrons, 75 deputy neutrons, and 11 assistant deputy neutrons, giving it an atomic mass of 312.

These 312 particles are held together by forces called morons, which are surrounded by vast quantities of particles called peons. Since Governentium has no electrons, it is inert. However, it can be detected easily, as it impedes every reaction with which it comes into contact. A minute amount of Governmentium causes one reaction to take over four days to complete when it would normally take less than a second.

Governmentium has a normal half-life of three years; it does not decay but instead undergoes a reorganization in which a portion of the assistant neutrons and deputy neutrons exchange places.

In fact, Governmentium's mass will actually increase over time, since each reorganization will cause some morons to become neutrons, forming isodopes (a new kind of isotope). This characteristic of moron-promotion leads some scientists to speculate that Governmentium is formed whenever morons reach a certain quantity in concentration. This hypothetical quantity is referred to as critical morass.

tHe WoRLD is Waiting foR tHe SunRise

To quote from a once familiar song, written by Toronto lyricist Ruth Lowe, "The world is waiting for the sunrise." That is because much of the world is enveloped in darkness. Canada is one of the world's bright spots—in the eyes of people everywhere. The world is patiently waiting for more of Canada's values (well, maybe) and valuables (yes, for sure).

Meanwhile, we Canadians are busy distinguishing ourselves from Americans (all that business about "the narcissism of minor differences"). So busy are we doing so that we seldom venture forth to face greater, global possibilities and adventures.

The jokes and lore here suggest that the adage "The grass is greener somewhere else" is a manifest absurdity. Greenest is here— well, much of the year, anyway.

Canadian Facts and American Opinions

Basic Information

Fact: 80 percent of Canada's population is located near the border of the United States.

Opinion: Canada may invade the United States at any given moment.

Fact: Some Canadians speak French.
Opinion: Canadians speak French so that Americans can't understand them.

Fact: Canada is the second largest country in the world (after Russia).
Opinion: Canada feels the need to become the largest country in the world (and in fact was probably behind the recent split up of Russia).

Fact: Canada has maritime boundary disputes with the U.S.
Opinion: Canada will try anything to increase its size.

Fact: Canada's population growth rate is higher then that of the U.S.
Opinion: Canadians are trying to overpopulate the world.

Fact: Canadians have a longer life-expectancy rate than Americans. (Canadians have a public health care system.)
Opinion: Canadians may not be human.

Fact: In Ontario (the province that is home to the capital of Canada), it is now legal for women to go topless in public.
Opinion: Canada is sliding down the slippery slope of immorality and plans to drag the U.S. along with it.

Fact: Canada has 6,522,092 men fit for military service.
Opinion: Canadian soldiers are all prepared to give their lives for the betterment of their country.

Fact: Canada owns more of America than Americans do.
Opinion: Canadians may be trying to buy our country out from under us, and they have the power to do so.

Fact: The popular FOX-TV show *The X-Files* is filmed in Canada. *Opinion:* Canadians are actually alien invaders from another galaxy.

Conclusion: Canadians hate Americans and have plans to over-take the U.S., and they have the power to do so.

What Can We Do to Help?

In October 2001, I found on the web the Anti-Canada website, with its motto, "Canada is evil." It's an amusing site established by Americans with a keen interest in Canadian affairs. The question to ask is why are they so interested in us? Is it that they have "caught on" to our shenanigans and scheme for world dominance?

Don't buy Canadian goods. Our economy is weak as it is, and if you give the Canadians your money, our great country will fall!

Don't travel to Canada. If we don't send any tourists there, its economy will crash and burn!

Tell your congressperson that you support stronger borders to the North!

Tell everyone you know about this site!

Link to this site from your own web page!

Oil vs. Water

The Saudi Arabian Oil Minister Ahmed Zaki Yamani awaited the arrival of Pierre Elliott Trudeau at Riyadh. There was banter with the visiting Canadians, one of whom noted, "When our people drill for oil in Canada, they often strike water."

Sheik Yamani sighed, "When we drill for water, we strike oil. You see how unlucky you are."

Then Paul Desmarais, chairman of the Power Corporation of Montreal, slapped his Saudi friend's back and made him an offer: "Tell you what, Zaki. We'll give you 50 percent of our water and you give us 50 percent of your oil. That's a fair deal, isn't it?"

Inventors of Radio

Guglielmo Marconi, an Italian inventor who erected wireless transmission towers in Ireland and Newfoundland in 1901, is generally credited with the invention of radio. However, scientists and inventors from all over the world had to make their contributions before radio as we know it could become a fixture of everyday life.

For instance, Joseph Henry, an American, and Michael Faraday, an Englishman, proved that currents in one wire could produce currents in another. Edouard Branly, a Frenchman, invented a device that could receive Marconi's transmissions and ring a bell. John Fleming, an Englishman, invented the vacuum tube, which was necessary to receive radio waves. The tube was later improved by another American, Lee de Forest. Reginald Fessenden, a Canadian, pioneered the world's first radio broadcast.

But none of this would have been possible in the first place without there being a means to collect the sounds for transmissions. The common belief is that the microphone was invented by an Irishman. But this is purely a patent mike story.

Two Men, One Woman

There are two men and one woman. Here is how various nationalities would solve the problem of which man gets the woman.

If the people are American, the two men will play poker, and the winner will get the woman.

If they are French, the men will fight a duel, and the winner will get the woman.

If they are Italian, one man will murder the other one, and the survivor will get the woman.

If they are English, the men will play whist and will ignore the woman because they haven't been properly introduced.

If they are Canadian, the two men will spend such a long time trying to come to a compromise acceptable to all parties that the woman will get bored and go away with an American.

In the U.K.

A Canadian couple on a holiday in the United Kingdom were on a bus touring the English countryside.

When the bus stopped at Runnymede, the man asked the tour guide, "What's so important about this place?"

The guide explained, "This is where King John signed the Magna Carta."

"When did that happen?" the man asked.

The guide replied, "1215."

The man looked at his watch and said to his wife, "Damn! We missed it by just twenty minutes."

Canadian in an English Country Home

A Canadian visiting England goes to spend a weekend at the country home of an aristocrat. He really wants to make a good impression, but by the first afternoon he notices that people are giving him the cold shoulder. He asks the butler what he could have done wrong.

The butler tells him, "Well, sir. It was this morning's fox hunt. When one sees the fox, it is customary to say, 'Tally ho!' Not 'There goes the little son of a bitch.'"

Canadian Soldier on Leave

A Canadian soldier was in London during World War II. He was going out on the town for the first leave he had had in many weeks.

Because there were so many servicemen in London, all the buses were packed. He was standing in the aisle of a bus and noticed a woman, seated, with a little dog on the seat beside her. He was pretty footsore after his weeks of training and drilling, so he asked politely, "Ma'am, could you hold that little dog on your lap so I can sit down?"

She gave him a dirty look and said, "No!"

Five minutes went by, and the soldier was getting tired. He said, "Please, ma'am. Pick up your dog so I can have a seat."

Once again she refused. A few more minutes passed, and the soldier was so weary he thought he'd fall down if he didn't sit down. He was also angry at the woman's lack of consideration. So he picked up the dog and dropped it out the window. The woman screamed. She yelled for the conductor, who stopped the bus so she could retrieve her dog. Then he ordered the Canadian off the bus.

An English gentleman sitting in a seat across the aisle said, "You Canadians can't do anything right, can you? You drive on the wrong side of the road. You hold your fork with the wrong hand. And now you throw out the wrong bitch."

Meeting the Queen

A man walks into Joe's Barber Shop for his regular haircut.

As he snips away, Joe asks, "What's up?"

The man proceeds to explain he's going to take a vacation in England.

"England!" Joe exclaims. "Why would you want to go there? It's a crowded, dirty country full of Brits! You'd be crazy to go to London! So how ya getting there?"

"We're taking TWA," the man replies.

"TWA!" yells Joe. "They're a terrible airline. Their planes are old, their flight attendants are ugly, and they're always late! So where you staying in England?"

The man says, "We'll be at the downtown International Hotel."

"That dump!" says Joe. "That's the worst hotel in the country! The rooms are small, the service is surly and slow, and they're overpriced! So whatcha doing when you get there?"

The man says, "We're going to go see Buckingham Palace and we hope to see the Queen."

"Ha! That's rich!" scoffs Joe. "You and a million other people trying to see her. She'll look the size of an ant. Boy, good luck on this trip. You're going to need it!"

A month later, the man returns for his regular haircut.

Joe says, "Well, how did that trip to England turn out? Betcha TWA gave you the worst flight of your life!"

"No, quite the opposite," explains the man. "Not only were we on time, in one of their brand-new planes, but it was full and they bumped us up to first class. The food and wine were wonderful, and I had a beautiful, twenty-eight-year-old flight attendant who waited on me hand and foot!"

"Well, I bet the hotel was just like I described."

"No, quite the opposite! They'd just finished a $25-million remodelling. It's the finest hotel in England now. They were overbooked, so they apologized and gave us the presidential suite for no extra charge!"

"Well," Joe mumbles, "I know you didn't get to see the Queen!"

"Actually, we were quite lucky. As we toured the palace, a royal guard tapped me on the shoulder and explained the Queen likes to personally meet some of the visitors, and if I'd be so kind as to step into this private room and wait, the Queen would personally greet me. Sure enough, after five minutes the Queen walked through the door and shook my hand. I bowed down as she spoke a few words to me."

Impressed, Joe asks, "Tell me, please! What'd she say?"

"Oh, not much really. Just 'Where'd you get that awful haircut?'"

News Report

Dominion Press—Security officials at Pearson International Airport reported that late last night they apprehended a Canadian citizen trying to enter the country legally.

Cultural Obsessions

A professor of anthropology at a major Canadian university is delivering a lecture on how to identify the dominant features of various cultures.

"It's quite simple," she says. "Just look for the things to which, or for which, people make great sacrifices.

"In medieval Italy, look at how much money the people gave to the Catholic Church in their devotion to Jesus and the Virgin Mary.

"In pre-Columbian Mexico, look at the sacrifice of humans on the Aztec altars of their gods.

"Even in modern India, look at the outrageous burdens placed on people in their remarkable veneration of cows.

"When people let something dominate their entire lives, to the extent that they don't even notice it any more, that's the key sign of cultural obsession.

"As a final note," she goes on, "it's striking that Canada is free of any dominant cultural obsession. That may be one of the hall-marks of a true democracy."

She begins to pick up her books. "I'm sorry, but that will be the end of the lecture for today. My car's in the shop to have its radio repaired, and I need to get my rental car out of the parking lot before I get a fine, buy some gas, get across town before the rush hour traffic gets too bad, and pick up my car before the garage closes. I'm sure you all want to beat the traffic, too. Class dismissed."

Dominican Republic

I have this joke from Ed Butts, a Maritime-born author whose novel Buffalo: A Fable of the West *is a minor classic. For seven years Ed was a resident and teacher of English in Sousa in the Dominican Republic. This joke (complete with its Canadian reference) is current there.*

A man died and went to Hell.

When he got there, the Devil met him and told him that Hell, like earth, had many countries; the man could spend his eternity of damnation in the country of his choice. The Devil showed the man a row of doors and suggested that he browse a bit before making a decision.

The man opened the door marked Canada. He saw a desolate Arctic wilderness in which poor souls were freezing amidst ice, snow, and howling winds.

He didn't like the looks of that, so he went to the next door, which was marked Saudi Arabia. There he saw agonized souls burning in a hot desert under a relentless sun. That didn't appeal to him either.

The third door was the Dominican Republic. There the man saw happy souls playing on a beautiful beach with a lovely ocean in the background and a warm tropical sun shining down on them. Everyone was laughing and singing.

"Wow!" said the man. "I'll choose this one."

After the man had told the Devil he'd chosen the Dominican Republic as the place to spend his eternal damnation, the Devil laughed and said, "Well, you've made your choice and now there is no turning back. This is what's going to happen to you here: Every morning, someone will come to torture you with electric shocks. Every afternoon, someone will come and pour boiling water on you. Every evening, the police will come and beat you to a pulp."

Then the Devil laughed and slammed the door.

The man was scared, but when he looked around, he saw that all the other damned souls were still laughing and singing and having fun. "How can you be so happy," he cried, "with all the terrible things that happen here?"

One of them smiled and said, "Amigo, is not so bad here. In the morning, when they come to give us the electric shocks, the power is out. In the afternoon, when they come to pour boiling water on us, the water is shut off. And in the evening, when the police come to beat us up, we just give them twenty pesos and they go away."

Couple in London

A couple, strolling through Kensington Park in London, England, sat down on a bench next to an elderly Briton. The Brit noticed that their lapel pins sported tiny Canadian flags. To make conversation, he said, "Judging by your lapel pins, you must be Canadians."

"That's a good guess," replied the gentleman.

"I hope you won't mind my asking," said the Brit, "but there are two red bars on the flag. What do they represent?"

"Well," replied the gentleman, "the left bar stands for the spirit of endurance displayed by the explorers of the land and the pioneers who settled the broad expanses of the country. The right bar represents the spirit of integrity and community for which Canadians are well admired the world over."

The Brit mulled this over and nodded. Having poor eyesight at his advanced age, and not immediately recognizing the image of the maple leaf, he then asked, "And what's that red figure between the two bars?"

"Oh," the lady piped up. "That's the maple leaf. It's the national emblem, and it has eleven points. Its points are there to remind us of the first eleven syllables of the country's national anthem."

The Brit asked, "And what are those eleven syllables?"

The gentleman smiled and replied, "O Canada, you know we're Americans..."

Languages

A European gentleman was on a cruise ship that docked at St. John's, Nfld. He went ashore for a stroll around town and became lost. He approached two locals, George and Clancy, who were on a street corner.

First he said, "*Parlez-vous français?*"

They looked at each other quizzically.

The he said, "*Hablan ustedes español?*"

They just shrugged. Next he said, "*Sprechen Sie Deutsch?*"

They just replied, "Huh?"

Finally he said, *"Parlate italiano?"*

Still nothing.

Exasperated, the man stalked off.

Clancy looked at George and said, "Do you think we ought to learn a foreign language?"

"What for, b'y? That fella know four of them and it didn't do him any good."

Neighbours

In the early 1980s, the deputy head of Moscow's Institute of the United States and Canada, a division of the USSR's Academy of Sciences, came on a fact-finding mission to Canada.

In the faculty lounge of the University of Toronto, he was introduced to a visiting American political scientist of some eminence. The American expressed surprise that the deputy head of such an important institution in Moscow would visit Canada.

"What are you doing in Canada?" the American asked. "I'm surprised to find you in Toronto rather than in New York or Washington."

"Canada is our neighbour, you know," the Russian replied.

The American said nothing, then walked away.

Why We Can't Stand Americans

This list likely dates from the 1980s. It is said to come from "The Beginner's Guide to Canadian Humour." I found it on the internet in September 2001.

1. Because they come up here in the summer, wearing funny clothes and carrying skis on the tops of their station wagons.

2. Because they never have anything but American money with them, and they never change it at a bank, and they complain about the exchange rate they get at stores.

3. Because they refuse to vote for Blue Jay or Expo ballplayers on their all-star game ballots.

4. Because of their tacky local newscasts in Buffalo and other crummy border towns.

5. Because they elect judges and have stupid TV commercials for them.

6. Because they're used to getting their booze almost for free and complain about our prices when they come here, and we can't argue because they're right.

7. Because their dollar is so high that it costs us a fortune to go down there for a few days and take advantage of their cheap booze.

8. Because they don't know the first thing about Canada, like who our prime minister is—or even that we have a prime minister or a different currency. And they glaze over if we try to explain it to them.

9. Because they don't even know that people like Lorne Greene, William Shatner, Rich Little, and Monty Hall are Canadian.

10. Because the only time they pay attention to hockey is when they win something.

11. Because they make terrible, weak beer and spend so much money advertising it that every seventeen-year-old in the Western world craves it.

12. Because before Vietnam they used to claim they'd never lost a war, even though we stiffed them in the War of 1812.

13. Because they think Wayne Newton is a great entertainer.

14. Because, although we're their leading trading partner and share the world's longest undefended border, they keep dropping cruise missiles on obscure bits of Alberta.

15. Because they still haven't seen through Ron and Nancy, and they actually think that people like Teddy Kennedy are left wing.

Stranded on a Desert Island

A Mexican, an American, and a Canadian were stranded on a desert island after their ship sank in a storm.

A few weeks passed and a strange bottle washed ashore.

The Mexican picked it up and rubbed the sand off its surface. Suddenly there was a flash and a large genie appeared before them. The genie granted each man one wish.

"Oh, please," said the Mexican, "I miss my family so much; I want to go back home to Mexico!" In an instant he was gone.

"I miss my office; I want to go back to New York City!" the American pleaded. In a flash he too disappeared.

There stood the Canadian, alone with the genie. "Gosh, it sure is lonely around here," the Canadian said. "I wish I had my two friends back!"

American Woman in France

An American woman travelling in France is accosted by a Frenchman unimpressed with her homeland.

"You Americans killed off the Natives of your country, you stole half of Mexico, you pillaged the rest of the world, and now I've heard you want to take over half of Canada if Quebec splits away from that country! Have you no shame at all? Haven't you made enough of a mess already?"

The American quickly shakes her head and says, "No, no, no, you've got it all wrong. Are you joking—with our terrible health care system, with our education system in disarray, with our entire social fabric torn apart, we aren't looking for new territory. We're just waiting for Ontario to annex us!"

CSBs

Some bank managers are dumb.

I took some Canada Savings Bonds into the bank, and the manager asked me, "Do you want them redeemed or converted?"

A bit put out at his ignorance, I replied, "What are you, a bank or a church?"

Banking on It

One day a little old lady entered the Bank of Canada building in Ottawa. She was carrying a bag of cash. She insisted that she must speak with the governor of the bank to open a savings account because, as she explained, "It's a lot of money!"

After much hemming and hawing, the bank staff finally ushered her into the governor's office. The governor asked her how much money she would like to deposit.

She replied, "$165,000!" and dumped the cash out of her bag onto his desk.

The governor was, of course, curious as to how she had come by all this cash, so he asked her, "Ma'am, I'm surprised you're carrying so much cash around. Where did you get this money?"

The little old lady replied, "I make bets."

The governor then asked, "Bets? What kind of bets?"

The little old lady said, "Well, for example, I'll bet you $25,000 that your balls are square."

"Ha!" laughed the governor. "That's a stupid bet. You can never win that kind of bet."

The old lady challenged, "So, would you like to take my bet?"

"Sure," said the governor. "I'll bet $25,000 that my balls are not square."

The little old lady then said, "Okay, but since there is a lot of money involved, may I bring my lawyer with me tomorrow at 10:00 a.m. as a witness?"

"Sure!" replied the confident governor.

That night, the governor remembered the challenge and, feeling a sense of nervousness about the bet, spent a long time in front of a mirror checking his balls, turning from side to side, again and again. He thoroughly checked them out until he was sure that there was absolutely no way that his balls were square and that he would win the bet.

The next morning, at precisely 10:00 a.m., the little old lady appeared at the governor's office with her lawyer.

She introduced the lawyer to the governor and repeated the bet: "$25,000 says the governor's balls are square!"

The old lady then asked the governor to drop his pants so they could all see. The governor complied.

The old little lady peered closely at his balls and then asked if she could feel them.

"Well, okay," said the governor. "$25,000 is a lot of money, so I guess you should be absolutely sure."

Just then, he noticed that the lawyer was quietly banging his head against the wall. The governor asked the little old lady, "What the hell's the matter with your lawyer?"

She replied, "Nothing, except I bet him $100,000 that at 10:00 a.m. today, I'd have the Bank of Canada's governor's balls in my hand."

U.S., Canada to Merge

Fifty-nine Million Layoffs Expected

U.S. and Canadian leaders announced today that their two countries are merging in order to reduce operating costs and increase production efficiencies.

"We're simply following the trend created by corporations which find this a quick way to increase market share and reduce expenses," explains the government's new architect, 23-year-old M.B.A. and investment banker Billy Smurtz. "We've created the first multinational country."

The new country, which will be named Canadusa, is expected to reduce both governments' operating costs by 30 percent, with fifty-nine million Canadusians expected to be laid off.

"Yes, there will be some disruptions," explains Smurtz, "but they're nothing we can't overcome. We've got to crank out some new flags, constitutions, money, and stuff like that. But the long-term cost savings far outweigh the disadvantages. We'll save

$3 billion a year just by closing down all those border crossings, not to mention shutting down that whole Washington, D.C., thing. Who can argue with that?

"There are already so many similarities," he adds. "They've got baseball, we've got baseball. They've got hockey, we've got hockey. They drive on the right side of the road, so do we. If we hadn't told you about it, you wouldn't even know we did it."

And the plan doesn't stop there. "We'd like to get Mexico into the operation as soon as possible," he says. "But that whole language, heritage thing they have down there is causing problems with the takeover."

Citizens in both countries are divided about the plan. One Canadian explains: "They've got that great military superpower thing going for them down there, eh? We've got to love becoming part of that." One American surfer remarked, "Yeah, I guess it's okay. But it's cold up there, isn't it? Couldn't we find a warmer country with better beaches, like Australia? Now that would be cool."

Some U.S. critics of the plan argue that there are more important issues at stake than just saving money. Like patriotism. But Smurtz argues that they're just being sentimental. "You watch. They'll get over it the first day they see a cut in their taxes. Besides, they're gonna get their own province."

One Nation

The United States Court of Appeals for the Ninth Circuit ruled in July 2002 that it was unconstitutional to require American school children to recite the Pledge of Allegiance because it contains the words "one nation under God, indivisible."

An editor from The New Yorker magazine phoned Robin Williams and asked the comic actor if he could suggest an alternative.

Williams replied, "Why don't they change it to, 'One nation under Canada'?"

Marxism in Practice

An American Marxist, a Russian Marxist, and a Canadian Marxist are discussing Communism in their respective countries.

The American Marxist boasts, "The United States is the most Communist country in the world because everyone—whether rich or poor—owns an automobile. That's Communism!"

The Russian Marxist claims, "The Russian Republic is the most Communist country in the world because everyone—whether rich or poor—stands in queues to purchase shoddily manufactured goods. That's Communism!"

The Canadian Marxist exclaims, "The Dominion of Canada is the most Communist country in the world because—as everyone knows—the state has withered away."

Those Clever Canucks

We Canadians have been secretly brainwashing Americans for years. We started by sticking extra vowels in our everyday vocabulary, like adding a "u" to words such as "labour" and "colour," and adding an "eh" sound to the end of every sentence we say.

The U.S. retaliated by making everyone south of the Mason-Dixon Line talk like a bunch of hicks so that Canadians could not understand them when they drive through to Florida vacations each winter. Thus, the first infiltration was thwarted.

We then started sending down our singers, actors, comedians, and writers to Hollywood to take over the industry: You control the media, you control their simple American minds. So far, this has been successful—look at how California has been changed.

This had led to further inroads throughout the States, using the National Hockey League's continued expansion of teams as a front. Where do most of these jobs for secret agents go? To Canadian hockey players.

Where will the clever Canucks strike next? First the U.S. and then someday Canada will take over the entire world!

26
two dozen classic Canadian jokes

Are there any Canadian jokes that may be described as classic? Are there jokes and stories that are told and retold across the country (in the English language) that have stood the test of time and repeated retellings so that they could be considered favourites?

If there are some, are there very many? Are there as many as twenty-four?

I think there *are* classic Canadian jokes and that there *are* at least two dozen of them. At least that is the number I am including here. I may not be an objective witness—after all, I have a vested interest in collecting our ephemeral humour and compiling it in book-length collections—but the expertise that I possess is based on wide reading, much listening, and broad-minded collecting.

Here is my selection of the jokes and anecdotes that Canadians have enjoyed the most. The two dozen jokes are arranged in rough chronological order, and the selection features a fair number of anecdotes and jokes about historical figures. The earliest joke is an anecdote that is more than one century old.

The majority of the jokes, however, date from the decades of heady nationalism—the 1960s and 1970s. Those that follow I first heard in the 1990s; whether these are "keepers"—whether they have staying power—is a matter yet to be settled.

Here, then, are the jokes and anecdotes that English Canadians are telling and retelling one another right across the country.

A final note: I have omitted from my list of twenty-four classic Canadian jokes two jokes that are internationally known and lamentably associated with this country. They come courtesy of anonymous users of the internet. Websites identify these jokes as being of Canadian origin. In my opinion they are awful, so I made the decision to include them here in the introduction to the chapter rather than in the list proper. They are jokes "so bad they're good," if you like.

In the version of "The Case of Beer Joke" reproduced here, celebrated TV comics Bob and Doug McKenzie are featured. They go unidentified in other versions. These other versions usually specify the setting as North Bay, Ont.

"Canadian Joke?" is my title for this specimen of "humour" that a British university research team in December 2001 declared to be "the funniest Canadian joke." It proved to be a joke that was new to me and to all my informants across the country. The only reason I am including it here is because from time to time people ask me about it. I have yet to meet a Canadian who finds it the least bit funny.

The Case of Beer Joke

Bob, a Canadian, is walking down the street with a case of beer under his arm.

His friend Doug stops him and asks, "Hey, Bob. Whatcha get the case of beer for?"

"I got it for my wife, eh," answers Bob.

"Oh!" exclaims Doug. "Good trade."

Canadian Joke?

What do you call a woman who can balance four pints of beer on her head?

Beatrix. (beer tricks)

Enough bad jokes. Now for the classics.

1. Party Loyalty

The stories told about Sir John A. Macdonald, Canada's first prime minister, are legion. Many of them concern his alleged alcoholism, but the best of them make much of his sharp wit and presence of mind. Here are two that were recorded by E.B. Biggar in his *Anecdotal Life of Sir John A. Macdonald,* published in 1891, the year of Sir John A.'s death. The book is dear to at least one of his successors, Conservative prime minister John G. Diefenbaker.

Sir John A. was arguing with Arthur Dickey, Conservative lawyer and Nova Scotia member of Parliament, about party loyalty. Dickey felt that he had to distinguish between the leader and the party. "I am still a Conservative," he told the prime minister, "and I shall support you whenever I think you are right."

Sir John A. looked down at Dickey with disbelief. "That is no satisfaction. Anybody may support me when I am right," he spat out contemptuously. "What I want is a man who will support me when I am wrong."

2. Mounted Police

The classic story told about the Royal Canadian Mounted Police took place before the turn of the nineteenth century, during the days when the newly created force was still known as the North West Mounted Police. The incident in question occurred in present-day Saskatchewan, along the Montana border.

An entire regiment of U.S. Cavalry accompanies over two hundred Crees to the border, where they are met by a single

Mountie. The American commanding officer looks around with surprise and dismay. "Where's your escort for these dangerous Indians?" he asks.

"He's over there," answers the Mountie, pointing to a fellow constable tending their two horses.

3. The *Habitant* and the Irishman

There is a *habitant* story told about the French-Canadian wood-carver who is hard at work when a friendly Irishman interrupts him.

"I love your figures of *habitants* and saints," the Irishman says. "But why don't you ever carve the figure of an Irishman?"

The woodcarver, a sage peasant, replies, "I would, if only I could find wood thick enough."

4. Sir Wilfrid Laurier

An amusing story is told of the French-Canadian *habitant* living in almost total isolation on his farm. Coming to the village to pick up supplies, he accosted the first acquaintance he met and proceeded to ply him with questions.

He was told that Queen Victoria had died. At once he was all sympathy and concern.

"*Non? Sacre! Mais* dat wan beeg shame. Who get dat job of Victoria?"

"The Prince of Wales," his friend informed him.

The *habitant* thought about that for a moment, then replied, "*Par Dieu!* Must be good frien' to Laurier!"

5. Saskatoon

Two English ladies are crossing Canada by train. At a brief stop in Saskatoon, the older turns to the younger and says, "I wonder where we are."

The younger replies, "I have no idea, but I will find out."

She steps onto the platform and spots the dispatcher. "Excuse me, could you tell me where we are?"

"Saskatoon, Saskatchewan," he replies.

She boards the train and the older lady asks her, "Well, where are we?"

The younger one replies, "I still don't know. It's obvious they don't speak English here."

6. W.L. Mackenzie King

A classic story involves Mackenzie King, the new prime minister, and the Leader of the Opposition, R.B. Bennett. It occurred in the House of Commons in 1928 but seems not to be part of the official proceedings.

Bennett was baiting King: "I would like to know what the prime minister would think," Bennett asked, "if he went into his garden in the morning to pick pansies or violets and was confronted by six naked Doukhobors."

Without a moment's pause, King rose and replied, "I would send for my Honourable friend the Leader of the Opposition."

7. Royal Visit

It was the official duty of Camillien Houde, the ebullient, bilingual, and controversial mayor of Montreal, to welcome King George VI and Queen Elizabeth to his city on May 18, 1939, and accompany them on their drive through the streets of Montreal in an open car.

The King and Queen were delighted to see such large and enthusiastic crowds, and so was Houde. He turned to the King and said, proudly, "You know, Your Majesty, some of this is for you."

8. Elizabeth and Philip

This tale is too good to exclude on the word of Prince Philip, who denied that it ever occurred, maintaining that no one who served him would dare address him so informally. Peter Gzowski, host of CBC Radio's Morningside, tracked down the amusing story. Apparently the incident occurred to the governor general, the Duke of Connaught, at a Board of Trade dinner in a small community in the Peace River district of British Columbia between 1911 and 1916. A good story is never, ever effectively or definitively debunked.

Not long after the royal wedding in 1947, Princess Elizabeth II and Prince Philip, Duke of Edinburgh, toured Canada. One evening they dined on humble fare in a lumber camp in the wilds of northern Ontario.

They were served a hearty dinner, and when the dinner plates were collected, prior to the serving of dessert, the waitress serving Prince Philip leaned over to him and said, "Save your fork, Duke. You'll need it for the pie."

9. Paul Martin Sr.

The following story is a true one. It concerns Paul Martin, long-time Liberal, cabinet minister in many Liberal administrations, and later High Commissioner to the Court of St. James. His son, long-time Finance Minister, is Paul Martin Jr. I know the story is true because I asked Paul Martin Sr. if it was true and he said, yes, embarrassedly, it was.

Martin was fabled for his photographic memory. He never forgot a name or a face—or almost never. Once, at a campaign picnic in rural Quebec, his gift failed him utterly. Upon arrival, he shook hands with several people, including a young boy.

"And how is your father?" Martin asked.

"Dead," the boy replied.

Martin attempted to overcome this gaffe by talking about the consolations of religion. Then he moved on.

A few hours later, leaving the picnic grounds, he again shook a row of hands, including the hand of the same youngster. Martin heard himself asking, again, "And how is your father?"

"Still dead," the lad shot back.

10. History Lesson

A primary school teacher was relating how Laura Second made her way through the woods at night to warn the British troops of an impending American attack. Mrs. Secord's bravery thrilled the little charges, as they had never before heard about her heroic episode in the War of 1812.

"Now, what would have happened had Mrs. Secord not succeeded?" the teacher asked.

One little fellow shot up his hand: "If she hadn't made the trek, we'd be eating Martha Washington chocolates today."

11. Consolation Prize

Everyone has heard about the national contest that advertised its first prize as one week in Toronto, its second prize as two weeks in Toronto, and its third prize as three weeks in Toronto.

But not everyone has heard about the Montrealer who claimed that he once spent a weekend in Toronto one day.

12. Essay on Elephants

Four students from four countries—Britain, France, the United States, and Canada—are asked to write an essay on the subject of the elephant.

The British student titled his essay, "Elephants and the Empire."

The French student naturally called his, "*L'Amour* and the Elephant."

The American student gave his essay the title, "Bigger and Better Elephants."

And the Canadian student, after much scratching of head, titled his essay, "Elephants: A Federal or a Provincial Responsibility?"

13. Canadian in Heaven

A Canadian dies and finds himself walking along a heavenly pathway. He comes to a fork in the road and halts.

There are two signs. One points one way and says "To Heaven." The other points the other way and says "To a Seminar on Heaven."

The Canadian follows the sign that says "To a Seminar on Heaven."

14. Multilingualism

Q. What do you call someone who speaks three languages?
A. Multilingual.

Q. What do you call someone who speaks two languages?
A. Bilingual.

Q. What do you call someone who speaks only one language?
A. English Canadian.

15. As Canadian as Possible

I am indebted to Peter Gzowski, who offered these details in his collection This Country in the Morning *(1974).*

Details are scarce, but apparently in the early 1960s, the producers of a CBC radio show held a write-in contest that required listeners to complete the following statement: "As Canadian as possible . . ."

Radio listener E. Heather Scott won the contest. She completed the statement by adding the words ". . . under the circumstances."

16. Best Newfie Joke

The best Newfie joke of all time is the one told by Silver Donald Cameron, writer and resident of D'Escousse, N.S. It's the best because with it he won the top award for the Great Canadian Joke contest on CBC Radio's Cross-Country Checkup *in 1974. It goes like this.*

A Newfie is jumping up and down on a manhole cover on Yonge Street in Toronto, shouting, "Forty-two, forty-two!" Along comes a Torontonian, who asks him what he's doing. The Newfie says that it's a great sport in Corner Brook to jump up and down on a manhole cover and shout, "Forty-two, forty-two!" and that the Torontonian should try it.

After much persuasion, the Torontonian gives in and does so, but without much enthusiasm. "Put your heart into it," the Newfie encourages him. "Leap high, yell it loud." The Torontonian shrugs, leaps twelve feet in the air, and screams, "Forty-two, forty-two!"

Suddenly the Newfie snatches away the manhole cover and the Torontonian drops down the manhole and disappears into the darkness. The Newfie replaces the cover and again jumps up and down on it, shouting, "Forty-three, forty-three!"

17. Getting Even

Q. What's black and blue and floats in the bay?
A. A Mainlander who tells Newfie jokes.

18. Put-down

A patron in a New York restaurant is choosing his lobster for dinner and notices that the tank labelled "U.S. lobsters" has a lid on it, while the tank labelled "Canadian lobsters" has none.

"Why does the American tank have a lid and not the Canadian tank?" he asks.

"Well," the waiter replies, "the American lobsters are so feisty we have to keep them down, but the Canadian lobsters keep each other down."

19. Crossing the Road

Q. Why does a Canadian cross the road?
A. To get to the middle.

20. Accident

An American, a Scot, and a Canadian were involved in a terrible automobile accident. An ambulance sped them to the emergency ward of the nearest hospital, but they were pronounced dead on arrival.

Just as the orderlies were about to put the toe-tag on the American, he stirred and opened his eyes. Astonished, the doctors and nurses who were present asked him what happened.

"Well," said the American, "I remember the crash, and then there was a beautiful light, and the Canadian and the Scot and I were standing before the Gates of Heaven. St. Peter approached us and informed us that we were all too young to die, and that for a donation of $50 each, we could return to earth.

"So, of course, I pulled out my wallet and gave him a $50 bill, and the next thing I knew I was back here."

"That's amazing!" exclaimed one of the doctors. "But what happened to the other two?"

"Last I saw of them," replied the American, "the Scot was haggling with St. Peter over the cost, and the Canadian was waiting for medicare to pay for his."

21. The Quebec Wall

There are three guys walking together on a beach: one is from Newfoundland, one is from Quebec, and one is from British Columbia. They come across a bottle, and when they uncork it, out pops a genie.

The genie says to them, "I will give each one of you a wish. That's a total of three wishes. One each."

The Newfie says, "I'm a fisherman, my dad's a fisherman, his dad was a fisherman, and my son will be one, too. I want all the oceans full of fish."

The genie waves his arms and—phoom!—the oceans are full of fish.

The Quebecer is amazed. He says, "I'm *pure laine, de souche,* and I want there to be a wall around Quebec so that nothing will get in."

The genie waves his arms and—poof!—there is a wall around Quebec.

The British Columbian turns to the genie and says, "Tell me more about this wall."

The genie replies, "Well, the Quebec wall is about 150 feet high and 50 feet thick. It completely surrounds the province of Quebec so that nothing can get in or out. Now tell me your wish."

The British Columbian says, "Fill it with water."

22. Three Wishes

An unemployed Glace Bay miner goes fishing and hooks an antique-looking bottle that is bobbing in the water. He reels it in and removes the seal and cork. Out pops a genie, who offers him three wishes.

"For my first wish, I want all the beer I can drink," the delighted miner says. In an instant he is transported to a brewery in Amsterdam, where he is surrounded by kegs of the best brew in the world.

"For my second wish, I want the most beautiful women ir world," he says. In an instant he is transported to a tent in Ara. full of the most desirable women in the world.

"For my third wish, I want never to have to work again in my life," he says. In an instant he is transported back to Glace Bay.

23. Canadian Coast Guard and U.S. Navy

Pat Carney rose in the Senate on May 30, 1996, and related the following story.

We are told it has been authenticated by the U.S. Navy. I have in my hand the alleged transcript of a radio conversation between a U.S. Navy ship and a Canadian source off the coast of Newfoundland last fall. It reads like this:

Ship 1: Please divert your course 15 degrees to the north to avoid collision.

Ship 2: Recommend you divert your course 15 degrees.

Ship 1: This is the captain of a U.S. Navy ship. I say again, divert your course.

Ship 2: No, I say again, divert your course.

Ship 1: This is an aircraft carrier of the U.S. Navy. We are a large warship. Divert your course now!

Ship 2: This is a lighthouse. Your call.

24. Creation

Once upon a time in the Kingdom of Heaven, God went missing for six days.

Eventually, on the seventh day, Michael the archangel found Him resting in a quiet spot.

He inquired of God, "Where have You been for the past six days?"

od heaved a deep sigh of satisfaction and proudly pointed
wnwards through the clouds. "Look, Michael," He said, "see
vhat I have made."

Michael looked puzzled and asked, "What is it?"

"It's a planet," replied God. "I've put life on it. I am going to
call it Earth, and it's going to be a place of great balance."

"Balance?" inquired Michael, still confused.

God explained, pointing to the different parts of earth. "For
instance, Northern Europe will be a place of great opportunity
and wealth, while Southern Europe is going to be poor. The
Middle East out there will be a hot spot. Over there I've placed
a continent of white people, and over there is a continent of
black people."

God continued, pointing to different countries. "This one
will be extremely hot and arid, while that one will be very cold
and covered in ice."

The archangel, impressed with God's handiwork, then
pointed to a landmass in the top corner and asked, "What's that
one?"

"Ah," replied God, "that's Canada, the most glorious place on
earth. It has beautiful mountains, lakes, rivers, streams, and
exquisite coastlines. The people from Canada are going to be
modest, intelligent, and humorous, and they're going to be found
travelling the world. They'll be extremely sociable, hard
working, and high-achieving. They'll be known throughout the
world as diplomats and carriers of peace. I'm also going to give
them superhuman, undefeatable ice-hockey players who will be
admired and feared by all who come across them."

Michael gasped in wonder and admiration, but then
proclaimed, "What about balance, God? You said there will be
balance."

God replied wisely, "Wait until you see the loud-mouth
people I'm putting just to the south of them!"